D1304728

FIREPOWER

in Limited War

FIREPOWER

in Limited War

★ ★ ★ ★ ★

Revised Edition

Robert H. Scales, Jr.

PRESIDIO

The opinions expressed in this book are those of the author, and do not reflect those of the Department of the Army or the Department of Defense.

Copyright © 1995 by Robert H. Scales Jr.

Published by Presidio Press
505 B San Marin Drive, Suite 300
Novato, CA 94945-1340

This edition printed 1997

First publication in paper by National Defense University Press, 1990
Revised edition first published in cloth by Presidio Press, 1994

Library of Congress Cataloging-in-Publication Data

Scales, Robert H., 1944–
    Firepower in limited war / by Robert H. Scales, Jr.—Rev. ed.
        p.   cm.
    Includes bibliographical references and index.
    ISBN 0-89141-533-5 (cloth)
    ISBN 0-89141-650-1 (paperback)
    1. Limited war. 22. Firepower. 3. Military history, Modern—20th century. I. Title.
UA11.5.S27   1994
355.02'15—dc20   94-36607
                                                  CIP

Photo on page 222 reproduced courtesy British Aerospace Aircraft Group. Photo on page 267 reproduced courtesy *Army Times*.

Printed in the United States of America

*This book is dedicated to my mom and dad,
Colonel and Mrs. Robert H. Scales.*

Contents

Preface

Place yourself in the boots of a young infantry soldier lying prone in some trenchline or treeline waiting for the signal to advance. He probably suffers from some considerable discomfort: cold, dampness, hunger, or thirst. He is most certainly frightened nearly to death. His stomach is tied in knots, his lips are thin and white, and his hands are shaking so badly that he is barely able to hold his weapon steady. He knows that to survive he must cross the killing zone to his front and kill or push away some enemy soldier who is probably as frightened and as miserable as himself. He carries very little with him to ensure survival: a rifle, some ammunition, and hopefully a wellspring of courage filled by confidence in his leaders and a pervasive desire not to let his buddies down. The empathy we share with this young soldier evokes in us a desire to do everything to help him across the killing zone. In American society in particular, we have in the past been generous in our willingness to expend firepower to save manpower.

Since most of the casualties suffered by American servicemen in war in this century have occurred among infantrymen, this book seeks to shed some light on how effective the expenditure of supporting firepower has been in preserving the lives of these soldiers. I examine five case studies derived from recent conflicts to suggest changes in the traditional way of employing firepower that might better suit the unique requirements of limited wars. The book is, above all, a history of firepower doctrine. Battles, weapons, and personalities are mentioned incidentally and only as they relate to the methods for employing mortars, artillery, helicopter gunships, and tactical airpower—the tools of war traditionally dedicated to helping soldiers make it across the killing zone alive.

Recent military history can be unpleasant reading, but it clearly demonstrates that limited wars are a reality and are increasing in frequency, in destructiveness, and in the importance of the international issues that they resolve. Wars of the nuclear age have mainly involved Third World countries but, on occasion, have drawn great powers into participation. The specific justifications for such involvement have been as varied as the conflicts themselves, but the exigencies of the changing world economic order seem to spin a common thread. As it has since the beginning of recorded history, conflict will continue to follow commerce. The incidence of wars beneath the nuclear threshold fought to gain economic advantage or deny it to others will, in all probability, increase in proportion to the increase in global economic interdependency. To protect its interests, therefore, the United States has no choice but to acknowledge the growing significance of limited wars and to undertake prudent and necessary preparations to fight them.

Limited war ranges in intensity from acts of terrorism, at the lower end of the spectrum, to larger conflicts with intensities somewhat less than full-scale conventional war, such as Desert Storm. In the modern era, limited wars have taken two distinct forms: wars of attrition and wars of intervention. I examine both forms in this book. A war of attrition is commonly characterized as a conflict without front lines, often fought in a lesser-developed region of the Third World, frequently in harsh conditions of climate and terrain. Such a war has often pitted a modern military force against a relatively primitive insurgent, as in the former Soviet Union's conflict against the Afghan resistance. The obvious technological and materiel advantages of the former have been more than offset by political and practical limits placed on the use of modern firepower, the unfamiliar and hostile character of the regions, and the often extremely long lines of communication between the developed nation and the battlefront. The insurgent's task has been made easier by sanctuary and materiel succor given by a powerful ally, knowledge of the battle area, and support from local populations. Powerful friends have often supplied an insurgent with modern tactical weapons and equipment as capable as that of his opponent. The level of an insurgent's materiel sophistication has been limited only by his ability to operate, transport, and maintain these complex weapons.

The natures of the enemy, terrain, and climate in a war of intervention are usually similar to those in a war of attrition. However, the forces of the intervening power are more limited and the expected duration of combat is only weeks or months rather than years. The intention—as in the cases of the Falklands, Grenada, Panama, and Desert Storm—is to intervene quickly to achieve a political or military objective, and then to withdraw once the objective is secured.

In both styles of limited war, the military objectives and tactical methods are influenced by internal and international politics. The insurgent seeks to maintain support of the people and to foster political support abroad for his cause. The intervening power, sensitive to political realities, must circumscribe its use of force. It must end the conflict quickly, before political pressures force termination under unfavorable circumstances.

The first four of the following case studies are reprinted from the first edition of this volume, originally published by the National Defense University Press in 1990. The chapter on the Gulf War is excerpted in part from my recent volume, *Certain Victory: The U.S. Army in the Gulf War,* published in 1993. Together, the case studies provide useful insights on how American firepower might be employed in a wide variety of future circumstances. Such insights are necessary, I believe, because leaders must have a realistic perspective on what firepower can and cannot achieve. I hope this study will help those leaders gain that perspective.

Robert H. Scales, Jr.
Camp Red Cloud
Republic of Korea

FIREPOWER
in Limited War

1
Firepower in the American Way of War

The Civil War was the first American conflict observed closely by professional European soldiers. Beginning in 1862, members of the Greater Prussian General Staff, as well as representatives from Great Britain and France, visited Union and Confederate field commands. The views of these men were remarkably alike—and uniformly unkind. They were appalled by what appeared to be a singular lack of field discipline on both sides. Colonel G. F. R. Henderson, eminent nineteenth century British military thinker and writer, noted in his biography of Stonewall Jackson,

> Neither was the fire of the Confederate infantry under the complete control of their officers, nor were their movements always characterized by order and regularity. It was seldom that men could be induced to refrain from answering shot for shot; there was an extraordinary waste of ammunition, there was much unnecessary noise, and the regiments were very apt to get out of hand.[1]

Observers noted that the Americans would rarely close with the enemy but chose instead to fight at ranges of a quarter mile or more and throw enormous quantities of lead at each other, often for hours without end. What these observers witnessed first hand has become immutably associated with the American way of war—the willingness of Americans to expend firepower freely to conserve human life.

Americans have routinely emphasized the value of firepower in their military method for a number of reasons, some of them based on a continuing military practice that began in the Civil War, others, more complex, arising from the essence of American national character. America's preoccupation with preserving the lives of its soldiers is deeply rooted in its liberal democracy. Jefferson's elevation of *life* as one of the inalienable rights of an individual underscored the obligation felt by American political philosophers in the new republic to provide for the protection of its citizenry. The inherent value of human life has become a political and moral imperative carried down and amplified through generations and passed into the ethic of American military men.

General Eisenhower, in his conversations with Marshal Zhukov, was struck by the different value that Soviet and American leaders placed on their soldiers' lives. In one instance, Zhukov explained that minefields were best cleared by marching soldiers through them, reasoning that a few losses to mines were acceptable to maintain the momentum of the attack. Eisenhower noted in his memoirs that such methods, regardless of their tactical utility, had no place in the armies under his command. "Americans assess the cost of war in terms of human lives," he wrote, "the Russians in the overall drain on the nation."[2] Throughout American history, from Antietam to Hamburger Hill, a victory won with too many lives was not considered a victory at all.

The proclivity to conserve lives in combat has been made all the more difficult by a parallel distinction of the American military tradition—the distrust of large, standing armies. Reliance on the citizen soldier to fight its wars has customarily given America a strong militia—but a less strong military. It has meant that American armies have had to learn to fight by fighting. Firepower lessened the price of this education. Americans learned as early as the Civil War that firepower steeled and coalesced unsteady troops and lessened the harm done by an enemy far out of proportion to its killing effect.

S. L. A. Marshall, in his pioneering studies on the personal qualities that made Americans fight, noted, ''Artillery fire which is promptly delivered is like a shot in the arm. It moves the man mentally and sometimes bodily, thereby breaking the concentration of fear.''[3]

In its major wars, the United States has been willing (and rich enough) to compensate in materiel wealth for what it lacked in preparedness for war. Once mobilized, America's war industry in the 20th century overwhelmed its enemies with weaponry. The challenge for strategists and field commanders was how to translate quickly the huge quantity of war materiel into the most destructive machines of war. Artillery and aircraft have been best suited for this purpose; bombing and shelling from great distances have proven to be the most efficient and cost effective means of delivering explosive power while avoiding direct, bloody contact with the enemy.

The appearance of an effective long-range muzzle-loading rifle in the mid-19th century led to the beginning of modern field artillery. In previous centuries, cannons were simply trotted in front of converging lines of infantry, pushed to a range of approximately 300 yards, and fired point blank into ranks of enemy infantry. This ''assault artillery'' was relatively safe in such maneuvers because the muskets of the opposing infantry were accurate only to about 50 yards. But a Civil War muzzle-loading rifle in the hands of a marksman could hit an area target such as a gun crew at 1,000 yards. Outranged by the rifle, artillery of the attacking force was pushed back beyond effective range. Without protective artillery, infantry were faced with charging across a half-mile of bullet-swept terrain against an entrenched, unshaken enemy. Technology thus favored the defense, and in the American Civil War and the Franco-Prussian War four years later, the cost of the attack quickly became prohibitive.[4]

The Prussians, although victorious, suffered terribly from French rifle fire.[5] They sought immediately to improve their artillery as a means of reducing the destructiveness of defensive firepower. Their solution was to adapt conventional siege artillery techniques to light field guns supporting the infantry. To protect itself from the fire of a besieged fortress, artillery of

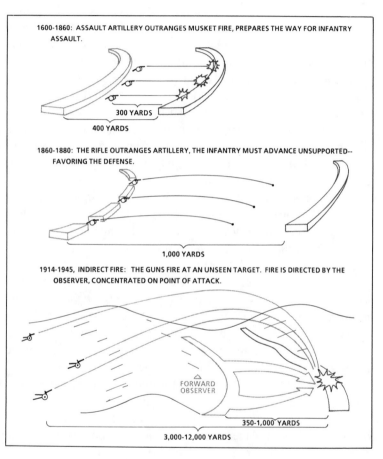

1600-1860: ASSAULT ARTILLERY OUTRANGES MUSKET FIRE, PREPARES THE WAY FOR INFANTRY ASSAULT.

300 YARDS

400 YARDS

1860-1880: THE RIFLE OUTRANGES ARTILLERY, THE INFANTRY MUST ADVANCE UNSUPPORTED-- FAVORING THE DEFENSE.

1,000 YARDS

1914-1945, INDIRECT FIRE: THE GUNS FIRE AT AN UNSEEN TARGET. FIRE IS DIRECTED BY THE OBSERVER, CONCENTRATED ON POINT OF ATTACK.

FORWARD OBSERVER

350-1,000 YARDS

3,000-12,000 YARDS

Evolution of indirect fire, 1600–1918

the siege train developed the means to fire from behind cover. Siege guns fired in a high-arcing trajectory that permitted the shells to clear protective cover and plunge down into a fortress. Since the gunners could not see the target, they aimed indirectly, by measuring bearing and distance to the target from a map and then calculating the azimuth of aim using a compass and the proper elevation necessary to raise the tube so that the projectile would reach the target. An observer placed on a flank spotted the fall of the shells; he used flags to telegraph corrections back to the guns.

Indirect fire remained with the siege train until late in the 19th century because firing was slow and imprecise, and because siege guns were too heavy and immobile to accompany a field army.[6] But the Germans recognized that new technologies could overcome many of these problems. The development of wrapped steel gun tubes and efficient breech loading lightened artillery to the degree that siege-caliber guns could be taken to the field. Gun cotton, or nitrocellulose, replaced black powder propellants for artillery in the 1880s. Nitro burned more slowly and lessened recoil shock. Less recoil made possible the development of a pneumatic device to halt the rearward movement of a gun and to return the tube to the same spot after each round was fired. This change permitted guns fired indirectly to be aimed with greater precision.[7] Because gun cotton was smokeless, artillery hidden behind a hill no longer gave away its position when it fired.

Other technologies applied to artillery at the turn of the century permitted "fire support artillery" to be as flexible and mobile as assault artillery had once been: modern instruments made indirect aiming an exact science; improvements in topography made possible shooting from map measurements with enough precision to hit unseen targets; the field telephone freed the artillery observer from the guns, allowing him to move forward with the infantry and adjust fire from the front; and the introduction of trinitrotoluene (or TNT) and improved metal fuzes made artillery shells tremendously more lethal and reliable.[8] By 1914 all of the elements of fire support artillery had been developed; they have remained essentially unchanged to the present.

In the process of this transformation, the nature of artillery combat was fundamentally altered. The direct-fire muzzle-loader was replaced by the field gun and howitzer, capable of accurate curved fire, which with their precise machinery and optical devices became more instruments than weapons of war. The general adoption of this instrument by all modern armies after the turn of the century symbolized acceptance of the reality that science and industry had replaced the ubiquitous, dashing gunner of Napoleon's day with a sophisticated yet sinister technician.

The American Army remained until the end of the 19th century a coastal and frontier garrison force. Modernization came slowly, particularly in the technical branches. By the time World War I began, American artillery consisted of an amalgam of various obsolete types. Safe behind its protective seas, the artillery arm was content to watch that conflict unfold and follow the tragic course of ruinous war with curiosity and growing concern.

America entered the Great War after three years of destructive trench warfare had caused enormous suffering among European armies. The small-bore rifle and machinegun continued to make the defense predominant. The tactical problem faced by military leaders of the untried American Army was how to restore tactical mobility to the battlefield without suffering the same fate as the Europeans.

By reputation the most innovative of senior American tacticians was a gunner officer, Major General Charles P. Summerall. He believed that the deadlock could be broken by perfecting cooperation and communication between artillery and the infantry. Attacks faltered when the infantry went "over the top" and immediately lost contact with the guns. Infantrymen had no way to shift or concentrate firepower on unexpected areas of resistance, or to stop and start a preplanned barrage to keep pace with the momentum of the attack. Summerall also observed that even when attacks were successful, a fatal pause occurred as the guns attempted to move forward across a shell-scarred no-man's-land to stay within range of the infantry. All too often, the enemy chose this vulnerable moment to counterattack and restore the defensive line.[9]

To improve communications, Summerall greatly increased the number of telephones and pyrotechnic devices in use. He streamlined the system of signaling between the guns and the infantry. With these improvements, American artillery soon gained a reputation for its ability to be shifted and concentrated to support the attack. Not satisfied, Summerall experimented with means of pushing light divisional guns forward with the infantry to ensure continuous fire support. All of his measures were effective to a degree, but, without field radios and motor transport, artillery firepower was unable to achieve the mobility necessary for a decisive breakthrough on the Western Front.[10]

From his appointment as Chief of Staff in 1926 until his retirement in 1930, Summerall continued to apply emerging technology to the problem of the infantry-artillery team. His efforts were carried forward by Lieutenant General Lesley McNair, Chief of Army Ground Forces, who was responsible for developing equipment, organization, and doctrine for the Army in the Second World War. Together the two men created an American artillery arm second to none.[11]

Because of the emphasis by Summerall and McNair on the artillery-infantry team, the American approach to mobile warfare was fundamentally different from that of most other Western armies in World War II. The German system of blitzkrieg melded together infantry, armor, and tactical airpower into a flexible, mobile arm. Aircraft, principally in the form of light and medium dive bombers, replaced artillery as the source of heavy indirect firepower. In effect, the German Air Force was exclusively a tactical arm and was designed for support of ground forces.[12] Tanks provided lower-level punch and shock effect. These three elements were linked together with a superb system of radio communications. But German artillery was too slow, and its doctrinal employment too inflexible, to provide mobile forces with firepower necessary to achieve the decisive breakthrough.[13]

The United States, on the other hand, relied on artillery to provide breakthrough firepower. Unlike German artillery, which was predominantly horse drawn, American guns were motorized, either towed behind trucks or mounted on modified tank chassis.[14] The American fire support communications network contained several times as many radio sets as the German, allowing a forward observer with an infantry company to maintain constant contact with the guns to his rear. Fire commands from observers were received by fire direction centers, or FDCs, located with gun batteries. FDCs used map grids, firing tables, and instruments to compute the aiming data necessary to hit an unseen target. An officer in each FDC had the communications necessary to bring all guns from division through corps to bear on a single target.

The science of fire direction had particular appeal to the technical proclivities of American soldiers, and it was the equipment and extensive training of FDCs that gave American artillery unsurpassed flexibility, speed, and accuracy.[15] The quality of artillery materiel was updated and improved. The 75-mm divisional gun of World War I was replaced with a more powerful 105-mm howitzer. Also, heavier models (including the 155-mm howitzer, 155-mm "Long Tom" gun, and 8-inch howitzer) were developed or modernized in time to be deployed in large numbers.[16]

The American style of blitzkrieg began by concentrating the fires from guns scattered throughout the front on a narrow point of attack to demoralize the enemy and punch a hole in his defenses for the infantry and armor to exploit. Mobile guns kept up with the exploitation force and ensured that continuous firepower was available to destroy pockets of resistance that might slow the advance.

Comments of friend and foe alike proved the wisdom of the American style of blitzkrieg. German field commanders were not much impressed with the quality and effectiveness of American armored forces, but they uniformly expressed a grudging respect for American artillery and tactical airpower during the last eight months of the war.[17] General Marshall wrote,

> We believe that our use of massed heavy artillery fire was far more effective than the German techniques and clearly outclassed the Japanese. Though our heavy artillery from the 105 mm up was generally matched by the Germans, our method of employment of these weapons had been one of the decisive factors of our ground campaigns throughout the world.[18]

The breakthrough firepower of the infantry-artillery team was considerably enhanced late in the war when the practical exigencies of combat had overcome many prewar doctrinal prejudices against the use of airpower in support of ground troops. The doctrinal dispute began with the trial of General Billy Mitchell and continued through the interwar years as Air Corps officers sought to create a separate air force capable of action independent of other services. On the other side of the controversy were the ground force proponents who sought to keep the air arm clearly subordinate to the Army commander for all airpower functions except strategic bombardment. During the early years of World War II, the conflict became personalized between General H. H. Arnold, Chief of the Army Air Forces, and General McNair. Because McNair openly opposed an independent air force, Arnold perceived McNair's efforts to create an efficient mechanism for Army Air Force support of ground forces as an overt attempt to undermine the capability of the Air Corps to wage a decisive strategic air campaign.[19]

The doctrinal struggle between these two factions effectively halted progress toward a system of close air support until the opening campaign in North Africa when the Luftwaffe provided a painful lesson on how it was to be done. At the battle of Kasserine Pass, American units were badly mauled by an air-armor team perfected by the Germans in Poland, France, and North Africa. Stuka dive bombers, designed specifically for ground support, continually bombed and strafed American defensive positions.[20] There was little evidence of Allied airpower. Major General Omar Bradley lamented the poor state of air support:

> We can't get the stuff when it's needed and we're catching hell for it. By the time our request for air support goes through channels the target's gone or the Stukas [German dive bombers] have come instead.[21]

After the disastrous opening campaign in the Northern Desert, a British air officer, Air Marshal Sir Arthur Coningham, instituted a system of control of Allied tactical airpower by grafting to the out-of-date American doctrine a system established and proven by the British Eighth Army in North Africa.

Coningham preached that communications was the key to successful air-ground operations. He insisted that air and ground field headquarters be located together and demanded that effective liaison be established between them from Army Group down to division.[22] Following the British example, the ground forces devised various signals using colored smoke and panels to identify friendly units from the air. Similarly, the Air Corps put more easily recognized markings on its planes in early 1943 to lessen the frequency of aircraft receiving fire from friendly units.[23]

Another procedure borrowed from the British during the Sicilian campaign was the use of a forward air controller, or "Rover Joe," normally an Air Corps officer in a jeep equipped with an aircraft radio. At Troina in Sicily, the air commander himself went into the battle area to direct his planes to the target. A year later in Italy, the Fifth Army and the XII Air Support Command placed air controllers in Army light observation aircraft to lead fighters to targets in the path of advancing troops.[24] The most significant technique developed in the Mediterranean theater was a streamlined system of air requests. Prewar doctrine required that a request for air support be passed by radio and approved at each level of command—a procedure that often took a full day. Through the use of radio nets, and by circumventing intermediate headquarters, the request time was reduced to hours.[25]

The American system of air-ground cooperation came into its own during the Normandy campaign in 1944. In part, effective use of air-delivered firepower was made necessary by the shortages of artillery ammunition that occurred when storms swept away beachhead resupply facilities shortly after the invasion. The previous Air Corps concept that fighter aircraft should not be used against targets within range of artillery was forgotten momentarily. The result was extraordinary. Ninth Air Force fighter-bombers concentrated on key points of resistance within very close range of friendly troops. Soldiers in contact discovered that these attacks were more effective at destroying close-in targets than heavy artillery normally used for this purpose. Pilots of fighter-bombers armed with 500-pound general purpose or 260-pound fragmentation bombs quickly became adept at attacking enemy-held foxholes, pillboxes, and hedgerows, sometimes within 300 to 500 yards of forward American elements.[26] Ground commanders favored an air preparation over artillery if they could be sure that the aircraft would be on time and if the infantry could exploit the psychological shock effect of bombardment with a follow-up attack.[27]

Cooperation between air and ground forces increased as both combat elements became more familiar with each other. Although AAF doctrine dictated that the two should remain separate, tactical air and ground forces in fact drew closer together as the war continued—and as the exigencies of combat dictated that both operate in harmony to save lives. Artillery units developed counterflak programs to suppress deadly ground fire while fighter-bombers attacked. After the breakout at St. Lo, aircraft VHF radios were installed in lead tanks of armored columns to permit ground elements to communicate directly with fighter-bombers circling overhead. Four to twelve aircraft became "flying commandos" that ran interference by destroying opposition in front of columns. Flights operated on a rotational basis to assure continuous cover.[28] During the breakout, this system was responsible for destroying more that 2,000 vehicles and tanks in a single week. After the sweep across France, the commander of a leading armored division commented, "The best tank destroyer we have is a P–47."[29]

Operations in the field far exceeded the theoretical limits imposed on close support aviation by strategists and doctrine makers in the War Department. Army Air Force manual FM 100–20, *Command and Employment of Airpower*, placed air-ground support last in priority behind the air superiority (or air-to-air) mission and interdiction (the attack of enemy troops behind the battle area). The Air Staff feared that too great a reliance on the ground support mission might jeopardize movement toward total separation of the ground and air services.[30] Opposition from the top took many forms: resistance early in the war to joint training between combat units of both services; Air Corps opposition to ground force efforts to introduce the light liaison planes flown by Army pilots (which later proved

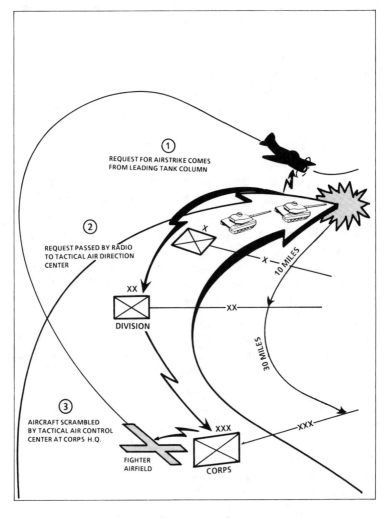

Tactical air control system,
Normandy Campaign, July–September 1944

successful as platforms for forward air controllers); and introduction by the AAF of VHF aircraft radios unable to net with any ground radios, which ultimatly delayed effective air-ground communication until June 1944.[31]

But in spite of opposition from the top, practical soldiers in the field did what was necessary to make close air support effective. General Bradley's disparagement early in the war turned to praise after the Normandy campaign. He found that even though close support was third in priority, it accounted for a third of all fighter missions flown by General Quesada's Ninth Air Force.[32] More than one in five medium bomber missions were flown in close support. General Quesada stressed the particular pride that skilled fighter-bomber pilots had in their ability to attack enemy ground forces threatening friendlies. "Close-in air-ground cooperation is the difficult thing, the vital thing," he noted, "the other stuff is easy."[33]

With the doctrinal disputes resolved by practical experience, the Air Force sought after the war to derive a usable tactical method from the many ad hoc systems used during the war. Both the AAF and the Army were pleased enough with the European system to adopt it unchanged as FM 31–35 in August 1946. Flexibility and responsiveness in the new system were guaranteed by the presence of a "shadow" Air Corps element at each level of Army field command down to regiment. Taking a page from the Luftwaffe, Air Force forward air controllers, usually fighter pilots themselves, were to be collocated with forward regiments and were provided with VHF radios similar to those carried in "convoy cover" tanks during the Normandy campaign.[34]

The early battles of the Korean War were fought using the ground and air firepower doctrine perfected in the European theater during World War II. In later campaigns in Korea, however, the distinct nature of the war again caused practical men in the field to modify these methods to suit the unique demands of a limited war fought in inhospitable terrain against an Oriental enemy. Air Force doctrine was dramatically affected. During World War II, US strategic bombing severely crippled German and Japanese industry. But the North Koreans were careful to shield most of their vital strategic targets across the Yalu in

Manchuria. The interdiction campaign in Korea made resupply more hazardous and laborious for the enemy, yet never effectively destroyed his ability to fight. The North Koreans and Chinese, much like the Viet Minh, moved enormous quantities of materiel at night, often using a transportation network no more sophisticated than the backs of their soldiers. For the first time in the history of modern warfare, an enemy force was able to conduct major ground campaigns successfully while never for a moment achieving air superiority.[35]

Two very difficult, related problems faced both air and ground fire support planners in Korea. The first was the need to achieve limited military objectives on the ground at the least cost in lives; the second was to achieve these objectives against a skilled, determined enemy who possessed unlimited human resources and unbounded political resolve. As the war dragged on and began to take the form of a World War I–style stalemate, it became increasingly difficult to maintain cohesion among combat soldiers in the field as well as popular support at home. Faced with these realities, General James Van Fleet, the Eighth Army Commander in Korea, gradually changed his method of operation so that the primary task of engaging the enemy fell upon artillery and airpower. A new term, "The Van Fleet Load," appeared in the media to describe huge tonnages of munitions expended by the United Nations Command to compensate for the enemy's superiority in manpower and to hold down its own losses.[36]

Firepower was relatively ineffective when the enemy dug himself into caves and bunkers, but when he chose to attack, the destructiveness of airpower and artillery was overwhelming. During the Chinese attack on the so-called No-Name Line in May 1951, American infantry dug themselves into bunkers with overhead cover and called in tons of artillery on top of their positions to annihilate the attacking enemy. In one infantry battalion, the troops huddled in their positions while 2,000 shells were fired in less than eight minutes. A single artillery battalion fired 10,000 rounds of airburst artillery in six hours.[37] General Edward Almond, who commanded the corps that bore the brunt of this attack, recalled instances when entire battalions were saved from annihilation by firepower alone. He spoke of "time on target'' concentrations in which as many as 14 battalions fired more that 2,500 rounds of differing calibers timed to land on a single point within two minutes.

In one case an infantry battalion was extracted using a "box barrage." With the battalion under "heavy pressure from three sides and with a road block to its rear, an artillery barrage was placed around the unit. At an opportune time, the curtain of fire in the rear of the unit was lifted and the friendly force fought a withdrawing action in that direction protected still by artillery fire on the other three sides.''[38] In desperate battles like these, allied ground commanders could never get enough fire-power. General Almond turned tanks into artillery by constructing ramps or using embankments to emplace the tanks on an elevated slope so that their direct-fire cannon could be fired over the high Korean mountains using indirect artillery gunnery techniques.[39]

Not unexpectedly, field commanders in Korea continually badgered the Air Force to commit more of its resources to the tactical battle. General Almond conceded the usefulness of interdiction during routine ground operations, but he argued that once the enemy concentrated forces near the front, the preponderance of bombing effort must be shifted to close support missions.[40] Under pressure from Army commanders and the Army Chief of Staff, the Air Force shifted its effort from rail and bridge interdiction to the direct support of ground troops. During the battle of the Soryong River, aircraft flew continuous close support missions. The Air Force supported Almond's corps with radar-guided blind bombing strikes at night close to friendlies. The Air Force flew over 4,500 sorties to beat back Chinese attacks on UN defenses in October 1952. Large numbers of aircraft overhead punishing the enemy across the front served to raise troop morale and reduce casualties.[41]

Problems remained. Most ground commanders desired to extend forward air controllers, or FACs, one level lower, from regiment down to infantry battalion. The Air Force resisted this initiative throughout the war (although FACs would be part of each forward battalion in Vietnam). Delivery accuracy remained poor, principally because the Air Force came to Korea inexperienced in the art of close support.[42] Jet pilots in particular had problems because their aircraft flew too fast to find the target and keep it in sight while making a bombing run. The Air Force solved this problem to some extent by placing tactical air controllers in propeller-driven trainer aircraft to direct jet aircraft to the target. Early in the war, many forward air controllers gave up their vulnerable jeeps for artillery liaison light aircraft from the Army, and equipped them with VHF radios to talk to fighters.[43] This change qreatly improved close-in target identification and reduced the incidence of fighter-bombers attacking friendly positions.[44] In spite of the best efforts of both Army and Air Force staffs to decrease response times, close support missions took too long to execute. The average response time was one hour, with a quarter-hour taken by the battalion or regiment to pass the request to the Joint Operations Center at Eighth Army.[45]

The poor responsiveness of close air support and the inability of the Air Force to integrate its fires with those of other fire support means remained a problem until the end of the war. A succession of senior Army generals wanted to solve the problem by copying the Marines' practice of assigning an air squadron to each corps. The Army insisted that this was the only way to achieve complete integration of air and ground fires.[46] In previous wars when airpower was considered ''nice to have,'' it was acceptable for it to be outside the direct control of the ground commander. But now Almond, Van Fleet, General Mark Clark, and others argued that close air support was a necessary ingredient for the success of the ground battle, and they could not assure success without some control of fighter-bomber aircraft.[47] The Air Force resisted this move successfully, but they did make some tactical concessions to improve responsiveness and fire support coordination.

The UN Command experimented late in the war with set-piece attacks in which artillery and air fires were delivered simultaneously or, in some cases, sequentially with no delay between them. For the most part, the experiments failed because the maneuver commander lacked the communications and control to apply both means in unison.[48] To some degree, ground commanders in 1953 faced the same tactical problem that Summerall faced in 1918—how to create a flexible, reliable system of firepower delivery effective and destructive enough to restore mobility on the ground.

The frustration of static warfare in Korea caused a few professional military men to question the soundness of the traditional American assumption that firepower would prove the decisive element in future battles. They argued that in past wars Americans possessed the potential for maneuver as complete as any opponent, yet the suspicion grew that a fixation on firepower never permitted the full potential of maneuver warfare to be realized. Another concern was the growing American distaste for expending huge volumes of firepower without proper regard for accuracy or the appropriateness of munitions to the target. The Korean War provided many disturbing examples in which thousands of artillery rounds were fired at hardened targets without effect when a single, accurate, direct-fire weapon might have done the job.[49]

In spite of these problems, a generation of military men came to rely on firepower alone for tactical success on the battlefield. The role of the infantry in the Korean War increasingly became that of a "finding and fixing force." The infantry held a thin defensive perimeter and patrolled aggressively to ensure that an enemy attack was detected in time to destroy it with artillery and airpower. Large-scale operations such as the battle for the No-Name Line became carefully orchestrated battles of attrition, the objective of which was to slaughter thousands using hundreds of thousands of bombs and shells with the least loss to the American side. Imperfect as it may seem today, the firepower system developed during the Korean War became accepted by Western armies as the proper tactical mechanism for dealing with an intractable Oriental foe.

The Korean War demonstrated to the US Army the potential value of vertical envelopment. Veterans recalled the endless toil and bloodshed necessary to assault and seize steep mountain peaks. Those with foresight recognized that many lives could have been saved by using helicopters to transport and support soldiers fighting in mountainous terrain. The decade between the American involvement in two Asian wars witnessed a growing effort by the Army to pioneer development of an entire family of vertical-lift aircraft. By 1960 the Army was committed to the modernization of its aviation fleet to include an all-turbine-engined family of medium- and heavy-lift helicopters and fixed-wing aircraft. Within two years, the ubiquitous UH–1 "Huey" appeared in the first of its many variations and testing was well underway on the Boeing Vertol HC–1B "Chinook" cargo-carrying helicopter.

Overshadowed by these major developments was a lesser effort begun at Fort Rucker, Alabama, as early as 1956 to arm Army aircraft. Crude machinegun mounts and rocket-firing devices were attached to an unlikely assortment of light and medium aircraft. The Air Force viewed these colorful early efforts with increasing discomfort. Discomfort turned to alarm during the early 1960s when the Army began a program to arm its fixed-wing Mohawk aircraft with bomb racks and machineguns. The Mohawk was not a helicopter and its performance, particularly its speed and carrying capacity, placed it in a league with light fighter aircraft. The Air Force perceived the armed Mohawk as a threat to its monopoly on the close air support mission and responded with a concerted effort in Washington to keep the Army out of the business of aerial fire support.

In the ensuing interservice debate, the Army argued that the Korean War demonstrated clearly that neither artillery nor Air Force systems could provide the surgical precision and direct observation necessary to engage a fleeting or entrenched enemy. The Army also argued the value of using troop-carrying helicopters to conduct combat assaults from the air and contended that the armed helicopter was the only fire support platform compatible with helicopter-borne or "airmobile" infantry formations. The Air Force responded that the Army's requirements for aerial fire support could be met with the current family of multi-role fighter aircraft.[50]

The debate might have continued fruitlessly for decades had practical experience in Vietnam not supported the Army's case for armed helicopters and the airmobile concept. Beginning in 1962, the unreliable and ungainly H–21 "Flying Bananas" began ferrying Vietnamese troops into combat. Later in that same year, armed Hueys began escorting the vulnerable transports into landing zones. The Air Force insisted that the Huey gunships be used only for "defensive" purposes. They could only engage when the H–21 transports were fired upon and could not wander off on their own to engage ground targets.[51] In spite of these restrictions, the Hueys proved their worth by markedly reducing the loss rate of escorted transports from ground fire. Thanks to the war, the gunship was here to stay.[52]

While early wartime experience kept the airmobility concept alive, the Army began a remarkable program at home to develop modern equipment and doctrine for helicopter-borne fighting units. Not since the German effort to perfect its style of blitzkrieg in the 1930s had an Army so focussed itself on creating an entirely new dimension in land warfare. From a historical perspective, similarities between the efforts of the two armies are striking indeed. After a decade of preliminary work, the Army created its first full-scale experimental airmobile unit, the 11th Air Assault Division, in 1964, commanded by Brigadier General Harry W. O. Kinnard. It was a conventional light division, in size and structure similar to other light divisions, except for its 434 aircraft, four times the normal division complement. The Hueys of two light helicopter battalions provided the lift to carry infantry. Firepower was provided by three conventional light artillery battalions that could be lifted by Chinooks and an aerial artillery battalion consisting of rocket-firing Hueys.[53]

General Kinnard built and employed his division in a manner as unconventional as its birth. Terrain-bound doctrine was ignored; bureaucracy was transcended. New ideas arrived continuously in the kitbags of pilots and staff officers returning from Vietnam. These ideas were evaluated and grafted to existing practices. By the fall of 1964, the 11th Air Assault Division was ready to be tested, and for two months it exercised continuously throughout the Carolinas under the close scrutiny of almost 2,000 tactical and technical evaluators.[54]

Parallels between German and American experiments with new concepts of war were also evident in the frustrations and obstacles that inhibited the progress of both. More traditional Army officers, although acknowledging the utility of vertical assault in Vietnam, doubted the helicopter's survivability in conventional war. Other services, particularly the Air Force, argued that a conventional Army division could be just as effective as the 11th if augmented by Air Force C–130 transports and dedicated fighter and reconnaissance aircraft.

In spite of these obstacles, the Carolina exercises justified years of work by the Army and vindicated General Kinnard's style of aerial warfare. However, it took the increasingly serious military situation in Vietnam to keep the 11th Air Assault Division alive. Fortuitously, although the division was tested in a conventional war environment, it happened to be particularly well suited to war in Southeast Asia. On 1 July 1965, the new division became part of the Army's permanent force and was redesignated the 1st Cavalry Division (Airmobile). General Kinnard remained in command. Two months after its activation, the division arrived in Vietnam.

Seldom has an American military unit been thrown so precipitously into combat; never has one experienced such an abrupt change in climate or terrain. Waiting to do battle with the 1st Cavalry was an enemy inured to combat in Southeast Asia and confident in the knowledge that they had defeated a first-rate Western army on the same ground just a decade before.

2
The First Indochina War

Colonel Charles Piroth, the commander of artillery at Dien Bien Phu, had fought his way through North Africa, Italy, France, and Germany as an artillery commander in World War II. In Italy he lost an arm to a German mine, and his martial image and authority were enhanced by the sight of an empty sleeve tucked into his belt. He complained often to his officers that he spent far too much time shepherding a seemingly endless procession of dignitaries about the camp. To many visitors, the French position seemed vulnerable; the firepower available for its defense, inadequate. Piroth however, was adept at assuaging the fears of French officials. He was certain that the few guns scattered about several strong points would be adequate to repel any attack by the Viet Minh. Firepower had proven the decisive factor in the defense of similar French positions in the past. Only the previous August at Na-San, an entrenched camp similar to Dien Bien Phu, French guns and bombers had broken the back of the Viet Minh ground assault and slaughtered thousands.

When the camp commander, General de Castries, cautiously suggested that 30 medium and heavy guns seemed rather a small complement of firepower, Piroth replied that the Viet Minh would not be able to drag more than a few light pieces through the jungle to oppose him. Supplying them over mountainous terrain bereft of roads or trail networks would be difficult, if not impossible. The hills surrounding the camp were too high for shells to be fired over them accurately, he insisted, and no enemy would be foolish enough to place guns on the exposed forward slopes of these hills and risk detection and destruction by air strikes and direct fire from Dien Bien Phu. He pointed out that the number of guns alone was not the sole measure of French firepower. Twenty thousand rounds of artillery airlifted into Dien Bien Phu at great effort would be more than enough to crush any attack before it formed. De Castries respected his gunner's advice and consoled himself with the belief that the airpower retained under his command would more than compensate for any shortage of artillery.

The French Union Forces occupied Dien Bien Phu for four months without serious threat. Piroth's confidence seemed justified. But beginning in March 1954, the French suddenly found themselves besieged by a force far larger and more powerful than anyone in the high command had previously thought possible. Piroth came to realize that the enemy had miraculously ringed the camp with enough firepower to destroy it, and after three days of merciless bombardment and ground attack, he knew that the garrison was doomed. Instead of crushing enemy guns, Piroth was unable to find them. Neither counterbattery fire nor sorties by bombers and fighters could silence a methodical bombardment by 200 guns and mortars firing over 2,000 rounds each day.

The communists quickly silenced the French guns inside the largest artillery position. Field guns positioned by Piroth at outlying strong points were beyond effective range of each other, thus incapable of taking up the fires of the silenced guns in the main artillery position. As he witnessed the destruction of his guns one by one, Piroth became increasingly depressed. He apologized to his commander and to some of the troops who were obliged to endure terrible shelling in poorly prepared, densely packed trenches and dugouts. "I am completely dishonored," Piroth said as he turned to leave the command bunker. "I have guaranteed that the enemy artillery couldn't touch us—but now we will lose the battle. I'm leaving." He retired to his own bunker. With only one arm, he was unable to cock his service pistol, so he found a grenade, pulled the pin with his teeth and held the grenade to his chest. His suicide presaged the sacrifice of the French garrison.[1]

When viewed again after thirty years, the tragic course of the siege at Dien Bien Phu unfolds like a microcosm of the greater Indochina War. During eight years of conflict, the Viet Minh experienced tactical defeat and often suffered terribly when forced to face the killing destructiveness of French firepower. But the Viet Minh accepted their losses and learned from their tactical mistakes. Methodically, over time, they succeeded in dominating all of Indochina except for a shrinking French "safe area" restricted to Hanoi and its immediate environs. The French Union Forces fought back with occasional motorized and airborne forays from their protected regions, only to grow weaker with each thrust as the Viet Minh grew stronger. Looking back, one cannot help being struck by the futility of the French military effort in Indochina. The Viet Minh in fact held most of the strategic and tactical cards.

Immediately after the Second World War, the Viet Minh enjoyed a ten-month respite from French colonial rule. During this time, the Viet Minh established a republic and began the process of building an army of resistance unimpeded by outside interference. Even after the return of French military authority, Viet Minh forces continued to grow in regions of Vietnam sympathetic to the insurgency. They were aided in great measure by the Communist Chinese, who provided arms, advisors, and sanctuary across the international border. After 1949, Chinese assistance became a flood that the French were unable to stem. Modern arms including anti-aircraft guns, machineguns, recoilless rifles, artillery, and vehicles made the Viet Minh increasingly capable of standing up to major French mechanized formations on equal terms.[2]

Mao Tse-Tung wrote of the peasantry as a friendly sea in which the insurgents, like fish, are protected and nourished. As the war progressed, the Viet Minh gained increasing allegiance from the Vietnamese people, particularly in northern Vietnam (or Tonkin). The local population, for example, provided the

Viet Minh high command with exact details of French movements and intentions. As long as the French Army remained
roadbound or relied on massive support bases and airfields to
launch airborne assaults, they were never completely able to
surprise the enemy. The Viet Minh owned the night and,
increasingly, the countryside. They were able to elude the
French and could at will close secretly around their objectives
and strike the French without warning. Finally, and perhaps in
the long run most importantly, the Viet Minh cause had about it
the certainty, indeed the inevitability, of history. France was the
last of the European imperial powers to resist the loss of its
colonies by force. The image of a European giant attempting to
crush a movement for independence gave the Viet Minh a moral
advantage in the world that made continuance of the war
increasingly unpopular in France and made full support by
allies, particularly the United States, less and less certain.

From the beginning, the French Army in Indochina realized that its mastery of and ability to conduct European-style
machine warfare was its greatest, and perhaps only, military
advantage. To the end, they believed that the enemy could be
crushed and Indochina subdued by concentrated firepower.
Experience early in the conflict also taught the French that artillery and airpower had little effect against an elusive enemy who
avoided a fight. What the French sought was a large-scale battle
of attrition—a showdown, if you will, which would grind the
Viet Minh to dust under a final massive avalanche of bomb and
shell.

This strategy had two telling flaws. First, the French soon
became frustrated by their inability to find and fix an enemy in
an inhospitable environment. The Viet Minh maintained the initiative throughout the war, choosing when and where to fight.
Fruitless searches, cordons, and mechanized forays into the hinterland usually resulted in either nothing or, all too often toward
the end of the conflict, terrible losses to the French in large-
scale ambushes and attacks on isolated perimeter forts. The
French in desperation changed their strategy to one that sought
to lure the enemy into attacks against exposed but heavily
defended positions with the hope of destroying them in a defensive battle of attrition. Successful at first, the French Army

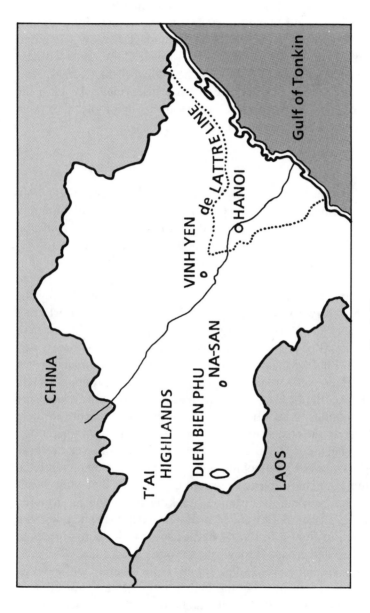

North Vietnam

chose defensive killing grounds farther and farther from their base of support. Their final choice was Dien Bien Phu.

The second French mistake was the assumption that they alone possessed the ability to apply massive firepower in a battle of attrition. Thanks primarily to their Communist Chinese allies and the respite gained by the ending of the Korean War, the Viet Minh soon became adept artillerymen. By 1953 the French had lost the contest for firepower superiority; they were out-gunned five-to-one at Dien Bien Phu.

Outpost Artillery Versus the Guerrilla

The first phase of combat action in Indochina lasted from 1946 until the beginning of the Communist Chinese involvement in 1950. This period witnessed mutual force escalation and increasingly greater losses on both sides. The French forces, hampered by budgetary constraints and the growing unpopularity of the war at home, sought simultaneously to secure the territories surrounding Hanoi and to locate and destroy the enemy in two key base areas hidden in the forest north and northeast of Hanoi. General Giap, the military commander of the Viet Minh, realized the importance of these base areas, particularly during the early phases of the guerrilla campaign when his forces were weak, untrained, and poorly equipped. Giap relied on the bases for unimpeded access to Chinese advisors and supplies. Viet Minh main force units could retire to them whenever threatened to rest and prepare for the next operation.[3]

The French challenged Viet Minh control over the base areas in 1947 by launching their first large-scale conventional offensive. Their objective was to capture the Viet Minh headquarters between an airborne blocking force and an armored column pushed northward from Hanoi. Giap was not yet strong enough to fight a full-scale battle, so he ordered his forces to disperse and escape through the porous French lines. The year-long operation yielded some supplies and several thousand Viet Minh dead, but by 1948 the French retired to the protection of the Red River Valley, leaving the base areas and the tactical initiative to the enemy.[4]

As he was building a conventional force, Giap maintained pressure on the French by infiltrating a steady stream of forces into the Delta lowlands surrounding Hanoi. His objective was to tie down French forces, destroy as many as possible, and create havoc in the colonial heartland by initiating numerous local attacks on isolated garrisons. To counter this tactic the French High Command sought to seal off the Delta from Viet Minh incursion. The French began a massive program to strengthen and expand their string of regional forts, outposts, and guard-houses inherited from the colonial period. They hoped that the defensive strength of these positions, and the protective fire-power available to them, would make the garrisons reasonably secure with as little manpower as possible. The forts were to be an economy-of-force measure to permit the creation of a mobile force capable of maneuvering the enemy into a decisive, large-scale battle of attrition. This task became a race against time. Fortresses had to be modernized to keep pace with the growing ability of the Viet Minh to destroy them with their increasing numbers and firepower.[5]

Most forts, particularly those in outlying areas, were ancient "Beau Geste" structures of little military value. The French hastily abandoned most of these and replaced them with rudimentary barbed wire entanglements and weapons emplaced in bunkers. Rarely would these crude posts, strung like beads along roads and canals, be manned by more than a platoon or two of Vietnamese Army troops led by a lone French officer and a few French NCOs. Several key villages would also have forts. Larger towns might be garrisoned by a mobile battalion or regional headquarters.[6]

To cover these widely spread garrisons, the High Command was forced to alter significantly many long-held tactical concepts about the employment of artillery. Since the days of Napoleon, the French had adhered to the doctrine that artillery could be decisive only when used in mass. Now artillery was intended to assist in the pacification and control of large areas. Consequently, it had to be scattered checkerboard fashion among widely separated garrisons throughout a region. An iso-lated post might have had only one or two guns at most. The smaller posts had to be content with a section of mortars. Guns so widely scattered were unable to provide destructive fire. For the most part, static artillery became merely an assurance of

French outpost artillery. To cover the greatest area, French batteries were often split into pairs of guns, stationed in isolated outposts.

French presence and had only limited psychological and harassing effect on the enemy.[7]

French artillerists quickly learned and practiced principles of employment that helped to enhance the effectiveness and lethality of position artillery. Isolated gun sections were emplaced and crews trained to fire in all directions, giving each fort a protective lethal area out to the firing limit of its guns.[8] Forts were constructed so that protective umbrellas of fire overlapped with other forts to ensure that each provided the other mutual support if attacked. In Tonkin, area commanders also had a number of "semi-mobile" sections of two guns and three trucks to provide some limited means of massing fires in an emergency.

Until the end of the war, position artillery remained the poor sister of the French Army in Indochina. In Tonkin alone, fixed guns accounted for over 400 weapons of mixed calibers, including US 105-mm and 155-mm howitzers and British 3.7- inch and 25-pounder guns. Artillery employed in static roles was not organized into traditional artillery batteries and battalions, however, but was collected in ad hoc groupings of 30 to 40 pieces under a small headquarters staff responsible for their administrative and logistical support.[9]

Such small forts often proved easy prey for a determined attack. After the Viet Minh began receiving mortars, artillery, and rocket launchers, only a very lucky or well-prepared outpost stood a chance of survival. Artillery was normally the only reinforcement the regional command could provide at night. The enemy assault invariably came just after dark. Once the attack was discovered, all of the surrounding garrisons within range would shift their guns toward the garrison under attack. Without detailed instructions, all guns would begin to concentrate fire on pre-selected targets just outside the perimeter wire of the threatened fort.[10] If the fort was near a large cantonment in Tonkin, local artillery fires might be augmented by a battery of 155-mm Long Tom guns, which could throw a 100-pound projectile 15 miles in any direction. Centers of resistance within the fort, built with concrete, offered the defenders a last-ditch chance to survive by withdrawing inside sturdy bunkers and calling for concentrated artillery air bursts over their position.[11]

If the garrison could hold out until daybreak, relief might arrive on the scene in the form of a mobile column or tactical air support. Too often, however, the small, isolated forts along lines of communication suffered overwhelming attack and were soon lost.[12] Bernard Fall, a sympathetic observer of the plight of the "area security forces," wrote,

> Perhaps the sector's operations officer would say, over the morning coffee, to one of his colleagues: "Did you hear about what happened to PK 141? Got clobbered last night. The Morane [aircraft] flew over it this morning and nothing stirred. Also looked a bit charred around the ports, the pilot said...." "Damn! This is the third bunker this month. There goes another 57 [recoilless rifles], two machine guns, ten grenades and the radio set. Hanoi is going to bitch like hell." And that was all the recognition PK 141 ever got.[13]

Why were the Viet Minh so often successful when attacking fortified places in the face of superior French artillery and airpower? Success came from a sense of cold pragmatism engendered by practical experience. Giap conceded to the French their firepower predominance and willingly spent lives, first to maintain his offensive and second to buy time in order to create a firepower arm powerful enough to challenge the French in open warfare. Giap, however, did instruct his "suicide commandos" to take precautions to lessen the effect of French firepower. Surprise and secrecy on the part of the attacker were essential.

The Viet Minh learned from experience that under no circumstances should a column be caught in the open by French aerial or ground observers. The Viet Minh travelled at night in small groups to lessen the probability of detection. They moved through areas firmly in their control and limited exposure outside of their protective base areas by planning attacks carefully and by moving to and from the objective with no delays. The Viet Minh learned from the Chinese the fine art of camouflage and practiced it so well that aircraft rarely identified troops marching directly under them.

If caught in the open by French firepower, the enemy would scatter and hide before the French were able to adjust in and mass artillery fires on their position.[14] Adjustment of fire was necessary because the first shots fired by the guns most often fell some distance from the target due to inaccuracies by the gunners in predicting the gun's trajectory and map location errors by the observer. The initial burst forewarned the enemy and a race against the clock began, immediately pitting the fleetness and cunning of the enemy against the technical skill and speed of the gunners. All too often the Viet Minh won. The French High Command commented,

> Neutralization was often jeopardized because certain artillerymen spent a relatively long time on adjusting prior to firing [a great many rounds] for [killing] effect. In the case of an enemy as elusive and as quick to disappear as the Viet Minh infantryman, the advantages of a careful adjustment of fire were often nullified because the target had the time to escape before he could be fired upon.[15]

The fleeting, elusive enemy and difficult terrain greatly reduced the killing power of artillery and airpower. Firing tables inherited from World War II understated the number of rounds necessary to kill or neutralize an Oriental force. The Viet Minh would stay and "hunker down" under a hail of fire that would have demoralized and scattered a European enemy.[16] The French general commanding the artillery in North Vietnam "was astonished to see that a burst of 24 light howitzer blasts did not neutralize the Viet Minh foot soldiers crouched on a road embankment at the outskirts of a village or else that a final protective fire of two or three salvos (10 to 24 shells) only brought about a short delay in the enemy attack of a fort."[17]

During the early years of the war, a French aircraft diving on an attacking force was enough to frighten the green insurgents and force them to break off the attack. But before 1950 the French could rarely send more than a single aircraft to turn back a local attack. Often the only aircraft available were old British-built Spitfire fighters. The Viet Minh quickly learned that airpower employed in penny packets possessed little destructive power. Aircraft moved too fast to isolate and aim at individual targets, and fighter aircraft could rarely make more than a couple of passes before returning to base for fuel. The Viet Minh soon learned to take cover, engage the plane with rifles and machineguns, and continue the attack after the aircraft departed.[18]

The enemy's tactics for the close attack effectively served to dissipate French firepower. Attacks were preceded by concentrated recoilless rifle, mortar, and machinegun fire intended to kill as many unwarned defenders as possible and, with luck, knock out the defender's radio, the sole means of calling for friendly fire. Often, if shells were available, the enemy engaged other nearby forts with mortar fire. This tatic served to confuse the French and caused them to divide their artillery response among several forts.[19]

The attacking force practiced what was commonly called the "hugging technique." Instead of attacking in depth, the entire force would crawl silently through barbed wire outside the fort and compress their formation into a single, tightly packed line of infantry. Invariably the defenders, relying on their European experience, and unable to see anything but faint glimpses of the enemy, would place final protective concentrations of artillery harmlessly behind the enemy.[20]

Not all French efforts to defend a static position ended in failure. Given a sturdy, modern concrete position, an alert outpost, and some luck, fortress soldiers could give a good account of themselves. Should the Viet Minh "commandos" be discovered passing through the barbed wire, the garrison often halted the advance with small arms fire. The defenders would use the radio to call in artillery immediately and would then adjust the impact of the shells to form a protective barrier of exploding steel between themselves and the enemy. Distant guns fired "star shells," essentially artillery-delivered illumination flares suspended by parachutes, to light up the fort and permit the defenders to locate and target the enemy.[21] Should the enemy be trapped outside the perimeter at daybreak, a competent defender would call for air support to complete the destruction.

Close air support of isolated garrisons became more effective later in the war as the quality of aircraft improved and as airmen became more familiar with their assigned sectors of responsibility. Bombing and strafing runs in defense of outposts were particularly destructive because a pilot did not have to guess the location of friendly troops. He could attack without time-consuming aerial reconnaissance and long radio conversations with unseen troops in contact. He was assured that the garrison was protected by concrete and anything moving outside was fair game.[22]

In spite of occasional successes and numberless sacrifices, the French were never able to secure the Red River Delta from Viet Minh infiltration. Ironically, what was intended as an economy-of-forces effort to secure the area around Hanoi eventually cost the French more in resources than it did the enemy. By 1954, 82,000 troops were immobilized behind the wire of 920 posts of varying sizes. Mobile units, intended for offensive operations, had to assign on a continuous basis one-quarter of their infantry and tank units to protect artillery, command posts, and other heavy equipment. As many as half of all infantry formations, either fixed or mobile, were used for guard duties.[23]

The surveillance of a 12-mile section of road cost the French the equivalent of an infantry battalion and a battery of artillery. The enemy could render that same stretch of road insecure with a single company of regular soldiers. In the entire Delta region, Viet Minh strength never exceeded 37,000 combatants. This manpower was enough to maintain the initiative, and the enemy exploited this advantage relentlessly to defeat French local security forces. Fortresses and firepower were no match for cunning, patience, courage, and a willingness to sacrifice many lives to achieve an objective. As one French general remarked, "We are the ones who are infiltrated in the Delta, not the Viet Minh."[24]

The French lost the opening round of the war when they lost effective control over most of the territory and population in North Vietnam. The French failure provides an unmistakable lesson for a Western army confronting a large-scale insurgency. No amount of firepower or fortification can be effective against an insurgent without first gaining the support of the people who inhabit the countryside. The French never fully realized the importance of winning popular support. Even if they had, it seems unlikely that as a colonial power they would have been able to present the peasantry with a long-term alternative more attractive than the independence promised by Ho Chi Minh. In such a situation, bombs and shells proved a long-term detriment to the French military effort. A senior French artillery commander writing immediately after the war understood the ambivalent role that firepower plays in the guerrilla phase of a revolutionary war:

> The evolution of a minor police action to full-scale military operations occurs almost imperceptibly. But the curve of this evolution becomes discontinuous at the moment when artillery appears on the scene, for, while this serves to create fear, it also often makes it difficult to identify rebel elements from within peaceful populations. Once artillery joins in ground warfare ... then the game is quickly compromised, for success ... is fundamentally more dependent upon political action than upon firepower.[25]

Giap Tries Open Warfare

With much of the countryside in his control, Giap was prepared to escalate the conflict to open, conventional warfare. He was secure in the knowledge that even if his attempt at direct confrontation with French firepower failed, he still would retain the allegiance of most of the people, and would be able to continue guerrilla warfare indefinitely until final victory was achieved. Time was on his side.

In 1950 Giap ordered Viet Minh forces in North Vietnam to the offensive. His objective was nothing less than to capture Hanoi and to push the French into the sea. The recent tide of war seemed to justify his decision to attack. The Viet Minh then controlled all of North Vietnam except for the Red River Delta. Giap had even succeeded in placing two crack regular regiments inside the Delta under the noses of the French.[26] The Chinese Communist victory in 1949 had provided Giap with a fully secure sanctuary from which to launch and support the attack. The Chinese provided the Viet Minh modern, sophisticated arms and advisors skilled in their use. With this Chinese assistance, Giap transformed his disparate guerrilla bands of 1946–1949 into well-armed conventional units. Five new 10,000-man divisions appeared, armed with Soviet rocket launchers, automatic weapons, and mortars, as well as several calibers of recoilless rifles captured by the Chinese from the United States in Korea. Giap also formed the 351st Heavy Division and patterned it on a Soviet artillery division. It was composed of two artillery regiments equipped with an assortment of Soviet light artillery and captured American 105-mm howitzers.

Because the peasant guerrillas had little experience with the technical complexities of artillery gunnery, the Chinese opened to them the extensive artillery school and firing range at Ching-Hsi in South China. This cooperation began a relationship that would grow rapidly in the next four years. Viet Minh gunners would never match the French in the rapidity, precision, and flexibility of their fire.[27] Nor could they "mass" or concentrate an entire group of available guns of different calibers and units simultaneously and precisely on a single target. One French gunner noted that Viet Minh artillery "never massed by battalion and even at Dien Bien Phu it did not appear that enemy artillery had effected massive concentration of firepower. Their action was primarily undertaken in the form of sustained harassment at a very slow pace."[28] For technical skill, however, the Viet Minh substituted a full measure of bravery, tenacity, and the ability to move guns through trackless jungle and employ them unseen.

To maintain the illusion of control, the French left a string of large isolated camps on the periphery of North Vietnam and in the midst of the enemy. These outposts contained more than 6,000 troops and were separated from the French main line of resistance by 300 miles of communist-held jungle. The Viet Minh offensive opened in October 1950 with startling success. They methodically overran and destroyed all of the overextended frontier posts. The French lost 6,000 men, 100 pieces of artillery and mortars, and several thousand tons of ammunition. It was the worst French colonial defeat since Montcalm died at Quebec in 1759.[29]

Spurred by his early victories, Giap pushed his forces toward a decisive showdown in the Red River Delta. But his hopes for final victory were proven premature by a new and formidable opponent: General Jean de Lattre de Tassigny, appointed Commander-in-Chief in December 1950. De Lattre was dispatched to turn the fortunes of the war and restore waning French morale. He accomplished the latter immediately upon his arrival. "In his first address de Lattre promised little: no improvements, no reinforcements, no easy victories. But he made one promise that he kept to his dying day: No matter what, you will be *commanded*."[30]

De Lattre realized that the Viet Minh could not be stopped unless French Union Forces took the offensive. He began immediately to rebuild and expand the two offensive elements within the Army that, if wisely handled, promised to be decisive: the mechanized mobile groups and the airborne. Mobile groups were essentially motorized infantry regiments, organized on the European pattern, consisting of a regimental headquarters, three infantry battalions, an artillery battalion, and other occasional attachments such as engineers or tanks.[31] They were employed like combat command or regimental combat teams in World War II and Korea. Operating independently as self-contained forces of all arms, mobile groups (or GMs, to use the French initials) were intended to roam freely about the countryside seeking out the main-force Viet Minh units and destroying them with concentrated firepower.

The quality of soldiers and materiel varied widely. Some GMs were manned almost entirely by colonials with French officers and NCOs; others had a more substantial leavening of professional soldiers from Metropolitan France.[32] Early GMs were poorly equipped, but with American aid, which began in quantity after 1950, they became increasingly more powerful. A group most often consisted of several hundred armored half-tracks as troop carriers, accompanied by a dozen tanks and artillery pieces, with a hundred or more trucks and light vehicles providing logistical and administrative support. The groups were kept in large garrisons when not deployed and were dispatched like "flying columns" to clear major routes, to relieve besieged garrisons, or to encircle suspected Viet Minh concentrations and destroy them with their substantial organic firepower.[33]

De Lattre knew how to employ mobile forces. He had commanded the Free French Army in its dash across Europe during the last nine months of World War II. He was wise enough, however, to understand that mobile warfare in Vietnam was fundamentally different from warfare in Europe. In a region of mountains, jungles, and rice paddies, mobile groups had little terrain for maneuver and were essentially road-bound; thus the tactical reach of mobile groups rarely exceeded a half-mile on either side of a major highway. A single roadblock or ambush could halt powerful convoys for hours. The Viet Minh often took full advantage of the French lack of off-road mobility by ambushing and harassing convoys.[34] During the Viet Minh siege of the city of Hoa-Binh, a French relief column took 11 full days to cover 25 miles. At one time the effort to keep open this small stretch of road consumed fully one-third of all mobile groups in North Vietnam.[35]

De Lattre expected artillery and airpower supporting the mobile groups to provide them a firepower advantage over the enemy. Artillery and airpower could range far away from the roads and destroy Viet Minh concentrations that his road-bound troops stretched along miles of convoy could not reach. Organized on the American pattern, the artillery battalion attached to each mobile group was smaller than most, having only 12 instead of the traditional 18 105-mm howitzers. Because all French artillery was "towed" as opposed to "self propelled," mobile group guns were unable to shoot while on the road and had to be unhooked from behind their towing trucks and placed into position before firing.

Although the French could not afford the 18 guns per battalion they preferred, gunners made a virtue of necessity by pointing out that restrictive Vietnamese terrain made smaller battalions more flexible and easier to employ in mountains and jungle. When it moved in convoy with the mobile group, the artillery was dispersed in battery segments of four guns and scattered throughout the column. This dispersal ensured that an ambush would not destroy all of the firepower supporting the mobile group. Also, since some columns stretched over several miles when moving on a single road, guns were spread to ensure all elements in the convoy remained under at least a portion of the protective artillery umbrella.[36]

De Lattre relied on the airborne forces as well as the mechanized mobile groups; 14 parachute battalions gave de Lattre a force not dependent upon roads for mobility. The French airborne was raised, organized, and tailored specifically for combat in Indochina. As the war gained in intensity, the size of the airborne forces grew rapidly from a few hundred in 1946 to over 10,000 by 1951. The force was mostly native with French and Foreign Legion leadership, although some units retained a high percentage of Metropolitan soldiers until the end of the war.[37]

A shortage of airlift, which persisted with little relief throughout the war, imposed a severe limit on the materiel that the airborne could carry with it into battle. For this reason, airborne combat formations were almost entirely infantry, armed with an increased allotment of small automatic arms and machineguns for close-in fighting. Each battalion had a few light mortars and recoilless rifles, which could be parachuted in door bundles from C–47 aircraft. Until just before Dien Bien Phu, airborne artillery consisted of only a few batteries of 75-mm recoilless rifles, flat-trajectory weapons normally employed by infantry soldiers.[38]

French airborne battalions tended to be larger than regular infantry battalions, led by better officers, and staffed and equipped with more sophisticated communications gear. These units were ''elite'' in the sense that all members, including native soldiers, were volunteer long-service professionals. The leadership tended to be more experienced, yet younger and more aggressive. They trained realistically and were proficient enough early in the war to challenge the Viet Minh in mountainous and jungle terrain without constant reliance on heavy firepower for an advantage.[39] The airplane gave parachute battalions unparalleled mobility when moving to the battlefield, but once on the ground their mobility was no better than the enemy's. The only escape from annihilation for units surrounded by a superior force in the jungle was to fight their way through Viet Minh to a friendly fortress or airfield.

The airborne depended upon the Air Force for reconnaissance, resupply, and, in large measure, fire support. Throughout the war, unfortunately, the French Air Force was operated on a shoe string. Obsolete German Junkers JU–52 transports were the only aircraft available for bombing early in the war:

> It amused the pilots to drop shells by hand through the doors of their Junkers onto any Viets they happened to see. They then got tired of tossing them out and asked the mechanics to fix home-

made bomb racks under the fuselage. The bomb racks usually worked, but one could never be quite sure of them—the bombs might still be there. Not that it mattered, for it increased the sporting side of things—landing was more fun.[40]

Fortunately for the French, American aid dramatically improved the ability of the Air Force to provide fire support for troops in the field before Giap began his general offensive in 1950. The Bell P–63 "King Cobra" was the first modern American aircraft delivered and was favored by the French because its accurate 37-mm gun proved effective as a powerful strafing weapon particularly well-suited to providing fires close to friendly troops. A shortage of cannon ammunition and spare parts forced the United States, over French objections, to replace the P–63s with Navy F–6F Hellcat and F–8F Bearcat fighter-bombers in 1950. These aircraft were more reliable and provided close support using guns and light fragmentation bombs.[41]

Close air support by the French Air Force became truly effective in October 1950 with the arrival of 24 B–26 medium bombers. These planes had fixed forward-firing weapons in the nose, superbly suited for close-in strafing. They could carry a single 1,000-pound bomb or an equivalent weight of small fragmentation bombs. Most significantly, the plane could fly from Hanoi to distant points in Vietnam and Laos with enough fuel to remain in the air above friendly troops and provide continuous close air support.[42]

All airpower in Indochina, including naval aviation, was subordinated to de Lattre and therefore did not suffer from inter-service doctrinal disputes and the presence of multiple air arms that hampered the United States in Korea. De Lattre split his air resources into three air command groups (or GATACs, for *Groupments Aerien Tactique*), each commanded by an Air Force general and each subordinate to one of the three regional ground commands in North Vietnam, South Vietnam, or Cambodia.[43] Both ground and air force headquarters were located together and remained in proximity throughout the war. Command and control was continually hampered by shortages of communications equipment and trained controllers, but the French went to great lengths to streamline the air request system to make it as responsive as possible to ground forces.

French close air support was provided mainly by F-8F Bearcat fighter-bombers, which flew from the airstrip at Dien Bien Phu before the final Viet Minh assault began.

Independent units, or even the smallest isolated posts, using an "emergency request net" tied directly to GATAC headquarters, were given unquestioned authority to call for immediate air support if attacked. This doctrinal concept was years ahead of its time.[44] Proximity and unity of command generally resulted in a smooth working relationship between air and ground components. However, it seems almost an axiom of modern war that minor frictions will arise between soldiers and airmen in combat. From the viewpoint of one French infantry commander,

> The pilot is a jealous animal who will not take off without orders from the Air Force. He is always ready to protect the autonomy of his service and to take the most inflexible approach.

The view from the air was predictably opposite:

> The infantry ... would like the Air Force to fly above them like tanks supporting the attack. It is a mission which we never will refuse when a comrade is in danger. But please do not ask us to attack targets protected with dug-in anti-aircraft cannon unless absolutely necessary.[45]

The French maintained a formal air request network based on the American system for routine air operations. The French, however, were rarely able to use the formal system because of the intensity of ground operations and the limited availability of aircraft. More often than not, a fighter-bomber enroute to a pre-designated target would suddenly be diverted to strike in support of an active ground engagement. The French believed such diversions to be unsatisfactory because often an aircraft in the air found itself armed with the wrong munitions for the strike. They preferred to keep a certain percentage of planes fueled and armed with differing ordnance on a ten-minute ground alert. Regional air headquarters then had the flexibility to choose the appropriate aircraft and bomb load for each strike.[46]

The most effective French innovation in the control of firepower was their use of "Moranes." These were small liaison aircraft, essentially French-manufactured versions of the German Feiseler "Storch" light liaison plane made famous by Field Marshal Rommel, who used his Storch as an aerial jeep during the campaign in North Africa. The Morane was a superb light plane for its day. It could operate from unimproved jungle air-

strips, was easy to maintain, and could carry a pilot and
observer with enough radio gear to communicate simultaneously
with the Air Force and artillery. The Moranes were flown by
both Air Force and Army pilots; the observers were equally
skilled at adjusting artillery fire and guiding combat aircraft to
their targets. Ground units with a friendly Morane overhead
were rarely ambushed. The little planes acted as radio relays
and helped lost units to locate themselves in the jungle.

To a ground unit in heavy contact, the ability of a Morane
observer to mass supporting fires often meant the difference
between victory and annihilation.[47] To do this well demanded
from the Morane observers coolness under pressure and the
utmost skill in orchestrating the deadly and complex fusion of
air- and artillery-delivered fire support. The normal procedure
for an aerial observer was to start artillery falling immediately
once on station and to call GATAC to dispatch aircraft on strip
alert or to vector aircraft involved in other missions to the contact. Aircraft arrived piecemeal, in ones and twos, often low on
fuel and armed with a variety of differing (and often unsuitable)
bomb loads. The Morane observer's critical task was to shift
quickly from artillery to airpower as it arrived on station and
back to artillery once the aircraft departed, ensuring that no
break occurred in the intensity or effectiveness of fire. A pause
of only a few minutes between delivery of the two might give
the enemy just enough time to regain the momentum of his
assault.

A skilled Morane observer could direct aircraft in "on the
deck" with artillery projectiles in the air fired on a time cue to
explode seconds ahead of and behind the aircraft. A miscalculation of a few seconds by the Morane might mean the destruction
of an aircraft by friendly fire. Since this process could only be
controlled from the air, ground commanders most often relinquished the responsibility for controlling firepower from their
ground observers to the Morane. This was just as well. In the
heat and confusion of battle, the Morane orbiting above was in a
better position to observe and make decisions than the observer
fighting for his life in the jungle below.[48]

Another essential skill demanded of a Morane observer was
the ability to place fires immediately in front of friendly troops.

The venerable Morane liaison aircraft functioned for both artillery spotting and control of tactical air strikes.

To do this effectively and quickly, a pilot needed an intuitive feel for the urgency of the situation, the destructiveness of the munitions at his command, the skill of the fighter pilots and gunners at his command, and some knowledge of the degree of protection afforded to defenders. An observer could not always rely on the judgment of the embattled commander on the ground whose problems were amplified by the fact that the enemy preferred to fight close-in. Only a few yards of jungle might separate friend from foe. In these circumstances "minimum safe distances" prescribed in regulations for bombs and shells were meaningless. To break a final charge, a French aerial observer would have to call in light artillery and napalm to within 40 yards of French troops, sometimes less if the sacrifice of a few friendly casualties might save the unit. Bombs were dropped within 100 yards; strafing by a skilled pilot could be brought in as close as a few feet from a position.[49]

American Air Force advisors were not particularly impressed by the French method of close air support. The sight of individual combat aircraft rushing helter-skelter across the countryside at the call of any small unit embroiled in a firefight appeared to be disorganized and without purpose or direction. Americans thought any air support system so decentralized to be incapable of supporting a decisive air campaign. To their minds, the French air arm had sold out to the Army and had become nothing more than aerial artillery.[50]

Brigadier General Albert Hewitt, in a letter to the Secretary of Defense written following a fact-finding mission to Indochina, noted,

> Perforce and because of the relationships existing between the French Air Force and the French Army, air operations are based primarily on ground operations. Because of the scattered nature of surface operations, air elements are usually employed in relatively small increments on independent actions that are separated by time, space or both. Under such circumstances it is difficult to take advantage of the shock effect and mutual support that results from concentration of force or to utilize effectively the inherent flexibility of airpower to achieve decisive results.[51]

General Hewitt was correct in one respect: the French effort to provide ground and air fire support was indeed "scattered." But the enemy was scattered. There were no large troop concentrations or supply depots conveniently available for attack by massed firepower.

The close air support system as it was improvised by the French proved adequate as long as enemy activity was restricted to low-level hit-and-run attacks on scattered garrisons. The real test came in early 1951 when Giap raised the firepower stakes and promised Ho Chi Minh that he would be in Hanoi by Tet.[52]

Encouraged by his success in isolating and destroying the French frontier posts, Giap undertook a full-scale attack to besiege Hanoi using newly formed regular divisions. On the 13th of January, Giap opened the campaign by throwing two of his divisions against the city of Vinh-Yen, which was defended by two understrength French mobile groups. De Lattre realized immediately that Vinh-Yen presented the opportunity he had long sought. Now he could use French firepower to best advantage in a set-piece battle of attrition. On 14 January de Lattre took personal charge of the battle. He ordered an airlift to reinforce Vinh-Yen and initiated a relief operation using fresh mobile groups to seize and hold strategic hills to the north of the garrison. Once these forces secured and fortified the hills, de Lattre intended to use them as a lure to draw the enemy into a "killing ground."[53]

Giap obliged with a vengeance. The French received their first taste of "human sea" attacks at Vinh-Yen—wave upon wave of Viet Minh infantry throwing themselves against the hastily dug defenses of the hill line. Lucien Bordard witnessed such an attack:

> The Viets attacked in spite of their increasing losses. They came in against machine guns as if they were drunk.... Groups of three linked their ankles, so that the dead or wounded would still advance, carried on by the others. And then there were those who blew themselves up with their yellow-powder bangalores with packets of sulphur tied to grenades. They died to smash the enemy.... In some places everything was so furiously burned that the French and the Viet Minh bodies could no longer be told apart.[54]

For three days the Moranes stationed themselves above the Viet Minh and dropped volley after volley of artillery fire into the enemy masses. The attacks intensified at night and Air

Force C–47 cargo planes orbited lazily over the battle dropping parachute flares to rob the enemy of protective darkness. De Lattre diverted all fighter-bombers in Indochina to Vinh-Yen. Transport planes were hastily converted to bombers and thrown into what became the most massive aerial bombardment of the war.[55] Aid from the United States arrived in the form of jellied gasoline canisters, or napalm bombs, which had proven effective in Korea. De Lattre acknowledged after the battle that the timely arrival of napalm helped in great measure to turn the tide. Napalm was not particularly destructive, but it could be dropped close to friendly troops in contact. Also, the exploding gasoline created a barrier of flame and smoke lasting two or three minutes, which gave the defenders a brief respite while it burned.

The sight of huge balls of flame appearing unexpectedly in their midst had an enormous psychological effect on the enemy. The diary of a Viet Minh officer found at Vinh-Yen evinced the terror produced by this first exposure to napalm:

> Another plane swoops down behind us and again drops a napalm bomb. The bomb falls closely behind us and I feel its fiery breath touching my whole body. The men are fleeing in all directions and I cannot hold them back. . . . I stop at the platoon commander . . . his eyes were wide with terror. "What is this? The atomic bomb?"[56]

By 17 January, the Viet Minh surrendered the battlefield at Vinh-Yen and disappeared into the forest. The battle had been a close call for the French, but it was a clear victory made all the more significant because it had been fought by brave soldiers and won with decisive firepower.[57]

Giap tried another major attack in March, this time with three divisions supported by artillery, mortars, and heavy anti-aircraft machineguns in the vicinity of the French outpost at Mao Khe. The Viet Minh were defeated more easily this time because the French were fighting in open territory and were defending a well-established series of outposts. A small French garrison reinforced by the 6th Colonial Parachute Battalion succeeded in beating off a force six times its size using prearranged artillery barrages and continuous strikes by B–26s and naval fighters.[58]

Still undeterred, Giap, after a two-month pause, launched a third multi-division attack along the Day River line in the South Delta region. Although this attack was accompanied by commitment of irregular forces to attack the French rear, the results were the same—devastation of the attacking force. Giap, facing the loss of nearly half of his combat divisions, had no choice but to withdraw to his sanctuaries in the north and evaluate the reasons for his failure.[59]

Both sides derived certain lessons from these battles. Giap's most important lesson was that his divisions were too lightly equipped to slug it out with French firepower in open combat. He would, therefore, revert to guerrilla and peripheral warfare, again employing irregular forces against enemy strength and his main battle forces against enemy weakness. He would commit his forces only when there was a high probability of success. For the next year he conducted low-intensity operations in the Thai highlands and in Laos.

The lessons that Giap learned from his defeat at the hands of French firepower were not altogether negative, however. Giap noted that the ability of his forces to stand up to firepower increased with experience. The terror effect of napalm and bombs at Vinh-Yen passed quickly when the Viet Minh learned that such weapons were not as destructive as they first appeared. When caught in the open during an attack, the Viet Minh learned to scatter quickly and press themselves against paddy dikes and minor undulations in the ground to protect them from strafing aircraft.[60] The Viet Minh also discovered at Mao Khe that a few well-hidden and bunkered heavy machineguns greatly lessened the effectiveness of French air attacks. Occasionally an aircraft was hit, less often destroyed, but the threat posed by these guns prevented destructive "on the deck" strafing, which caused most of the casualties at Vinh-Yen.[61]

Giap learned in later battles that he did not necessarily have to match French firepower gun for gun to lessen its effect. A few artillery pieces, mortars, and recoilless rifles, carefully hidden, protected, and fired discretely in small masses at a French column, proved effective far out of proportion to the relative size of the artillery force.[62] During Operation Lorraine, conducted in the narrow defiles of the Thai hills, the Viet Minh successfully used all arms simultaneously to destroy a French mobile group near Chiang Mai in 1953. Communist artillery and mortars opened fire on all elements of the convoy from both sides of the road on which the two-mile-long convoy was stalled. Artillery was dug in as close as 50 meters from French vehicles and could not miss. French soldiers who survived the battle noted that enemy waves attacked directly through their own exploding artillery and were on top of the vehicles before the shelling stopped. The ambush was broken only when French legionnaires charged artillery positions hidden in the hills. Ominously, they discovered that none of the enemy guns had been destroyed by French airpower or artillery fire.[63]

Giap realized that the infantry weapons he was receiving from his Soviet and Chinese allies were superior to the French weapons and better suited to close-in fighting. This meant that French battalions—particularly the lightly equipped airborne— would be at a disadvantage should their external fire support be suppressed or destroyed. Chinese supplies of heavy weapons were also becoming more readily available to help narrow the gap between French and Viet Minh firepower.

The Viet Minh developed a realistic tactical method for employing guns that made best use of what little firepower they had. A regular Viet Minh battalion attacking entrenched French troops late in the war could expect supporting fires from two batteries (each with three 75-mm Soviet mountain guns), three mortar companies (each with three 82-mm mortars), and seven recoilless rifles. During the preparation phase of the attack, the enemy fired the recoilless rifles into strong points and kept the French pinned down with up to 400 rounds from mortars and artillery. When the battalion reached the French lines and began firing machineguns, the supporting fires would be shifted to more distant targets. Captured Viet Minh documents admitted that this level of support was not sufficient to "wipe out" the French, but the presence of Viet fire support did effectively end the French monopoly on heavy firepower and gave the attacking force a momentary edge that the Viet Minh exploited through liberal use of fanatical waves of soldiers.[64]

Giap also realized that he had been too impatient in his first attempt at open warfare, and he was not going to repeat this mistake. His new strategy was not to avoid the big battle. Instead, he would fight it on his own terms. He sought to draw the French farther away from their bases in an effort to weaken their ability to project and supply large, firepower-intensive forces, and then strike when a combination of favorable circumstances involving weather, lines of communication, terrain, and available forces negated the French firepower advantage. In many bloody, inconclusive fights involving units from single regiments to divisions, Giap preferred to sacrifice some units hopelessly trapped by French offensive action rather than let himself be drawn into a "meat grinder" operation like those the Americans carried out so effectively in Korea.[65]

The victories against the Viet Minh in 1951 firmly convinced a succession of French Commanders-in-Chief in Indochina that the war could be won by fighting a decisive set-piece battle of attrition. To the end, they sought to lure the Viet Minh into attacking well-prepared positions—to create a series of small Verduns intended to let the enemy "bleed himself white" in the face of French firepower. The belief that this would happen became known as the "illusion of Vinh Yen."

In their haste to destroy the Viet Minh in a battle of attrition, the French made several critical miscalculations. First, they over-estimated the killing effect of their own fire support systems—particularly airpower and artillery.[66] To a forward observer standing on the ground, the destructive power of detonating bombs and shells appears overwhelming indeed. However, the Americans in Korea recorded many instances in which troops in contact worked over an area with tons of ordnance only to be fired on again when attempting to resume the advance. Eyewitness reports from these actions remarked consistently that, although the target area may have been torn up with craters and uprooted trees, there was painfully little evidence of enemy casualties.

Recent experiments and analytical studies done by the US Army and RAND Corporation tend to support earlier combat observations in Korea. The studies show that in the most favorable circumstances of terrain and enemy disposition an exploding 750-pound bomb has less than an even chance of causing a single casualty. Napalm is the least effective of air-delivered munitions: its destructive radius is less than 30 yards, and proportionately less if dropped in dense jungle.[67] Artillery killing power is equally unimpressive. A single 105-mm artillery round fired against dug-in troops has less than one chance in a hundred of causing a casualty.[68]

These odds were computed assuming the target to be European soldiers arrayed in a conventional attack formation. The destructiveness of modern firepower decreases even more sharply when the enemy, huddled in a jungle, cannot be seen or when he attacks silently at night, dispersed, skillfully using each crater or fold in the ground for cover. The frustration felt by European soldiers when confronted with such an enigmatic opponent was expressed vividly by a group of pilots immediately after the war:

> The Viets have adapted themselves at an incredible speed to napalm, to all forms of strafing and to the fire of heavy weapons. The effectiveness of the fortifications as well as their passive defense against napalm bombs or artillery shells are masterpieces of their kind.... They are a race of fighters who had become aviation and cannon proof.[69]

French firepower was effective early in the war because of its psychological effect and because it was often fired into masses of unseasoned infantry. As the enemy became more adept at avoiding French firepower, and as they began to possess firepower means of their own, increasingly more ordnance was needed to achieve significant results. Unfortunately, manpower constraints and a parsimonious government at home severely limited the Army's ability to deliver more firepower. With over 500 guns tied up in small, scattered outposts, French gunners were never able to increase the proportion of artillery supporting mobile operations. Had the French been able to release more guns to their offensive arms it seems unlikely that the tenuous supply situation in Vietnam would have allowed a corresponding increase in the supply of ammunition. It is instructive to note that in 1951, the year French mobile forces defeated Giap in open warfare, the artillery, both position and mobile, in all areas of Indochina fired *a third of a million rounds*. In 1969 American artillery of all calibers fired *ten million rounds* in South Vietnam alone.[70]

The Air Force, too, was hard-pressed to provide adequate aerial firepower for even routine air operations. Throughout 1951, the few available bombers and fighters were flown to the limits of endurance and managed, through herculean effort, to drop *8,621 tons* of bombs.[71] Compare this to the *110,000 tons* of bombs dropped by the US Air Force during a two-month period in support of a single operation.[72]

A second miscalculation made by the French was the very same made by the Germans when they chose to fight a war of attrition at Verdun in 1916: unless the attacker holds an over-whelming advantage in the means of destruction, casualties are likely to occur in equal measure on both sides. Ironically, the French attempt to ''bleed the Viet Minh white'' caused the greatest losses to French mobile forces, particularly among junior officers and NCOs. These were the men that France could least afford to lose. Casualties became so severe late in the war that the quality of leaders and led began to decline alarmingly. Training and morale suffered because infantry battalions spent months at a time in the field and returned to garrison decimated by battle casualties, disease, and exhaustion. The High Command found itself unable to replace losses with native Frenchmen and were obliged to fill the ranks with increasing numbers of North and Central Africans, Vietnamese, and legionnaires.

As a result of the cumulative effect of all of these factors, the combat reliability of the French infantry began to decline after 1951. It was then that the High Command saw a precipitous rise in the amount of artillery support needed for infantry operations. Since the days of the Napoleonic wars, shaken or green soldiers required greater concentrations of firepower to keep them effective. Where previously a French battalion might rush a strong point or maneuver against an ambush, it now pulled back and let artillery do the job. A zone commander in Tonkin commented late in the war, ''The infantry can no longer achieve the results obtained by artillery and aircraft fire.''[73] And another noted, ''The constant dependence upon artillery to counter the least evidence of resistance is also a classic sign of unit fatigue.''[74] The renewed dependence on artillery to substitute for a loss of infantry effectiveness was evident in munition expenditures. In a three-month period in 1952, the artillery in Tonkin expended 4,800 tons of munitions of all types. By 1954 this expenditure had increased to 8,900 tons while the number of guns in Tonkin had not increased in equal proportion, nor had enemy activity escalated. At the same time, the infantry used ever-increasing numbers of mortar shells. In Tonkin 850 tons of mortar ammunition were fired in a three-month period in 1952. In a similar period in 1954 the infantry fired 1,980 tons even though troop strength remained constant.[75]

The Lesson of Dien Bien Phu

Perhaps had de Lattre still commanded, the French would not have begun their fatal campaign at Dien Bien Phu. But de Lattre died of cancer in 1952. He was succeeded by a string of less competent men. The decision to occupy Dien Bien Phu was influenced in great measure by French success at the battle of Na-San airfield in November 1953. The French fought a particularly successful battle of attrition there by employing a ten-battalion garrison reinforced and supplied entirely by air. Giap badly miscalculated the strength of Na-San to be only five battalions and launched a regular division to crush it. Repeatedly Giap threw his forces in familiar mass attacks against the garrison only to be repulsed with a loss of over 1,000 men. Na-San seemed to show that an isolated garrison was capable of fighting the "big battle" supplied, reinforced, and supported by air transport alone.[76]

In the fall of 1953 General Navarre, the latest Commander-in-Chief, decided to repeat Na-San on a grand scale by building a fortified position deep in Viet Minh territory that would invite the decisive big battle. Operation Castor began with the seizure by airborne assualt of the village of Dien Bien Phu some 190 air miles from Hanoi. Dien Bien Phu is in a cultivated valley, 10 miles by 4 miles, surrounded by rugged, jungle-covered mountains rising 3,000 to 4,000 feet above the valley floor. The French quickly massed a division-sized force of airborne soldiers within the airhead. During the 55-day siege, over 4,000 reinforcements were parachuted into Dien Bien Phu. The strength at any one time, however, never rose much above 13,000.

The position was partitioned into a series of mutually supporting strong points organized for defense against ground attack only. The primary position, nicknamed Eliane, was centered about the airstrip and contained most of the artillery and mortars. One strong point was situated four miles to the south, and to the north were three outlying positions, each encircling low hills guarding the most likely approaches to the valley. The surrounding hills, which rose up to 3,000 feet from the edge of the French positions, were not occupied. Each of the strong points consisted of a number of mutually supporting, but poorly constructed, field fortifications. Fighting positions were shallow, the earthworks unrevetted, and the parapets made only from piled dirt. General de Castries, the commander at Dien Bien Phu, ordered all fighting positions constructed to withstand artillery bombardment. But local material was scarce, and there were too few aircraft available to fly in concrete, timber, and steel from Hanoi, so little overhead cover was constructed. The artillery sat on top of the ground with no parapets for the guns or covered bunkers for the gunners.[77]

Ostensibly, the French High Command occupied Dien Bien Phu as a base camp from which to conduct offensive operations in an effort to regain control of northwestern Vietnam and Laos. But, in fact, the few offensive sorties made from the camp resulted in no contact at all or occasionally heavy losses to ambush and counterattack. After five weeks of frustration, large-scale offensive operations ceased. French patrols ventured no farther than the jungle's edge in all directions. The enemy controlled the hills. Dien Bien Phu was surrounded. The loss of freedom to maneuver should have removed any justification for the French to stay longer. But the High Command could not shake its obsessive desire for a showdown with the Viet Minh. Dien Bien Phu became in fact, if not in intention, a base from which French firepower could lure and then destroy the enemy. The "illusion of Vinh Yen" persisted.[78]

Ironically, the French failed to provide more than a token volume of fire support to achieve this objective. Twenty-four 105-mm howitzers and four 155-mm howitzers were about one-third the complement of artillery normally associated with a force of this size. Hanoi held hundreds of guns in reserve, but

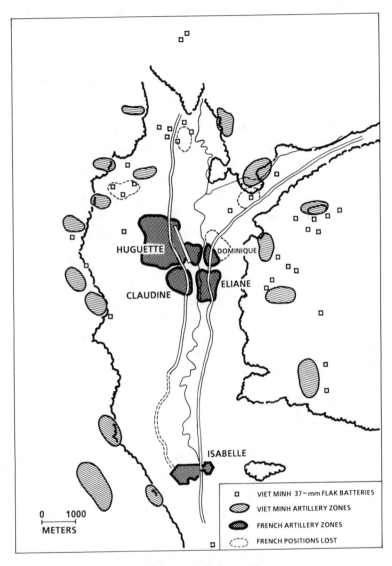

Artillery and flak positions,
Dien Bien Phu, March 1954

Colonel Piroth did not think them necessary.[79] The guns at Dien Bien Phu were poorly placed and unable to provide mutual support between distant positions. The fire coordination and control was poor and certainly not up to the standards practiced by the position artillery in Tonkin. As a result, there were numerous occasions when the artillery failed to intervene promptly to turn back a Viet Minh attack and all too many incidents of French shells falling on friendly troops.[80]

Four medium guns were all that Piroth had available for counterbattery fire. He had boasted that these guns would destroy any Viet Minh piece by the time it fired a third round. However, the artillery target acquisition procedures were primitive and counterbattery planning was extremely poor. There is no evidence that Piroth destroyed, or even silenced, a single Viet Minh gun during the siege. The Viet Minh eventually eliminated all of the French artillery by counterbattery fire.[81]

Reading after-action reports 30 years after the siege, one is struck repeatedly by the apparent lethargy and lack of aggressiveness and initiative among artillerymen at Dien Bien Phu. A young American Air Force officer sent to Vietnam to assist the French in photo interpretation visited Dien Bien Phu four days before direct Viet Minh assaults began, and six days before Piroth's suicide. He spent an afternoon watching the guns in action. His description of one mission is revealing:

> The firing of 105mm howitzer for approximately 30 minutes was observed by our party. During this time approximately fifteen rounds were fired. It is interesting to note that although there was an L-type plane [a Morane] aloft and also eight F–8F's [fighters], this firing was unobserved. The gun was firing at a target to the northeast of Dien Bien Phu. It was reported that the target was a small supply center of rice and food.[82]

This was one of only a few missions fired that afternoon; all were unobserved. At that very moment, however, three divisions and hundreds of guns were hidden in the jungle as close as a quarter-mile from the perimeter.[83]

The French expected the artillery to provide workmanlike, reliable fire support—but they expected their Air Force to do most of the killing. For close air support, some 130 combat aircraft were available. These included 47 B–26 bombers, 16 of which were newly arrived, on loan from Clark Air Base in the Philippines.[84] The balance were naval fighters that had been in continuous service for two years without adequate maintenance or overhaul. In spite of recent infusions of American aid, the French Air Force stretched itself beyond its limits to support Dien Bien Phu.[85]

The extreme distance from air bases near Hanoi to the target area required pilots to remain in the air at least three hours for each sortie. This left fighter aircraft only 15 minutes or less to find their targets and make a single pass before beginning the long trip home. Long air missions were further complicated by abominable conditions of terrain and weather. The siege was conducted in the monsoon season. Low clouds usually surrounded Dien Bien Phu during most of the day. It took the utmost nerve and skill for pilots to weave their planes between mountain peaks as they tried to fly under the weather.[86]

The French had hoped to lessen the burden on fighter pilots by stationing aircraft at Dien Bien Phu. The siege began on 10 March. By 14 March, communist gunners closed the airstrip, destroying seven Bearcats, three transports, four Moranes, and two helicopters on the ground. Air support from Dien Bien Phu no longer was a threat to the Viet Minh.[87]

The incessant demand for aerial support and difficult flying conditions soon began to take their toll on pilots and planes. French aircraft maintenance, never efficient under ideal conditions, found itself totally unable to keep planes in the air. Automatic cannon continually jammed or exploded on strafing runs. Aircraft experienced engine trouble repeatedly and crashed into the jungle. At the height of the battle pilots were flying two missions per day when weather permitted, some averaging 150 hours per month in the cockpit. Pilot fatigue became such a problem late in the battle that French doctors grounded whole squadrons to prevent further accidents and total pilot exhaustion.[88]

Enemy anti-aircraft guns were the greatest impediment to effective close air support. Giap realized that the high mountains surrounding Dien Bien Phu channeled supporting aircraft into two or three narrow approaches, and in bad weather aircraft could only approach from the northeast. He placed heavy 12.7-mm machineguns in dense collections along these approaches.[89] Aircraft flying low over the valley were suddenly deluged with fire. Many were lost. These "flak traps" made low-level bombing and strafing practically impossible. The final blow to effective air support came in early April with the appearance of 37-mm automatic anti-aircraft cannon. These guns were the best the Soviet Army could send. As early as February, French intelligence intercepted radio traffic indicating that the 37s had been dismantled and were enroute to Dien Bien Phu. The French High Command discounted the intercepted message as a poor effort at deception.[90] By the end of April 1954, the Viet Minh had succeeded in emplacing 24 37-mm guns and as many as 740 12.7-mm machineguns and 20-mm automatic cannon in dense clusters around the camp.[91]

The overwhelming demand for close air support left few aircraft to interdict the flow of soldiers and supplies from China to the battle area. Much has been written about the extraordinary efforts of 100,000 native porters organized by Giap to push forward thousands of tons of materiel over 600 kilometers of trails and primitive roads. Artillery and anti-aircraft cannon were hauled hundreds of kilometers by hand over rugged mountain passes and into positions overlooking the target. French intelligence detected the initial movement of these guns toward Dien Bien Phu from the base area almost as soon as it began. Giap achieved surprise because the French simply could not accept the reality that a siege conducted using first-rate materiel could be sustained on the backs of coolies.[92]

All of Giap's movements were meticulously camouflaged—an entire battalion could vanish into roadside ditches at the sound of an approaching plane. Jungle parking and maintenance areas were provided for trucks along usable roads. Elaborate trellis works were erected—tree tops were tied together to form spacious jungle cantonments. To pilots flying interdiction missions above the infiltration routes, the sight below was mystifying:

> In my career I have had the opportunity to fly over Moroccan, Italian, German, even English adversaries. I never had such a sensation of complete emptiness as above Viet Minh territory.[93]

American observers were most critical of the French for not conducting a more effective interdiction campaign. With

only a single squadron of eight Navy four-engine Privateer aircraft available for long-range surveillance, it seems unlikely that
the French Air Force could have done much better.[94] It seems
equally unlikely that, had many more aircraft been available, a
full-scale interdiction campaign could have been any more successful. The flow of supplies might have been slowed, but
bombers alone could not have halted 100,000 porters. Bernard
Fall, who was present in Vietnam during the siege, was more
objective than most American observers in his assessment of the
French use of air power:

> All in all the French Air Force in Indochina fulfilled its mission
> as well as could be expected. What it lacked in materiel it more
> than made up by the knowledge which most of its pilots pos-
> sessed of the terrain and meteorology ... and by the relative
> absence of friction between the ground and air force staffs. The
> latter knew that this was first and foremost a ground war, and
> adjusted its own sights accordingly.[95]

With its guns destroyed and its Air Force neutralized, the
French High Command knew that the fall of Dien Bien Phu was
a matter of time. The defenders did not give up easily, however.
They suffered terribly in poorly prepared, open fighting positions under the methodical bombardment of 200 guns and rocket
launchers firing 2,000 rounds per day.[96] They watched nightly
as enemy sappers dug attack positions within yards of their
strong points, and they fought furiously to repel fanatical
human-sea attacks that ultimately involved five divisions—over
50,000 combat troops. In April the heavy monsoon rains began,
limiting the already scant resupply efforts by Air Force transports. The rain crumbled fortifications and turned trenches into
miserable racing torrents.[97]

Giap attacked furiously. Practicing hugging tactics to avoid
the few remaining mortars in action, he rushed whole regiments
against the French entrenchments. Repulses were many, successes few. The Viet Minh suffered heavy losses and morale
problems appeared among the besiegers, but Giap persisted.
During the final phase, which began on 1 May, Giap resorted to
sheer weight of humanity to overwhelm the weakened garrison
and its few remaining guns. Fighting was bitter; Giap sustained
staggering losses. On the 7th of May General de Castries

surrendered, and with his surrender the French ended their colonial rule of Indochina. The French lost 15,000 men, of whom 6,500 were prisoners. This was less than four percent of the total French strength in Indochina. Giap suffered 23,000 casualties—more than *half* of his engaged combat forces, nearly one-quarter of his combat strength in all of Indochina. *But he won.*[98]

Western nations are all too anxious to put behind them unpleasant history. Were it not for reflective men such as Bernard Fall and Jules Roy, Americans might have ignored completely the French experience in Indochina once the painful image of victorious Viet Minh standing atop the command bunker at Outpost Isabelle disappeared from motion picture and television screens. But the lessons of the war were clear to those who cared to observe.

No amount of technology or firepower will make secure a region unless the support of the population has been gained. The French invested 500 guns and 100,000 men in a futile effort to control the Red River Delta. Yet, until the end, Giap retained the initiative and maintained a first-line regiment in the field not 20 kilometers from Hanoi. Without popular support, the French found themselves isolated in a hostile sea, able to move only with the greatest difficulty by day and locked in their garrisons nervously awaiting attack by night. An insurgent who controls the countryside, and is fortunate enough to have a sanctuary at his rear, can escalate a conflict from guerrilla warfare to conventional warfare at will. Confident in the knowledge that if the enemy's firepower proves too destructive, he can lower the level of conflict, the guerrilla retains the strategic initiative. Success indeed "is fundamentally more dependent upon political action than upon firepower."

3
The Second Indochina War

S*enior Colonel Ha Vi Tung was Chief of Staff of the North* Vietnamese Military Region IV in the Central Highlands, an area beginning in Cambodia and cutting across the midsection of South Vietnam, ending at the South China Sea. A small man with deeply weathered features, Ha was a practiced, proven veteran of many battles with the French. His task from the High Command in North Vietnam was to use the division of fresh soldiers at his command to conduct a sustained advance through the Central Highlands with the ultimate objective of cutting the country in two. From within a sanctuary hidden in the heavily forested Chu Pong Massif, which straddles the Cambodian border, Colonel Ha meticulously supervised planning for the campaign. He took care to caution his staff that an operation of this magnitude might oblige them to fight large American units for the first time.

His plan centered around the siege and eventual destruction of a Special Forces camp at Plei Me, located about 20 miles east of his mountain sanctuary and manned by a constabulary of 300 Jarai Montagnard tribesmen and 10 American advisors. Two first-rate regiments were available for the operation. One was to seize the camp and the other would ambush the column that the South Vietnamese would most certainly dispatch to relieve the camp. Just in case his initial assault was not immediately successful, Ha deployed a battalion of heavy anti-aircraft

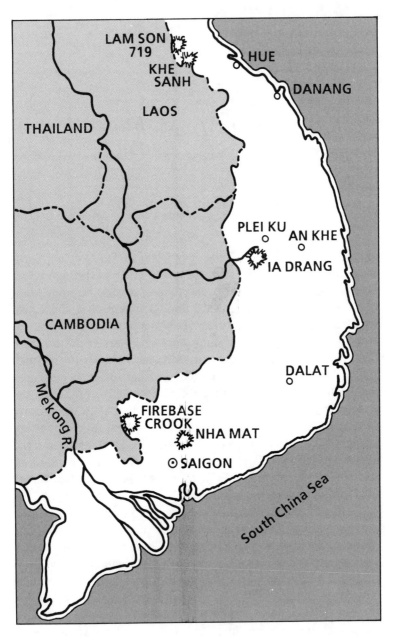

South Vietnam

machineguns along expected flight routes to protect his soldiers from marauding aircraft. By 19 October 1965, Ha and his staff had moved within a few miles of the camp and established a radio link to the attacking regiments. That same evening, his troops opened the battle by surrounding Plei Me and closing in for the kill.

By midnight on 19 October, Captain Harold M. Moore, the commander at Plei Me, knew he was in serious trouble. His camp was being hit from all directions by attacking troops skillfully using the darkness to draw unseen within yards of his perimeter. Mortar and recoilless rifle fire was continuous. With no friendly artillery within range, Moore radioed for close air support. Before dawn a forward air controller (FAC) aboard a C–123 flareship was orbiting above. The first air strike was delivered at 4 a.m., just as the enemy began his first coordinated assault. The outline of the camp could be seen clearly in the flarelight and a continuous procession of pilots was able to drop napalm and bombs within yards of the perimeter. Air Force Colonel Edsel Manning, air liaison officer for the II Corps Tactical Zone, scrambled US Air Force and Vietnamese airpower, as well as Navy and Marine fighters, from every corner of the central region and from carriers off shore. By early morning on the 20th the skies over the camp had become a very busy place. During peak hours, the FACs stacked up aircraft and sent them in singly or in pairs to ensure that bombing and strafing runs were coordinated, precise, and continuous. With four air forces flying eight types of strike aircraft, this was no easy task.

Senior Colonel Ha's "flak traps" scored their first kill that morning—a UH–1B "Huey" shot down east of Plei Me, all four crewmen dead. Later the same day, two B–57 Canberra bombers were engaged with heavy machinegun fire; one was downed and the other was forced to divert to Plei Ku airfield for repair. During the next two days, two fighters and another helicopter would go down. Just as Ha predicted, the South Vietnamese dispatched an armored column to relieve the garrison. It was summarily ambushed five miles from the objective; for two hours mortars, recoilless rifles, and automatic weapons took a heavy toll on the government troops.

From a tactical viewpoint, the siege progressed according to a plan long proved by practical experience in the first Indochina War. The enemy soldiers carried out their attacks with customary alacrity and precision. The American response held few tactical surprises. As the battle progressed, however, Colonel Ha became increasingly alarmed at the price exacted by airpower for each of his successes. From radio transmissions intercepted and from prisoners captured after the battle came a description of growing confusion and panic on the enemy side. Colonel Ha did not expect American aircraft to attack at night, nor was he prepared for such a furious and sustained aerial bombardment. Just maintaining pressure on Plei Me had cost him half a regiment in two days. Eighty tons of aerial ordnance steadily drained the strength of his force, to the point where a final assault became impossible. After four days of fruitless effort, Colonel Ha reluctantly pulled his battered regiments away from their exposed positions around Plei Me and ordered them westward, back to the sanctuary of Chu Pong Mountain. The enemy had experienced the effect of concentrated American firepower for the first time, and for the first time the siege of an isolated fortress had been broken by airpower alone.[1]

On the evening of 27 October, General Westmoreland visited An Khe, headquarters of the newly arrived 1st Cavalry Division, located in the Central Highlands not far from Plei Me. He discussed the recent siege and instructed General Kinnard to embark on a campaign to destroy Colonel Ha's soldiers as they retreated. Circumstances were perfect for Kinnard's style of airmobile combat. The trackless route back to Cambodia was no impediment to the division's complement of 476 helicopters. Kinnard proposed to devote one of his brigades to searching for the enemy systematically over a huge area. Individual companies and platoons would leapfrog by helicopter between suspected enemy locations to conduct brief searches and withdraw—all the while protected by armed helicopter gunships and artillery.

Instead of supporting safely from the rear, Kinnard moved his artillery batteries into the battle area by helicopter, often ahead of the infantry so that the maneuver force would be protected by firepower from the moment it touched the ground. In these isolated regions, guns were positioned in tight groupings, rarely with more than a platoon for local security. These were not the heavily sand-bagged and bunkered "firebases" familiar to artillerymen later in the war. Kinnard relied on surprise and frequent movement to safeguard his guns. Rarely would a battery remain in one spot for more than two days. Kinnard was convinced that the enemy could not plan and mass for a set-piece attack in such a short time. Whenever possible he positioned his batteries in pairs to give additional punch to the infantry and to provide mutual support between batteries.

At first glance it would appear that scattering infantry platoons and artillery batteries helter-skelter across a wide expanse might leave the total force vulnerable to defeat in detail. In fact, Kinnard hoped that the enemy would believe this, because he knew that the helicopter made every scattered unit not in contact a reserve that could be picked up and committed, often within minutes of a contact. He emphasized that contact was the name of the game. Terrain had little tactical value in this style of war. He instructed his soldiers to seek contact in any form—a helicopter receiving ground fire, a warm campfire, beaten down grass, any sign that would indicate the presence of the enemy. Platoons were intended to find the enemy. They were employed in the manner of a matador's cape: seemingly vulnerable and waved in the face of the enemy, their purpose was to draw the enemy into decisive combat. Firepower provided the sword behind the cape. Hidden carefully and raised at the final moment, guns and airpower in the hand of a skilled matador would do the killing.

Kinnard began his hunt on 28 October, landing helicopters in scattered clearings grown thick with waist-high elephant grass. Immediately, the ubiquitous and random helicopter assaults began to interfere with Colonel Ha's efforts to withdraw his regiments. Soldiers were continually harassed by rocket and machinegun fire from helicopters. Occasional airstrikes added to the growing confusion and panic. On 1 November, the Americans got their first major break when a platoon landed directly on the medical aid station of the 33d Viet Cong Regiment, just a short distance east of Colonel Ha's headquarters. In the ensuing firefight, the VC lost 100 soldiers dead and all medical supplies. On 3 November cavalry troops landed at the foot of Chu Pong Mountain. That evening the troops ambushed an unsuspecting enemy patrol, killing dozens, and held off a battalion counterattack with the help of rocket-firing helicopters.

By 10 November most of the remaining VC force had run the aerial and firepower gauntlet to reach the safety of Cambodia. The cost of the siege and the withdrawal had been enormous. The two regiments could assemble only half their original strength. However, a new regiment, the 66th, had only recently arrived from North Vietnam. It was fresh and unbloodied. Colonel Ha was too much the professional to surrender the initiative without another fight. In the relative quiet of his mountaintop refuge, Ha met with each of his regimental commanders on the evening of 10 November and planned a renewed attack. For reasons that remain obscure, they chose, incredibly, to mount another set-piece attack against the Plei Me Special Forces camp. Ha committed all three of his regiments to the effort. For additional punch he added a battalion each of heavy mortars and 14.5-mm twin-barreled anti-aircraft guns. The next five days were spent preparing for the attack. For the first time, the North Vietnam Army would employ a full three-regiment division in South Vietnam.

Unknown to the NVA, General Kinnard also decided to renew the offensive. On 13 November, 28 lifts by heavy CH–47 helicopters placed two artillery batteries at Landing Zone (or LZ) Falcon, miles ahead of the infantry and only five miles east of the Chu Pong Massif in the Ia Drang Valley. At 10:30 the next morning Lieutenant Colonel Harold A. Moore, commanding the 1st Battalion, 7th Cavalry, began landing three companies into LZ X-Ray, a small (100 by 200 meters) clearing at the foot of Chu Pong Mountain and right in the midst of the enemy division on its way to attack Plei Me. The ground around X-Ray was flat, with scrub trees up to 100 feet tall, thick elephant grass, and curious spouted ant hills scattered about, each up to eight feet high. The vegetation grew thicker and higher to the west as the ground began to rise toward the mountain.

The battle for LZ X-Ray began the moment the first helicopter touched down. By early afternoon all companies of the 7th Cavalry were heavily engaged. Arriving helicopters were taking hits, and the enemy was attacking the landing zone furiously from every direction. Colonel Moore knew by midafternoon that his battalion was in a fight for its life. Just before dark he pulled all of his forces, except for a single isolated platoon, into a tight perimeter. Incredibly, the lone platoon, with only 12 soldiers alive and unwounded, would remain isolated and survive for two days, surrounded by the enemy but protected by a barrier of firepower.

The NVA began attacking in larger formations the first evening and continued unrelentingly for two days. Wave after wave of determined soldiers threw themselves against the perimeter. During that night, the two supporting batteries from LZ Falcon fired over 4,000 rounds around the perimeter. Forward observers "walked" exploding rounds so close that hot shell fragments whistled over the heads of friendly troops.

The attack intensified the next morning. Enemy fire became so accurate that the forward observer with the most hard-pressed company was pinned down, unable to observe. Fortunately, the artillery officer located in Colonel Moore's command post could see the fight, and from his distant position he adjusted artillery and air strikes around the company. By mid-morning, tracers criss-crossed the battalion command post area and aid station, killing or wounding several men. Enemy fire became so intense that any movement resulted in more casualties. Combat became so confused that it was difficult to tell friend from foe. For a moment Colonel Moore feared that the landing zone would be lost. He was determined that history would not repeat itself: "It certainly entered my mind that we were the 7th Cavalry Regiment," he recalled, "and by God, we couldn't let happen what happened to Custer."

At 8:00 in the morning, Moore ordered each of his platoons to throw a colored smoke marker so that the precise outline of his perimeter could be seen by air and ground observers. Then he ordered all fire support brought in extremely close. In the confusion, some friendly artillery fell inside the perimeter and two cans of napalm accidently landed nearly on top of

A line of helicopters lands to pick up troops and airlift them to a new location in a search and destroy mission like those used by General Kinnard at the Ia Drang. The helicopter allowed movement of troops over long distances and hostile terrain in Vietnam.

Colonel Moore's command post. But soon the artillery formed a protective firepower shield too intense for the enemy to penetrate. With the perimeter clearly marked by smoke, helicopter gunships were able to bring machinegun fire even closer. Heavily loaded and clumsy ''Huey'' attack helicopters rolled in repeatedly, firing machineguns and rockets into the face of the enemy.

Throughout the critical 40 hours at X-Ray, the Air Force maintained tactical aircraft constantly on station with a fighter-bomber on a target run every 15 minutes. During periods of extreme desperation, aircraft risked destruction by flying through plummeting artillery shells and small-arms fire to deliver napalm and fragmentation bombs. Colonel Moore noted that on one occasion white phosphorus artillery shells proved particularly effective at halting the enemy. Apparently the 66th had never experienced the smoke and burning effect of ''WP,'' and its sudden appearance seemed to have a debilitating psychological effect.

In marked contrast to Dien Bien Phu, the heavy helicopter gave isolated defenders the reassurance that they would continue to be supported with an inexhaustible supply of artillery guns and ammunition. On 15 November enemy pressure slackened sufficiently to permit two more batteries of light artillery to be lifted into LZ Columbus, a firebase hastily cut out of the elephant grass only five miles northeast of the fight. Lifts of ''Chinooks,'' each carrying a hundred-round load slung underneath in a large nylon cargo net, shuttled continuously from base camp to firebase without interference from enemy or terrain.

Shortly after noon on the second day of the fight for LZ X-Ray, Colonel Ha and his staff witnessed a large area to their immediate south suddenly erupt with hundreds of thunderous explosions, moving inexorably across the ground like a giant fiery carpet being unrolled. The first B–52 strike in support of a tactical fight landed squarely on his rear area. Additional strikes continued along the Chu Pong Massif for the next five days. Rumors spread throughout Ha's three regiments that these ''carpets'' covered 20 square kilometers and that ordinary trenches and foxholes offered no protection.

Colonel Ha tried X-Ray once more on the 16th, and again suffered a blood bath. This time the Americans pushed outward toward his position, the advance preceded by a moving wall of artillery shells. After three days of fighting, Ha's death toll exceeded 1,000. Firepower once again had prevented his victory.

After the X-Ray fight, Ha realized that a prepared infantry perimeter with plentiful artillery carefully plotted and registered was too tough a target. He drew his attention to the real source of his failure, the supporting artillery batteries positioned in lightly defended landing zones to the east. An attack there might more easily kill American soldiers and eliminate the enemy's most devastating source of killing power. On 16 November he ordered the 66th regiment to move toward LZ Columbus and destroy both batteries of artillery positioned there.

Coincidence again played an ironic role in the battle. On 16 November, Colonel Moore's tired and battered soldiers were lifted out of X-Ray and replaced by two battalions, the 2/7th and the 2/5th Cavalry. In keeping with the tenet that terrain without enemy on it was of no value, General Kinnard ordered the two fresh battalions to abandon X-Ray and close on LZ Columbus to join up with and protect the artillery. The 5th Cavalry left X-Ray first and closed on Columbus at noon. But the 7th Cavalry left later by a different route, which led across the path of the 66th regiment. Unfortunately, the 66th had a 20-minute headstart.

Shortly after noon, the enemy commander halted his unit a mile or so short of LZ Columbus for a casual lunch break. Immediately, his outposts reported that a large American column was approaching. With no time to spare, he ordered his units into an improvised ambush. Quickly, the experienced NVA soldiers lay themselves flat in the elephant grass. Some climbed trees for a better shot. None were under cover. The Cavalrymen were practically within sight of Columbus when the enemy opened fire. The horror and heroism of the next six hours has rarely been equalled in American wars. Within seconds the enemy were in the midst of the Cavalry. Fighting was hand-to-hand. Within minutes, hundreds of intermingled Vietnamese and American dead and wounded littered the open meadow that came to be known as LZ Albany. Artillerymen only a short distance away listened to the frenzied radio calls for fire from artillery observers still alive, but were unable to fire for fear of hitting friendly soldiers. Aircraft and helicopters darted in and out of the kill zone but could not easily find the enemy partially hidden in the elephant grass.

By early evening the worst was over. A few leaders rallied the remaining soldiers into two perimeters. The survivors marked positions with smoke and called protective fires throughout the night. The next morning the enemy retreated, leaving behind 400 dead. But in only a few hours, the 7th Cavalry had suffered 157 killed—two-thirds of all those lost by the division during the campaign. To Senior Colonel Ha, the lesson was clear: surprise the Americans and separate them from their firepower and the battle becomes an even match.

The fight between regulars at the Ia Drang established a precedent that increasingly came to characterize American combat in Vietnam. To be sure, guerrilla style warfare was still common, and throughout the war the United States made a limited effort to assist the Vietnamese in training popular and regional forces to fight local guerrillas using guerrilla tactics. But by 1965, the enemy had coalesced into larger units capable of escalating the conflict to the conventional stage of revolutionary warfare. US strategy centered principally on the destruction of these larger VC and North Vietnamese units in the hope that the respite thus gained might allow the South Vietnamese Army to carry on less intense aspects of the war.

The protracted nature of the "war of attrition" that followed was the result more of political calculation than of the imperative of face-to-face combat on the ground. Much has been written about the strategy that sought through gradual escalation to increase the cost of the war until the North had no choice but to negotiate a settlement. To soldiers far removed from the subtleties of international politics, "gradual escalation" in practical terms translated into making the war too expensive for the enemy by killing his soldiers wholesale.

Success on these terms was made all the more difficult by a patient enemy willing to accept enormous battlefield losses to achieve political victory. The words of Ho Chi Minh to the French continued to haunt those who saw enemy casualties mount without appreciable progress at the peace table: "You will kill ten of us and we will kill one of you and in the end it will be you who tire of it." General Giap, again in the field directing the new war, stated unequivocally, "The minimum aim of the Viet Cong is not to fight to the bitter end but only to the point that the enemy can be brought to the conference table and there defeated."[2] So, ironically, both sides accepted the consequences of attrition warfare, but the enormous difference in political resolve and cultural stoicism between antagonists meant that US firepower had to maintain, or perhaps even better, Ho Chi Minh's ten-to-one ratio in order to stand any chance of strategic success.

Firepower and Maneuver

Infantry could not hope to achieve kill ratios as disproportionate as these without a great deal of outside support. The fighting ability of infantry on both sides was about even. The enemy's guile, capacity for hardship, and skill with camouflage was matched by the flexibility, initiative, and technical skill of the Americans. Infantry weapons carried into combat were about equal in quality on both sides: although the enemy may have had an advantage in the reliability and power of his automatic weapons, the Americans generally were able to carry and expend a greater volume of ammunition in a firefight.[3] Helicopters helped in great measure by freeing infantry from the "tyranny" of inhospitable terrain. But once the infantryman was separated from his carrier and on foot, one side was as mobile as the other.

The lesson of the Ia Drang was that the pivotal factor in the tactical contest would be firepower. If the Americans could bring artillery and airpower to bear quickly and effectively, the advantage was theirs. The enemy's objective was the same as it had been against the French: to separate the Americans from their source of firepower or to strike quickly and withdraw before incoming firepower shifted the odds against them.

The Ia Drang also taught that an enemy who wished not to fight could only be brought to battle by a methodical search using many small units, usually platoons, spread thinly over a wide area likely to conceal the enemy. This meant that a lieutenant, inexperienced and often isolated in the jungle with his platoon, became the leader most directly responsible for finding and fixing the enemy.[4] Major General William Depuy, commander of the 1st Infantry Division in 1966, understood the lieutenant's plight and published a simple yet comprehensive regulation that told small-unit leaders how to fight in Vietnam.[5] Variations of the 1st Division regulation soon became standard in other divisions, differing only in minor detail to accommodate local variations in terrain, enemy capabilities, weapons, and equipment.

The regulation warned leaders to take great care when searching dangerous territory, to move in a formation that exposed the fewest men to initial contact. A firefight would begin with a furious exchange of rifle and machinegun fire. It might be triggered by two opposing point men stumbling into each other. Most often the enemy opened fire first from point blank range. In the first, terrifying moments of the firefight, the lieutenant was expected to concentrate on keeping his unit alive and intact until reinforcement arrived. To avoid needless casualties, he was instructed to curb any unwarranted instinct to assault or outflank the enemy position. He was to collect together isolated elements and draw back from the enemy's "close embrace" to make easier the task of delivering close-in firepower.[6]

The survival of the platoon would then rest with the lieutenant's superiors. His battalion commander was responsible for building up overwhelming firepower superiority as quickly as possible. The battalion commander might choose to reinforce the committed unit with additional infantry. But though a light infantry company could arrive quickly by helicopter, its light organic firepower made it little better able to achieve significant killing effect than the unit already in contact. More likely, the sudden arrival of another unit into the fight raised the risk of additional casualties. An isolated platoon in contact might be reinforced by mechanized infantry reinforced with armor. But such units had to move by ground. The time necessary to collect and dispatch a mechanized unit would make its arrival untimely.

Also, as the battle for Plei Me demonstrated, a road-bound relief force might itself become a victim should it stumble into a carefully laid ambush.[7]

Unlike in a conventional war, the placement of additional maneuver forces in the enemy's rear would not cause the enemy to abandon his position. A double or single envelopment against an insurgent force might look good on a battle map, but infantry commanders soon learned that such maneuvers wasted manpower and in dense jungle did not prevent the enemy from breaking contact and slipping away. Unless an infantry commander really knew his business, the last-minute entry of more infantry directly into the heat of a firefight quite often created confusion and made the total defensive effort less effective by interrupting the coordination between maneuver and supporting fires.[8] Therefore, commanders soon learned, and most divisional instructions dictated, that immediate reinforcement of the firefight would come principally from artillery, attack helicopters, and tactical air.

Firepower became all the more important to an infantry unit obliged to pursue the enemy deep into his own sancturaries and base camps. The Viet Cong located such places in deep jungle, swamps, and mountains. Contrary to popular opinion, the VC disliked such miserable, debilitating places as much as any Western soldier, but he retired there because it offered the chance to fight the Americans on more even terms.[9]

The enemy was a master builder of field fortifications and tunnels, truly as accomplished as the Japanese had been at this type of warfare. He surrounded his underground fortresses with such diabolical devices as claymore mines and command-detonated shells and bombs. Even an extensive base camp could be so well camouflaged that a US unit might intrude well into its labrynth of tunnels and bunkers before triggering an ambush. Immediately, exploding mines and machinegun fire would inflict casualties so close to the bunkers that supporting fires could not be laid down without endangering friendly wounded.[10] A direct assault under such unfavorable circumstances would only cause more casualties.

The approved method for destroying a base camp was to determine its precise dimensions and isolate it by forming a loose cordon, taking care to keep soldiers away from prepared defenses and back far enough so not to inhibit the delivery of firepower. The commander then turned the battle over to his supporting arms to pound the fortification with air and artillery.[11] After the first application, a few soldiers would probe the position. If they received more fire the process was repeated again and again. "Doctrinal" assaults rarely occurred. Frontal attacks came only after the position had been devastated and the enemy so stunned and punished that the advance became a cake walk.[12] Commenting on the wisdom of this method, a commander from the 25th Infantry Division, and a veteran of numerous attacks against bunker complexes, paraphrased jazz singer Sophie Tucker:

> I've been rich and I've been poor and believe me, being rich is better. As an infantry commander I have assaulted fortified base camps both ways: the traditional closing with the enemy and the let-the-artillery-and-air-do-it, and believe me, the latter is better.[13]

As the quotation implies, experienced infantry commanders were the most vociferous proponents for fighting the battle with firepower. In a remarkable study, titled *The Dynamics of Fire and Maneuver*, done at the Army War College in 1969, a group of seven students (two of whom would become four-star generals) surveyed 200 returning commanders to determine their impression of the relative balance between firepower and maneuver in Vietnam. Overwhelmingly, these veterans concluded that firepower dominated the battlefield. An infantry commander maneuvered his units to achieve two objectives. The first was to find the enemy, and the second was to move his unit into the best position to ensure that firepower could do the killing. They agreed that the enemy should be engaged at the maximum effective range of organic weapons, usually 200 to 300 yards in thick terrain. To advance any closer would only cause more friendly casualties without a corresponding loss to the enemy.[14]

The study also criticized, to some degree, the training and indoctrination of new commanders, implying that many were unfamiliar with the true nature of the war and were unprepared to integrate and control the abundant fire support available. The

study remarked that young soldiers learned quickly on their own
how to survive the shock of contact. American soldiers in combat have traditionally been able to develop expedient methods
for getting the job done while assuring their own survival. Often
the lessons were learned and practiced before such methods
were taught by their senior commanders, and long before such
methods became accepted doctrine.

It would seem, in light of American experiences in previous wars, that too much reliance on firepower might affect
adversely the aggressiveness and elan of maneuver soldiers. The
study concluded quite the opposite—that, in fact, large doses of
firepower bolstered the confidence of the infantry by demonstrating the superiority of the killing weapons at their command.
The knowledge that so much support was available made soldiers all the more spirited and aggressive should tactical circumstance ultimately dictate that an assault was necessary. The
study concluded that massive firepower was one means of com-
pensating for the limited training of young infantrymen. Each
soldier came equipped with a "well of courage," which could
be drawn upon whenever necessary, but which could also be
conserved and used sparingly thanks to the killing power of supporting arms. In fact, the authors of the study noted, "Young
draftees are subjected to the moral effect of war and are sustained by our materiel advantage and the knowledge that it will
be used."[15]

Not all commanders in Vietnam agreed that a firepower-
intensive tactical method was appropriate for all occasions.
Colonel C. K. Nulsen had been an advisor to the South Vietnamese rangers, and operated with them in War Zone "D" two
years before the arrival of major American units. He succeeded
in influencing the regional Vietnamese military commander to
teach his rangers how to fight in the jungle using stealth and initiative rather than firepower. The ranger soldier was just as
good in the jungle as the Viet Cong, he insisted, and with training, experience, confidence, and leadership, he could meet the
enemy head-on and defeat him at his own game. Firepower was
important, but it was most useful as a last resort to tip the scale
in favor of the government forces once the battle was joined.[16]

Nulsen later commanded a US battalion in the 196th Light
Infantry Brigade attached to the 25th Division and attempted to

inculcate the same knowledge of field craft and self-reliance in his American soldiers. When given the opportunity, he slimmed his companies down to 70- or 80-man units able to move quickly and quietly through the jungle. He taught them how to hide from the VC and how to move at night and hit the VC in surprise attacks.[17]

Thanks to such training, Nulsen's battalion could operate without relying heavily upon helicopters and firepower. Most division "SOPs" (standard operating procedures) dictated that companies and platoons begin operations with helicopter assaults. Routinely, artillery, gunships, and tactical fighters softened up each helicopter landing zone with a "preparation" fired just before the lift helicopters set down. If given the chance, Colonel Nulsen avoided using this standard operational routine. Whenever possible he sent his companies into the combat area alone and on foot to melt unobtrusively into the jungle. Most division SOPs directed that units in the field halt in the late afternoon to prepare defensive positions for the night. Helicopters appeared overhead at about 4 p.m. each day to deliver mail, a hot meal, and defensive "kits" that included barbed wire, claymore mines, starlight scopes, mortars, and sandbags. Before dark, soldiers would "button up" by digging themselves in and by firing artillery concentrations close-in all around the perimeter.[18] Although such preparations virtually assured that an infantry position would not be overrun, Nulsen believed that such displays telegraphed intentions. Any subsequent contact would then be on the enemy's initiative, usually resulting in high enemy body counts, but with a corresponding rise in friendly casualties.

Nulsen kept his companies in the field for long periods without resupply and sent them back to the same general area time and again to ensure that each company knew intimately its area of operations. Whenever possible, he kept his companies hidden, moving them at night to set up numerous small-scale ambushes. The results were rarely spectacular. Infantry squads were sometimes able to surprise small enemy units and a short, vicious firefight ensued, lasting only a few seconds. The engagement was over before supporting fires could be delivered. Although not dramatic, the cumulative effect of numerous small skirmishes was a favorable kill ratio and an enemy force without the tactical initiative.[19]

Nulsen considered a well-disciplined rifleman to be the surest and most reliable source of firepower. His problem was not to get his soldiers to use firepower, but to restrain use of it until the unit was able to maneuver to tactical advantage. He noted that all too often units called in outside firepower simply because it was there. From his experience, the act of calling back soldiers from an assault just to bring in supporting fires sapped alertness and aggressiveness and robbed his men of the opportunity to close with and kill the enemy in decisive combat. But, disturbingly, if artillery and air were not requested, no matter how obscure the contact, an explanation was necessary. Unlike in other wars, a commander was now expected to justify why he did *not* choose to use firepower. This requirement led, Nulsen contended, to rigid adherence to SOPs and an automatic artillery response to every VC-initiated activity. Even a lone sniper, if his presence were reported to higher headquarters, would receive "the million dollar treatment."

As a student a year after he finished his second tour in Vietnam, Nulsen wrote in an essay,

> Firepower too easily becomes an acceptable and quick solution for commanders who have neither the experience nor the time to come to grips with the militarily elusive and politically sophisti- cated challenges of counterinsurgency operations. It is through overemphasis and over-reliance on artillery and aerial bombard- ment that commanders change effective military tactics into coun- terproductive operations.[20]

Nulsen's views and methods were shared by other com- manders. By mid-1969, battalions in the 9th Infantry Division in the Delta region began shedding conventional war accouter- ment and took to the swamps to fight the enemy on his own terms. The 4th Battalion, 39th Infantry, prided itself on being a "guerrilla battalion, US style":

> The US battalion readied itself for combat. Holes weren't bored in the sky by helicopters circling over the target. Nor was artillery and Tac Air placed blindly on red dots on the map marking VC locations. Helicopters weren't hastily assembled for an ill- planned airmobile assault. The battalion knew that the enemy

would be gone slick as a whistle before the lead ship set down on the LZ. Experience had taught this lesson well.... Only guerrilla tactics augmented by US firepower can defeat the enemy at low cost.[21]

Brigadier General Willard Pearson, commanding the 1st Brigade, 101st Airborne Division, employed Nulsen's "lighter touch" with firepower—but on a grander scale. He was convinced that excessive use of artillery in support of ground operations "doesn't do much good and discloses what friendly units are in the area."[22] Likewise, he taught his units that the helicopter made too much noise. Troops should enter a guerrilla battlefield on foot, stealthily, in small units. "We believe we should outfox him, out guerrilla him," Pearson said. "Once control is established, we can throw off our own guerrilla cloak and react violently, destroying him with superior firepower and mobility."[23] As the quotation implies, Pearson was not averse to using large doses of firepower whenever the enemy was found and fixed, but he certainly believed that restraint in the use of firepower was a virtue, not a vice.

Pearson's guerrilla style of infantry tactics would have been impossible for General Kinnard's 1st Cavalry when it came up against the concentrated mass of an NVA division or when faced with a well-armed foe bunkered and entrenched in a base camp. Small unit patrols and ambushes were effective only when the enemy operated in similar fashion, as happened later in the war, after the Tet offensive. However, Nulsen, Pearson, and other commanders who shared their views were concerned that the imperative to trade firepower for manpower had grown so pervasive among their peers that it interfered with the ability of the infantry soldier to do his job in *any* tactical circumstance, however favorable to maneuver. They understood that in American wars the balance between fire and maneuver has traditionally tipped in favor of the former. But in Vietnam this balance was profoundly affected by the overwhelming need to keep casualty rates to an absolute minimum. As General Kinnard noted many years later, by World War II standards, the battle for LZ Albany was a clear victory:

> The press got on us right away about Albany. I think that it was a victory for us ... they had higher casualties. They left the

battlefield, not us. But it was a loss in the sense that you're not looking for 2 to 1 losses, you're looking for 10 to 1 or 20 to 1. So Albany was not up to our standards.[24]

Commanders soon came to realize that any potential benefit derived from tactical experimentation and innovation with maneuver in the field carried with it the heightened risk of increased casualties. In Vietnam, more than in any other war in American history, the preservation of soldiers' lives was the overriding tactical imperative. Faced with these new and exacting standards, most field commanders were unwilling to deviate too far from the accepted firepower-intensive tactical method. They preferred the safer course and endeavored to keep a shield of protective firepower around their troops whenever possible.[25] In the battles to follow, these realities placed increasingly greater constraints on infantry maneuver. The only practical alternative was to employ firepower in massive quantities and give it primacy over maneuver.

Artillery, Fighters, and Gunships

A force groomed since 1945 to fight in Europe required radical alteration to prepare it for an Asian war. The artillery arm was fortunate in that it required fewer doctrinal and materiel adaptations. The guns and ammunition on hand in 1965 served adequately with only minor modification. Infantry divisions were equipped with the same 105-mm howitzer used in World War II and Korea. A light airborne version of the ubiquitous "105" developed during the early 1960s became the standard piece for airborne and airmobile divisions. The light version with its ammunition could be lifted into combat slung underneath a CH–47 helicopter with the gun crew riding inside.[26] Division and corps artillery units included the towed 155-mm medium howitzer, also of World War II vintage, which could be lifted by a heavy CH–54 helicopter, and the newer 8-inch howitzer and 175-mm gun, both of which were mounted on tracked carriages.[27] The 8-inch was best suited for precision fire. Its 200-pound projectile was particularly effective against bunkers and fortifications. The 175 was intended as a long-range "sniping" piece and shot a somewhat lighter shell with dubious accuracy out to a maximum range of 20 miles.

Helicopters, able to transport guns and soldiers on a moment's notice, provided the tactical advantage in Vietnam. Light artillery was lifted by the CH–47 Chinook (above), medium artillery by the CH–54 "Flying Crane" (below).

At the height of the war, the United States deployed 65 battalions of artillery to Vietnam, for a ratio of gun to infantryman not unlike that in Korea and somewhat less than the ratio in Europe during World War II.[28] As in Korea, however, battalions in Vietnam fired far more shells per gun; total expenditure for US units throughout the war exceeded 20 million of all calibers.[29]

As these numbers imply, artillery was the workhorse of the fire support system in Vietnam. The guns were always available to fire, day or night, regardless of weather, and their response was certain. In a general sense, artillery battalions were employed in a manner similar to French artillery's employment in Indochina. "Position artillery" consisted of the heavier sorts emplaced in relatively static fortress-like firebases scattered throughout more populated provinces. Employment differed from the French in that the Americans grouped guns by battery, or sometimes grouped numbers of batteries, and moved them from firebase to firebase more frequently.

Thanks to the helicopter, the American version of "mobile group" artillery was more agile; but the principle of its employment was the same. These guns, usually divisional pieces and a few light pieces from corps artillery, staged out of fixed firebases but moved constantly by air, sometimes as often as once or twice a day during peak operating months. Artillery extended its reach using raids in which a few guns would move into a distant position and engage targets outside of an established artillery fan for a few hours before returning home.[30]

Once in the field, artillerymen quickly modified conventional artillery tactics to accommodate the unique circumstances of terrain, weather, and the enemy. The Americans adopted and improved upon the French method for firing in all directions. Instead of using conventional linear firing formations, they arranged guns in circular patterns, which meant that shells from a battery in a "star" formation would impact in a circular pattern regardless of the direction fired. The guns themselves were emplaced in circular pits. Gunners developed ingenious techniques and devices to shift guns quickly and safely in any direction of fire.[31]

In the conventional, linear style of war common to Europe, guns were pushed close to the front so that the fires from many batteries could mass on a single point. But in a war without fronts, tactical necessity dictated that batteries be dispersed to cover the largest possible expanse of territory. Massing of fires can be done quickly only when the target is overlapped by the firing arcs of many batteries. The need to scatter batteries widely in Vietnam made it very difficult to concentrate overwhelming artillery firepower on any single point. In theory, mass could be achieved by firing many more rounds from fewer guns, but killing effect dissipated geometrically with the time it took to deliver fire. Eighteen rounds fired by eighteen guns landing at once without warning were far more effective than six guns firing three rounds apiece.[32] The difficulty of massing was lessened to some degree by careful planning and by the wealth of firepower available in Vietnam. Before particularly important operations, artillery commanders thickened coverage by inserting additional batteries into an area, each with more than its normal load of ammunition.

Every infantry battalion would have at least one, usually two light batteries at its command. Additional long-range fires might come from heavy guns in distant fixed firebases. Heavy guns were considered essential if a maneuver unit knew that it would be up against a bunkered or fortified complex. In particularly difficult fights, the medium lift helicopter permitted the artillery to "pile on" additional guns and ammunition unhindered by enemy action. Firepower reinforcement from Air Force and Army attack aviation ensured that an overwhelming mass of firepower would eventually be achieved. However, the instantaneous surprise effects from massed time-on-target fires, common in World War II and Korea, were rarely seen in Vietnam.[33]

Infantrymen called Vietnam a lieutenant's war. To artillerymen it was a captain's war. Battery commanders in widely dispersed firebases were often alone, connected to their parent battalions by a tenuous radio link and a weekly visit by the battalion commander. Geographic isolation created special problems. In a conventional war, the battalion headquarters tightly controlled the firing procedures of its subordinate batteries. But in a war without fronts, a young, relatively inexperienced captain was obliged to compute his own firing data and aim his guns at distant targets safely without the reassurance of outside checks. When the infantry battalion he supported came into heavy contact, his task was to sort out, from the confusion and panic coming through the radio, where the friendlies were and what type and quantity of firepower they needed. Lives depended on his split-second decisions. More often than not he made decisions alone.[34]

Artillery and its supported infantry maintained contact by a proven structure of gunner officers attached or assigned at each level of infantry command as forward observers and liaison officers. The key point to be understood is the remarkable difference in importance placed on the artillery liaison and observer structure before and during the war. In peacetime, infantry and artillery units tended to exercise apart. To an infantry commander, firepower was something seen at a distance during an occasional firepower demonstration. The greenest artillery lieutenants became forward observers for infantry companies, and a posting as a liaison officer to an infantry battalion or brigade was not eagerly sought by the keenest of artillery captains. But in combat, infantry commanders demanded effective firepower daily and were present to grade its performance from the very personal perspective of its receiving end. The forward observer became the infantry company commander's right-hand-man and rarely left his adopted company except for an occasional visit to the battery to collect pay and mail. The survival of the company often depended on the FO's skill in calling in and adjusting fire quickly and precisely. Good FOs were prized; bad ones rarely stayed in the field very long.[35]

Armed with map, compass, and radio, a skilled forward observer could use the fire from distant batteries for a variety of unique purposes in Vietnam. When moving through enemy country, an infantry unit most feared ambush. Cautious units investigated a suspicious area by firing artillery into it before sweeping through. When moving down a trail or stream bed, an experienced FO "walked" fire ahead of him by dropping an occasional round every hundred meters or so on each side of the route of march to flush out a possible ambush.[36] Patrols, uncertain of their position deep in the jungle, often asked for a white phosphorus marking round to be exploded in the air at a designated point to assist the patrol leader in locating himself. To protect a unit remaining in position overnight, the forward observer called in a series of defensive fires before dark. Starting a safe distance away, the observer would bring the exploding shells as close to the position as safety would permit. The distant guns would remain aimed at these targets throughout the night. Should contact occur, only a few seconds were needed for the battery to load and fire. Although this technique might make the unit safe, or at least feel secure, the radial lines drawn toward the position by each adjusted target told the enemy precisely where the unit was.[37]

As in all wars, the effectiveness of artillery fire in Vietnam depended on speed and accuracy of delivery. Ideally, an artillery unit firing in support of troops in contact was expected to have shells exploding in the target area within two minutes of receiving an FO's request. Delivery of fire often took much longer, averaging for light artillery almost six minutes under the best circumstances and for heavy artillery, which required repositioning of its pieces, 13 minutes.[38]

Delays were caused by a number of factors. All firing computations were double and often triple checked to prevent firing errors. Such caution reduced errors but cost time. Hesitancy and caution by inexperienced members of the gunnery team often resulted in processing delays. The most common delay of this sort came from forward observers who, when under fire, became confused or uncertain of their own position or the location of a target.[39] Politics and bureaucracy could delay fires even longer. In populated regions, permission from a local Vietnamese sector headquarters was required before firing. Normally, the fire direction center, or FDC, of the close support artillery battalion supporting a brigade obtained clearance for all fires in the brigade area. The FDC kept a current map showing all friendly troop locations as well as populated regions off-limits to artillery without clearance to fire from Vietnamese authorities.[40] Artillerymen developed methods to streamline clearance procedures and shorten fire mission delays. Areas known to be unpopulated or populated only by the enemy were declared "specified strike zones" or "free fire zones" into which fires of any sort could be delivered without clearance.

Generally, the artillery FDC expanded these areas at night after curfew, when anyone moving outside populated areas was sure to be enemy.[41] Later in the war, the military command in Saigon required regional artillery control headquarters to establish "Air Warning Control Centers" to broadcast warnings to aircraft in the area before artillery could fire. Although normally not a cause for long delay, the AWCC provided another source of friction in the system, which might add a minute to the artillery response time.

By late 1968, most higher artillery headquarters established combined Vietnamese-US coordination centers that included artillery, air, naval gunfire, and targeting sections from both countries. These centers helped to some degree, but clearance delays continued to be a problem throughout the war. It was common for missions to be delayed up to ten minutes to obtain all necessary clearances. The average delay was seven minutes. It was not uncommon for the artillery to be denied permission to fire at all near populated areas.[42]

Accuracy of fire was also a recurring problem. Artillery fires "off of a map" to hit an unseen target. Inaccurate maps meant inaccurate fire, and the maps in Vietnam were notoriously bad. Topographic surveys, inherited from the Japanese and the French, were so unreliable that points on the ground were commonly misrepresented on the map by a quarter-mile or more. Man-made structures and roads had long since disappeared or been moved since the maps were printed, causing terrible confusion for unwary soldiers who relied on temporary features for navigation.[43] Soldiers often became disoriented in thick jungle and, when caught in a sudden firefight, found themselves incapable of pinpointing their position accurately. To be safe, artillery batteries would fire initial rounds in a contact fire mission well away, as far as 1,000 meters. The first round might be a smoke or white phosphorus shell detonated high in the air so the FO could see it. Subsequent rounds would be "walked" methodically inward toward the enemy in contact at 100-meter and then at 50-meter increments.[44]

The patience of an infantry commander demanding fire on a target was often tried by what appeared to him to be needless delays. However, when soldiers were in serious trouble, gunners generally fired their rounds "close and quick" without a great deal of adherence to the letter of the regulation. This was the time when an artillery commander earned his pay. The decision to sacrifice safety for speed was his, and he alone accepted responsibility if friendlies were hurt by any misjudgment.

The real test of an FO's mettle was his ability to bring rounds in close. Contact at 100 meters or less gave the FO an all too infrequent opportunity to do real damage to the enemy. Skill was essential to be sure, but equally important was the infantry commander's faith in the FO's ability. With care, a battery of light artillery could be fired to within 50 meters as long as friendlies were behind cover. At this distance, concussion and blast were tremendous, and hot shell fragments would whistle over the heads of the infantry. The infantry commander knew that an error of only half the turn of a handwheel on a gun far to his rear would drop rounds among his soldiers.[45] The enemy, also knowing this, often would fire mortars or rocket-propelled grenades into the Americans when attacking in the hope that the infantry commander might think that he was taking casualties from his own artillery and order a cease-fire.[46]

The mortar is an indirect fire weapon that traditionally belongs to the infantry. It is nothing more complicated than a simple smooth tube connected to a baseplate. Because it fires at a high angle of elevation, the recoil shock is transferred directly to the ground, eliminating the need for a complicated recoil mechanism. Lighter mortars were intended to be carried by infantry soldiers, providing the rifle company commander with his own personal artillery.

Most infantry units failed to employ mortars effectively in Vietnam. Tubes, baseplates, and ammunition were too heavy to lug through jungle on the backs of soldiers already overloaded with personal gear and small arms. Such exertions were rarely worth the effort because artillery firepower was plentiful, responsive, and always available. Although mortars were simple in function, errors in laying and firing were easily made, particularly by infantry soldiers not accustomed to engaging unseen targets using indirect fire.[47] The problem of mortar firing safety was aggravated by the inadequate training that many mortarmen received. As often as not, mortar crews were scraped together

Artillery, such as 105-mm howitzers (firing from a 1st Cavalry Division "firebase" in 1966, above), provided the backbone of the US firepower system in Vietnam. With plentiful firepower available from guns, helicopters, and fighters, mortars (an 81-mm fires, below) were often left behind and neglected in Vietnam.

from riflemen no longer able to take to the field. For these reasons, most infantry commanders were content to leave their
mortars at firebases and rely on artillery to provide necessary
indirect fire support.[48]

A lesson the artillery re-learned from the French was the
value of spotter aircraft in jungle war. American artillery groups
and division artilleries had their own organic aircraft and a complement of knowledgeable artillerymen assigned to them as
aerial observers. Artillery spotter sections had changed hardly at
all from previous wars. While the turbine helicopter was a common means of transportation in Vietnam, artillery observers still
favored the light, single-engine L–19 "Bird Dog" inherited
from Korea. It was a simpler, quieter, and more robust aircraft,
and its slow speed was an asset when the mission was to loiter
above a point and observe patiently for any clues of enemy presence.[49] The artillery only complained that there never seemed to
be enough Bird Dogs to accomplish a myriad of routine (but
vital) tasks such as registration of batteries, convoy cover, and
aerial surveillance.

Early in the war, the 1st Cavalry Division Artillery
increased the effectiveness of its few attack helicopters by team-
ing them in pairs with a Bird Dog. Keeping the little aircraft
aloft permitted the helicopters, with their limited endurance, to
await a mission just minutes away at a friendly firebase. Unlike
the French Morane of the first Indochina war, artillery aircraft,
or any Army aircraft for that matter, could not communicate
directly with Air Force fighter-bombers.[50]

The attack helicopter proved its worth during the advisory
period in Vietnam. Although restricted initially, at Air Force
insistence, to the defensive role of escorting troop-carrying helicopters, its ability to destroy ground targets soon led to its
acceptance as an offensive weapon. By the time US forces were
committed to combat, the Army and Marine Corps employed
armed helicopters variously as escorts, aerial cavalry, and fire
support vehicles.

Air cavalry helicopters were dispatched in pairs ("pink
teams") to roam over large areas gathering intelligence. When
necessary, they employed on-board weapons to engage targets
of opportunity or to provide fire support to isolated ground

reconnaissance units caught by the enemy outside the range of supporting artillery. In the fire support role, armed helicopters were grouped together as a battalion of aerial rocket artillery (ARA) in airmobile divisions. ARA helicopters were employed like any artillery pieces. Their fires were requested and processed through normal fire support radio nets.[51] Consequently, mission response times for aerial artillery were comparable with those of cannon artillery. For an aircraft already airborne, a complete mission 10 minutes; aircraft scrambled on the ground took 24 minutes on average, of which 11 were consumed flying to the target.[52]

For the first three years of war, the Army and the Marines could field only an attack helicopter jury-rigged from an early-model Huey no longer suitable for duty as a troop carrier. "Huey gunships" were variously armed with combinations of 2.75-inch rocket pods, automatic 40-mm grenade launchers, and multiple forward-firing machinegun mounts. Imaginative and resourceful ground crews bolted on all manner of armament combinations depending on the specific role of the aircraft. Gunships were armed additionally with one flexible machinegun mounted in each side door, to be fired by a door gunner. Four crewmen, armament, ammunition, and crew armor brought the ancient bird up to its maximum gross weight, making take-offs in the hot, humid Vietnamese climate a sporting proposition at times. Excessive weight also made the aircraft slower than the troop ships it escorted, as well as sluggish and difficult to maneuver for a pilot trying to thread through jungle canopy or avoid enemy ground fire.[53]

Such an imperfect instrument made the growing reliance ground forces placed on it all the more remarkable. As so often happens in war, the real secret of success seemed to rest with the men who operated the machines rather than the machines themselves. Most helicopter pilots flying early in the war had experience in other arms. They understood the nature of close combat and the plight of troops in contact. They were able to fly their craft "in the weeds" immediately above the infantry. A request for helicopter support could come from any member of the maneuver chain of command. Once on station, attack helicopters talked directly to the infantry on infantry radios without delay or interference from intermediaries.[54]

In serious situations, the infantry expected their armed helicopters to take risks. During the opening moments of the bitter fight for LZ Albany, only the aerial rocket artillery and cavalry gunships could move in close and low enough to provide effective fire support. They were able to identify pockets of enemy intermingled with friendlies by observing the color of crisscrossing tracer streams—blue-green for the Viet Cong and red-orange for US ammunition. A heroic but bizarre incident occurred in the same unit that fought at LZ Albany when one pilot, after killing the crew of a heavy machinegun, landed in the midst of the enemy and grabbed the gun to prevent the enemy from putting it back into action.[55]

Although the Huey gunship was a makeshift system, it did possess certain qualities that suited the fire support mission. It was the only fire support system in Vietnam available for support to Army troops that contained the intrinsic ability both to detect and to engage a fleeting target immediately. Vision was virtually unlimited, and its slow speed and low-level performance allowed the four sets of eyes aboard to spot the slightest sign of the enemy. Attack helicopters occasionally were limited by weather, but because they flew lower and slower and could hover, their allowable ceiling was half that of fixed-wing aircraft.[56] The fact that it did not carry weapons of great destructiveness permitted the gunship to support with precise, discriminating firepower. It was (and remains) the only reliable means for delivering fire support closer than 50 meters from friendly troops; in some cases support could be delivered as close as 5 meters as long as friendly positions could be clearly seen from the air.[57] Not only could it shoot closer, but a gunship's rockets did not blow over trees or tear up terrain.[58] Pound for pound, aerial rockets were two or three times as lethal against enemy troops as artillery.

Not until late 1967 did the first true gunship appear in Vietnam. This was the AH–1G ''Cobra,'' a system designed in haste from the proven Huey engine and power train. The Cobra was accepted by the Army as an ''interim'' system until an attack helicopter could be designed and built from scratch. Although not all that the Army desired, it was far more capable than the Huey gunship: fast enough to keep up as escorts, and

Early in the war, a Huey gunship (above) carrying two mini-guns and rockets flies support cover. Beginning in 1967, the AH–1G Cobra (below) replaced the Huey in its gunship role.

having better armor and a far more capable assortment of armaments.[59]

In spite of the huge tonnages of aircraft bombs and artillery shells dropped in their midst, enemy soldiers in contact with US units most feared the gunship. The VC could hide from or avoid most other means of fire support, but a gunship overhead represented a close and constant eye from which there was far less chance for escape.[60]

Without question, the attack helicopter was the most popular aerial firepower system among ground commanders. Eventually, the popularity of the attack helicopter became its biggest drawback. The infantry came to expect a gunship on station to provide fire support for all contact. Increasingly, helicopters became aerial rocket platforms, leaving fewer of them available for equally important tasks such as convoy protection, route reconnaissance, and screening.[61]

Lieutenant General A. C. "Ace" Collins, commander of the I Field Force in 1970, noted that maneuver commanders tended to call for armed helicopters before artillery, even though artillery was the more responsive system. Collins credited this to the fact that gunships flying in the air around a commander's own helicopter gave the commander a sense of immediate control over his firepower. He could direct attack helicopters on to the target personally, without having to wait for clearance. He did not have to preoccupy himself with the complexities of turning artillery on and off to bring in air-delivered close support. Maneuver commanders came to prefer helicopters over artillery to such a degree in the 4th Infantry Division that the division commander, Major General Burke, prohibited any of his units from calling for attack helicopters unless they requested artillery first.[62]

The Marines had similar problems. Lieutenant General Victor "Brute" Krulak, commander of Fleet Marine Force Pacific, noted that between July 1966 and June 1967 two-thirds of the missions flown by the Marine helicopter observation force had been as armed helicopters, not in the observation role. Krulak was angered by this because he realized that war in jungle terrain demanded that best use be made of the few aerial "eyes" available to a field commander.[63]

Fixed-wing aircraft were available in abundance to provide close air support. But a study of US strategy in Vietnam conducted by BDM Corporation noted,

> Army gunships were often overused and misused. The ground forces became quite fond of them and at critical times occasionally employed them in lieu of tactical air and artillery. This unsound predilection was highlighted in Laos in 1970 when helicopters reportedly were employed against well defended hard targets.[64]

Dense jungle greatly reduced the killing effect of helicopter rockets and machineguns. Yet helicopters were all too often called upon to attack targets better suited to fixed-wing aircraft carrying more powerful weaponry.[65] Armed helicopters were never intended to take on hardened targets. Heavy artillery could be used against such targets, but the heavies were slow and success against small point targets problematical. Close air support from fighter aircraft was, and remains today, the surest way to deliver overwhelming firepower quickly and precisely against tanks, fortifications, and bunker complexes.[66]

The advisory period in Vietnam from 1962 to 1965 helped the Air Force to refocus attention on the need to fight limited wars and provided enough time to let these experiences sink in before US troops were committed to combat.[67] Some shortfalls were relatively easy to correct. Although the value of forward air controllers had been established in World War II and Korea, the Air Force possessed no forward air controller aircraft of their own before 1966. In 1963 this requirement was filled by borrowing 25 "Bird Dogs" from the Army.[68] Likewise, early experience in the war demonstrated the need for an aircraft that flew slower, stayed aloft longer, and carried larger ordnance loads than F–100 and F–4 high-performance fighters, neither of which were particularly well suited for close air support. In 1963 the Air Force reclaimed a number of previously obsolete Navy A–1 propeller-driven attack aircraft from storage to meet the close air support requirement, and initiated a crash program soon after to convert T–37 jet trainers to light, maneuverable ground support aircraft.[69] To the end of the war, many in the Air Force believed that these relatively unsophisticated aircraft remained most effective for supporting troops in contact.[70]

In 1965, the Air Force determined the need for a first-line fighter aircraft intended solely for close air support. The Air Force recommended the A–7D, a modified version of another existing Navy plane. The A–7 provided a sophisticated, computerized bombing platform, long loiter time, and impressive armament load at the comparatively low cost of $1.5 million each. Unfortunately, instead of purchasing the aircraft from the Navy "off the shelf," the Tactical Air Command insisted on substantial changes in the A–7, including a new engine and new avionics. The first flight of the modified aircraft did not occur until March 1968. It did not become operational in Vietnam until 1971. By then most US troops had been withdrawn from direct combat.[71]

Without the A–7, bombing in Vietnam was done using a "seat of the pants" system. Modern aircraft such as the F–100, F–4, and Navy A–4 had nothing more sophisticated than an "iron" sight, similar in principle to a rifle sight, which could be adjusted up or down before the attack to compensate for variations in bomb type, release altitude, and air speed. To hit the target, a pilot had to turn into a shallow dive and line up on the target so that he released his bombs at a prescribed speed, altitude, and dive angle, all the while offsetting the nose of the aircraft to the left or right to compensate for the estimated effects of cross winds. Like a good rifleman, an experienced pilot was more accurate because he knew intuitively how to compensate among the four flight variables and apply "Kentucky windage" during his attack run.[72] On-board computers and laser rangefinders would eventually take the art of bombing out of the stone age and result in a quantum increase in accuracy. But these improvements would come too late to improve the precision of close air support in Vietnam.

Bombing accuracy in close support missions was affected by other factors. High-speed fighters such as the ubiquitous F–4 required more area to turn and maneuver above the target area. Superior speed forced pilots to bomb from higher altitudes, further diluting accuracy.[73] Another more sensitive problem concerned pilot skill, particularly during the early years of the war. Training given to tactical fighter pilots before the Vietnam War reflected the mission priorities of the Air Force, which centered mainly on nuclear weapons delivery. Some conventional delivery training was required, but it was minimal. For hundreds of young pilots who found themselves in combat for the first time early in the war, the art of close support was learned slowly. Several years elapsed before the necessary pilot skills were adequately diffused throughout the Tactical Air Command.[74]

The most ingenious innovation in close air support in Vietnam was the transformation of a C–47 transport aircraft into a machinegun-firing gunship, affectionately known as "Spooky" or "Puff, the Magic Dragon." These unlikely warbirds were the brainchild of Ralph E. Flexman of the Bell Corporation. His concept was championed by an exceptional group of farsighted Air Force mavericks who overcame considerable opposition from within the fighter community to put Spooky to use in Southeast Asia. Guns on these aircraft fired to one side rather than to the front. This arrangement permitted Spooky to circle a fortress or village under siege and keep its guns trained continuously on the target, unlike conventional attack aircraft, which could aim and fire only while diving on the target. The earliest versions carried on-board flares to light up the target area, enough fuel to stay on station for hours, and sufficient ammunition to beat back all but the most determined attacker.[75]

A phenomenon of recent history has been the disturbing habit among Western nations, the United States in particular, to expect too much from aerial firepower. Perhaps this expectation has been the product of our search for a technical means to win wars without expending lives. Whatever the cause, the use of airpower in Vietnam certainly followed the historical precedent. Policymakers with an imperfect understanding of the true limitations of modern airpower concluded all too readily that those wondrously destructive weapons of aerial warfare would be able to persuade the enemy to come to terms with a minimum of human investment.

During the advisory period, airpower advocates contended that, although air forces made up less than 5 percent of the total military strength, aircraft were credited with 25 percent of enemy killed—and this was predominantly in support of defensive operations.[76] Much greater things were expected from airpower when the allies took the offensive. In 1965 Colonel

An Air Force F-100 Supersaber releases its ordnance on a close support bombing mission.

James P. Hagerstrom wrote of the greater role that airpower would assume as US ground forces were committed to the war:

> I think the whole essence of the US operation is *not* to fight a war of attrition—infantryman-versus-infantryman but to let airpower destroy the enemy once the ground has identified them and put his finger on them.[77]

The system for requesting close air support provided a "shadow" air staff at each level of Army command from battalion through corps (in Vietnam a "corps," was called a "field force"). This system was intended to process requests for air support up the chain of command, and to exert various degrees of command and control over aircraft formations once dispatched. Ground soldiers were concerned with two types of requests for air—preplanned and immediate. As the name suggests, a preplanned request was used routinely for such missions as airmobile landing zone preparations or the attack of relatively fixed targets such as bunkers, trails, and fortifications. An immediate request was time sensitive, usually called in support of troops in contact.

The system was complex and cumbersome.[78] A preplanned mission began the day before when an infantry company commander, for instance, might request an airstrike for a task such as an LZ preparation for the next morning. The request made its way up the chain from battalion to brigade, division, field force, and finally to the Military Assistance Command in Saigon for approval. At any level it might be refused, but in practice this occurred rarely in Vietnam. Strike planners in Saigon determined the number and type of aircraft, munitions, and time of attack. The forward air controller received this information back down through channels during the early evening of the day before the preplanned strike.

The FAC took off in his light aircraft before dawn and spent the next two hours coordinating the strike between many different agencies. First, he radioed to the air element at brigade or division to advise that he was on station and to determine if strike aircraft were on time; then he radioed the operations officer of the infantry unit to get a physical description of the target to aid in its location from the air.[79] Next came an often laborious and frustrating effort to gain clearance from the artillery firing at the target. That process might include as many as four or five clearances. Each clearance required the FAC to get friendly locations, confirmation of target location, and permission to engage. The FAC then contacted the ground commanders and, again, the laborious process of information exchange was repeated. The FAC told the company commander the type of aircraft and ordnance to expect, and the commander passed on the method he would use to mark his position and the target. Meanwhile, the strike fighters arrived, vectored in by Air Force ground control radar. Now the FAC was talking on three radios: Air Force Tactical Control and strike aircraft on UHF and ground commanders on FM.[80]

Once the FAC was sure that he had located the target, he fired a smoke rocket toward it just before the fighters rolled in to attack. He then talked the fighter pilots through the mission, not an easy task considering that it was unlikely the pilots had been in the area before. Fighter pilots circled faster and higher than the FAC, so they needed additional time to locate the target themselves and ensure in their own minds that the approach was safe.[81]

Nearly 70 percent of all missions flown in Vietnam were preplanned. Practical experience in two previous wars had shown preplanned missions to be the most efficient. Because the mission took a day or more to develop, there was time to brief pilots, plan in detail, and allocate the optimum aircraft type and bomb load for each target.[82]

The procedures for an immediate strike were essentially the same as for preplanned except that the call for fire was handled by radio and expedited through the system to field force. If possible, higher headquarters contacted fighters already airborne and diverted them from less important missions.[83] All of this took time. The system was subject to the friction that one would expect from professional, competent pilots faced with the difficult task of delivering lethal munitions at an unseen target in close proximity to friendlies. Mission response times varied. Early in the war, most immediate requests were answered in less than a half-hour, with approximately half in 15 minutes or less.[84] Additional delays—6 minutes each at battalion and brigade and 8 minutes at division—occurred later in the war when intermediate headquarters began to exert more control over the process in an effort to improve troop safety. Aircraft scrambled from the ground took from 40 minutes to an hour or more from the time of the initial request to arrive on station.[85] Diverted aircraft averaged approximately 40 minutes. These times were essentially unchanged from the Korean War.[86]

Once attack aircraft were on station, FACs required an additional 15 minutes to pass on final instructions and orient the fighters on the target.[87] To this must be added an additional hour, on average, between the moment of contact and the time that the commander on the ground initiated the request for air support. Such long delays occurred because infantry commanders tended to call for supporting fires in sequence, beginning first with the most responsive and escalating to close air support either as an afterthought or after organic weapons, artillery, and attack helicopters proved unable to do the job adequately.

Field commanders complained from the beginning that close air support was being requested too late to have any destructive effect. Of the 117 sorties flown for the 173d Airborne Brigade during Operation Hump in November 1965, only 36 were employed to support troops in contact.[88] Similarly, the 1st Cavalry noted that air strikes all too often were used as "blocking" fires behind the enemy or were dropped too far away because of the inability of FACs and fighter pilots to identify clearly the locations of friendly troops.[89] The tendency for units to escalate their fire support sequentially limited the participation of close air support to less than 8 percent of the total ground contacts, while artillery and armed helicopters provided fire support for 40 percent of ground contacts. More than half of the firefights were over so quickly that they did not generate any request for fire.[90]

The complexity of the air-ground control system proved to be a particularly serious problem in Vietnam. In a revolutionary war, the insurgent's greatest asset was his inherent mobility. Once spotted, he had to be attacked immediately. A preplanned mission against a day-old target rarely caused any damage. Even an immediate strike in support of a contact two hours past could do little unless the enemy intentionally chose to stand and fight, or the unit in contact somehow managed to fix a portion of the enemy force in place. Several minutes of aircraft circling overhead followed by an incoming smoke rocket from the FAC aircraft told even the dullest enemy that a strike was imminent and provided more than enough time to move out of harm's way.[91] As a general rule, tactical airpower was reserved by the ground commander for only large-scale firefights lasting for a long period, usually between three and six hours.[92]

Fire Support Coordination

Employment of combat forces as a "combined arms team" has been the immutable tenet of maneuver warfare. Infantry, armor, and artillery must be employed in concert and orchestrated by the maneuver commander to gain full advantage of each individual arm's potential. The same applies in principle to firepower. Artillery, helicopter, and tactical air are nothing more than varying means to deliver explosive power. Each has its advantages and disadvantages, and each contributes a measure of capability not possessed by the other: responsiveness and accuracy by artillery; precision and direct observation by helicopters; destructiveness by close air support.

The application of all in combination creates a synergism of effect that makes the whole of the system far more lethal than its component parts. To apply them properly requires as much skill in orchestration from a fire support coordinator as does the exercise of combined arms from a maneuver commander. In the past, fire support coordination at the tactical level rested with the commander of the artillery battalion assigned to support each maneuver brigade. Practically, the work was done by field artillery liaison officers, normally captains, assigned to each maneuver battalion.

Good battalion liaison officers were hard to find and even harder to educate. Most came to the job with no experience in fire support coordination. Many had never been forward observers, fewer still had served before in Southeast Asia. Try as it might, the Army school system was no more capable of teaching young artillery captains the intuitive sense of time and space necessary to orchestrate the complex firepower battle in Vietnam than it was of inculcating a similar intuitive feel for the relationship between fire and maneuver in young infantry commanders.[93] The commander of II Field Force Artillery lamented that the formal training his liaison officers received at the artillery school

> has not equipped them with the experience of operating a UH–1H console, of controlling preparatory fires over a PRC–25 radio from the back seat of a LOH [light helicopter] while coordinating with the infantry commander over the intercom, of simultaneously adjusting artillery fire and gunships and instructing an Air Force FAC in support of troops on the ground marked by a puff of smoke, or of coordinating fires in support of the maneuvers of two converging friendly forces who speak different languages. Formal training for artillery liaison personnel should go beyond the stage of learning artillery techniques that may be reduced to a paper solution of a paper problem.[94]

Supporting a unit in contact was a fire support coordinator's biggest challenge. In large-scale operations involving a company or more of enemy, the battalion commander would gather up his operations officer and artillery liaison officer, or LNO, to begin reinforcing the firefight. Most likely, the three would be airborne in the command and control helicopter, equipped with a bank of radios linking all participating maneuver and support units. Reinforcing by fire was complicated by the confusion of combat and the large number of objects flying through the air near the contact. Medevac helicopters had to be brought directly into the fight to take out the wounded; the infantry's own mortars might be firing from within the unit perimeter, although quite often neither the company commander nor his FO were aware of when and where the mortars were firing.[95] The FO was busy adjusting artillery close to his position. Artillery trajectories would be converging from all directions. Attack helicopters would be down low, trying to keep under artillery trajectories, but difficult to see. Air Force FACs and a continuous string of strike aircraft would soon arrive to further crowd the airspace, not to mention the occasional frightening appearance of enemy anti-aircraft fire.[96]

From the air, the LNO could see the complete outline of the unit under fire and could help the FO rapidly construct a protective wall of artillery around it. The LNO had to be careful not to get too deeply involved in the FO's business. He had enough to do himself, and his FO had access to plenty of other help, including an artillery aerial observer, an FAC, and his entire chain of command orbiting above asking for information and offering "helpful" advice.[97]

A liaison officer could only learn the intricate skill of firepower orchestration properly by doing it in combat. It required him to apply fire to a target continuously with each air or ground delivery means separated from the other by precise manipulations of space and time.[98] Separation by space alone, using clearly defined sectors on the ground for each means, simplified the process, but it also limited the variety of ordnance that could be delivered into a single area. Often one piece of ground required more than a single type of fire support. Fighter aircraft were comparatively more destructive, but could not drop close. A determined enemy under bombardment often used the dead time between aircraft passes to renew his assault. Artillery and helicopters, on the other hand, offered continuous support, but neither had the destructive power to kill an enemy entrenched in the jungle.

Separation by space also risked leaving wide gaps in firepower coverage. In clear weather, armed helicopters and fighters required separation of a kilometer at the very least. At night or in bad weather, helicopters and fighters could not be used together safely at closer than three miles.[99] With good visibility, experienced pilots, well-defined targets, and clearly marked friendly lines, strikes could be coordinated closer, but this process was dangerous for pilots from two services who could not talk to each other directly. Communications between Army and Air Force strike aircraft had to be relayed by voice over three radio nets from helicopter pilot to liaison officer to FAC to fighter pilot and back again. All the while, the two craft might be converging at a combined closure rate near the speed of sound. Likewise, separation between artillery and fighter aircraft normally left a gap of at least 750 meters.[100] In emergencies, this distance could be reduced, but placing artillery and air fires too close together ran the risk of fighter pilots mistaking smoke from exploding artillery rounds for the FAC's target-identifying mark.[101]

The doctrinal solution to the problem of simultaneous delivery of air and artillery ordnance was to create special flight corridors in the sky. In theory, as long as a fighter-bomber stayed within a prescribed aerial "box," it could safely fly underneath and above the artillery. As the illustration on page 108 indicates, the "restricted fire zone" method of control may have been a good idea in theory, but it proved a very complicated proposition to put together during the confusion of battle.

To establish a safe corridor for high-performance aircraft, a fire support coordinator first had to ensure that all information concerning his plan, such as altitudes, direction of flight, and length, width, and effective times of restrictions, was disseminated throughout all elements of the firepower system. Artillery fire direction centers then had to convert this information into firing safety data for the guns to ensure that no projectile strayed into the aerial corridor. The process took a great deal of time, and any unexpected development in the tactical situation caused this fragile and inflexible system to break down quickly.[102] Therefore, it proved effective and reliable only in a relatively static environment such as the defense of Khe Sanh combat base by the Marines.

Guns and artillery helicopters (or ARA) were the only two fire support means able to work an area simultaneously while supporting a maneuvering force in heavy contact. Guns and ARA both operated on the same artillery fire request net and could talk to the FO on the ground without the need for relay. Because artillery helicopter pilots were also artillerymen, they could sense the location of the gun batteries and, by keeping very low, could fly directly under the incoming shells.[103] Most importantly, ARA and cannon artillery worked together habitually. Pilots were not intimidated by the sight of artillery shells exploding underneath and artillerymen were confident of not shooting down a helicopter by accident. Separation between the two was measured as the ranging error of the guns plus the explosive radius of the shells—a distance for light artillery of approximately 100 meters.[104]

A variety of fires could be delivered in a single area by assigning flight paths perpendicular to the artillery trajectories and turning the artillery on and off between strafing runs. This style of time separation was the most effective means for ensuring close and continuous fire support, but it could be done only if the LNO knew his business—and if he had the complete trust of maneuver commanders and pilots. Flight paths and friendly locations were difficult to discern in featureless jungle, and it took a very convincing FAC to induce a fighter pilot to dive his aircraft toward a hillside erupting with artillery with the promise that the shelling would cease just seconds before the fighter released his ordnance and turned over the target.[105]

With training and time to work together, Air Force FACs and Army fire support coordinators lessened greatly the dead time between various applications of aerial and ground-delivered ordinance. But in even the best circumstances, time delays occurred ranging from two to eight minutes—often just enough time for a stunned enemy to collect his wits and continue the attack or for an anti-aircraft machinegunner to take aim carefully at the next wave of diving aircraft.[106]

For these reasons, firepower was most often coordinated into the battle using space rather than time. If conditions were right, it could be very destructive. Just a month after the fight at Ia Drang, a battalion of the 1st Infantry Division stumbled into an elaborate base camp near War Zone C in Tay Ninh Province, near the village of Nha Mat, 35 miles north of Saigon. The camp was a thoroughly fortified and superbly camouflaged underground city occupied by elements of two VC regiments. The US battalion commander, Lieutenant Colonel George Shuffer, was moving his battalion southward with a rifle company deployed on either side of a north-south jungle road.[107] Following traditional methods, the enemy allowed the battalion to penetrate well within the base camp area before initiating contact. The VC then rushed from their fortified camp and charged the battalion in waves.

Heavy machineguns mounted in trees covered the VC assault and pinned down the two lead companies instantly. Colonel Shuffer's B Company was forced west of the road by the heaviest attack. The trail company tried to flank the enemy from the west but it, too, was halted by withering small arms fire. Soldiers took refuge behind ant hills and road embankments. The commander formed his unit into a circular perimeter

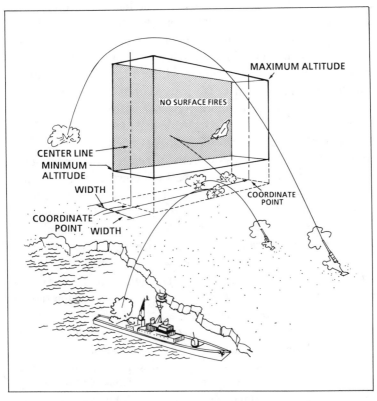

In theory, surface and aerial firepower could be delivered simultaneously on a single point by constructing an aerial "box" around high-performance aircraft. Helicopters could participate by flying at treetop level, below the artillery fire. In actual practice, the system was less precise and more complicated.

in the midst of the basecamp and began the process of destroying the enemy with firepower.

A light battery located to the south at Lai Khe had been firing all around the perimeter since a few minutes after the contact began. Colonel Shuffer narrowed its fires to the south and added an 8-inch and 175-mm battery firing from the same direction. The greatest threat came from east of the north-south road. Colonel Shuffer assigned this region to the Air Force, instructing his FAC to bomb anything east of the road. The B Company skirmish line was pinned down behind the road embankment. Bombs were dropped a safe distance away, but cannon fire and napalm were laid down parallel to the road just in front of the infantry hunkering behind the far embankment.

Armed helicopters were assigned the north flank, where the jungle was most dense. The enemy there was trying to infiltrate through the battalion perimeter in small groups. After the battalion headquarters section marked its position with colored smoke, the helicopters were able to fly just above the jungle canopy to spot and engage the scattered infiltrators with rockets and machineguns. Artillery was inappropriate for the north flank because shells fired over the heads of friendly troops from the south might have detonated prematurely in the high jungle canopy above them. For four hours, artillery, fighters, and armed helicopters worked continuously to lay down an impenetrable curtain of fire around the battalion. After suffering at least 300 dead, the enemy broke contact and deserted its base. US losses were 40 killed and 104 wounded.

Applications of firepower as efficient and decisive as in the battle of Nha Mat were relatively rare. In this instance, favorable circumstances of weather, terrain, and troop dispositions, as well as the level of training and trust between maneuver and fire support, combined to create a particularly favorable outcome. More often than not, frictions of war combined to limit the killing power of fire support as effectively as it limited the decisiveness of maneuver in the jungle. These frictions took many forms. Some of them could not be avoided.

Darkness and bad weather were the most pervasive. Artillery was affected least by darkness and weather, but the FO still needed some form of artificial illumination (either from artillery

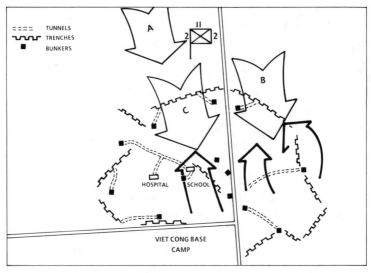

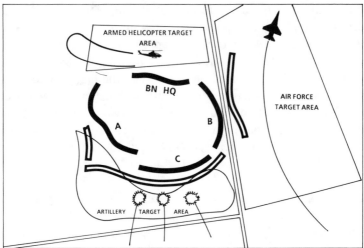

Battle of Nha Mat,
5 December 1965

"star shells" or aircraft flares) to spot the enemy. In poor visibility, separation distances between delivery systems increased from less than a kilometer to three miles or more. The pace and tempo of delivery was slowed considerably at night.[108] The Air Force could bomb at night in support of troops by using a ground-based radar beacon that vectored aircraft to the target and signalled them when to drop. Skilled "skyspot" operators could achieve accuracies of 200 meters or less in ideal circumstances, but safety regulations prohibited routine skyspots any closer than about 1,000 meters from friendly lines. On several occasions, notably at the siege of Khe Sanh, radar-controlled aircraft delivered ordnance as close as 250 meters from friendly troops.[109]

The confusion and uncertainties of close combat also impaired the delivery of fires. Inexperience was part of the problem, but the very nature of the war acted to limit the effectiveness of fires.[110] In previous wars, FOs and pilots could zero in on tanks, bunkers, buildings and other clearly defined subjects. But in Vietnam, targets were invariably diffused, hard to see, and quite likely were lost completely in a featureless carpet of green.[111]

Without exception, field commanders in Vietnam applauded the abundance, variety, and destructiveness of firepower available to them. But some became concerned that too much firepower was expended during periods of inactivity on less lucrative targets while too little was used in support of troops in combat. Most division SOPs dictated an elaborate firepower preparation of each helicopter landing zone. These were controlled and coordinated by a single artillery liaison officer.

Tactical airpower was first on the scene with two fighters lingering 20 to 30 minutes over the landing zone, making on average three bombing passes. When the Air Force was finished, the LNO began an artillery preparation that worked over the area for five to ten minutes, expending 200-300 rounds. The last round fired was white phosphorus to notify the helicopters then just beginning final approach that all artillery tubes were clear. If the LNO's timing was precise, attack helicopters would make a single firing pass over the LZ seconds after the last artillery round landed. The troop-carrying helicopters would follow immediately behind the gunships.[112]

The final approach by a Huey, heavily loaded with troops, into an LZ was a very dangerous moment. Infantry soldiers, greatly fearing a "hot LZ," rightfully insisted that the fire of an enemy nearby be suppressed until soldiers were on the ground and the helicopters safely away. When the risk of a hot LZ was high, no one questioned such elaborate displays of firepower. But some commanders believed that preps had become too automatic and too much for show rather than for effect. Some commanders often wasted too much time and ammunition prepping areas they knew to be free of the enemy. These preps served only to warn the enemy that a helicopter landing was imminent. All too often, a white phosphorus shell landing in an open field became a signal for the enemy to come out of foxholes and bunkers to open fire. Many aggressive infantry commanders violated the "iron rule" and landed troops in remote areas without a prep. Some "prepped" one obvious LZ and landed their Hueys in an unlikely LZ to catch the enemy off guard.[113]

Although a moderate application of firepower might frighten or turn back an enemy, a tremendous amount of ammunition was required to kill him in the jungle. The lethality of conventional "iron" munitions had not increased since the first Indochina War, but to soldiers on the ground iron bombs and shells appeared more lethal than they actually were. This fact led in turn to a pervasive tendency not to extract the greatest possible destructive effect from firepower systems once the enemy was found and fixed. Contacts were won at great cost and they provided the only sure means of locating lucrative concentrations of enemy. Yet only 15 percent of artillery and 4 percent of Air Force munitions were delivered in support of friendly ground actions.[114]

More fire support wasn't delivered primarily because it wasn't requested. After-action reports from routine contacts seem to indicate that once firepower secured the safety of friendlies and turned back the enemy, soldiers on the ground often failed to request enough additional firepower to achieve decisive killing effect. In most engagements, close support rarely exceeded a few hundred rounds of light artillery and a flight or two of fighters. Combat experience in previous wars as well as empirical data gathered in extensive experiments showed that light artillery shells expended in the thousands were relatively ineffective against entrenched, dispersed soldiers in the jungle.[115] It took one 105-mm light battery firing 2,000 rounds over a two-hour period to equal the lethality of a single pass by a flight of F–4 fighters against such a target.[116]

If the objective of close combat was attrition, then hundreds of bombs and many thousands of artillery rounds would have been needed to ensure the destruction of most VC formations. A study conducted during the war by the RAND Corporation noted the propensity of some ground commanders to call for only a token amount of firepower when in contact. The study concluded that troops in a firefight were often satisfied when supporting fires allowed them to extricate themselves from a serious situation. In the thick jungle, where the enemy could not be seen, the killing effect caused by additional ordnance poured into the enemy position remained unobserved and unappreciated.[117]

Not only were fewer rounds requested, but the fire support chain rarely delivered the more deadly varieties of munitions to destroy a force found and fixed by the infantry. Both the Air Force and the artillery possessed bomblet ammunition of one sort or another. Variously called cluster bomb units (CBUs) for aircraft or improved conventional munitions (ICMs) for artillery, these munitions spewed a large number of small, highly lethal grenades over a much larger area than a regular iron bomb or shell. An artillery ICM round could be up to 20 times as effective and an air-delivered CBU 7 to 9 times as effective against enemy soldiers.[118] Yet, during the most intense phase of the war, ICMs accounted for less than one round in a thousand of all artillery fired.

Bomblet munitions had drawbacks of course. Since their explosive effect covered a much wider area, they could not be fired close. Because they detonated in the air, the risk of causing friendly casualties was somewhat greater using this variety of munition. Any error in time setting might cause the bomblets to be ejected prematurely and land among friendly infantry.[119]

General W. R. Peers, commanding the I Field Force, was among the first to be alarmed by the reluctance of his subordinates to ''pile on'' enough firepower for significant killing effect. Throughout his tenure, Peers continued to preach the merits of concentrated firepower in support of a heavy contact. In his debriefing report he recalled asking a commander how many rounds he had fired in support of a company in contact with an enemy battalion. The commander's response was, "I put a TOT [time-on-target concentration] right on them, sir." In checking, however, General Peers discovered that this commander's interpretation of a TOT was 30 rounds. Peers remarked, "In my view ... it should have been somewhere between 800 to 1,000 rounds."[120] As a point of contrast, modern Soviet artillery doctrine calls for the expenditure of between 2,000 and 4,000 rounds of artillery to destroy a company entrenched in open terrain.[121]

Target Intelligence

Major General David Ott, Commandant of the Artillery School at Fort Sill immediately after the Vietnam War, once reflected that the greatest single failure of the firepower system in Vietnam was its inability to develop reliable, targetable intelligence.[122] Platoons were used to lure the enemy into a fight because intelligence was so seldom good enough to locate the enemy without a firefight. In a war without fronts, the insurgent controls his territory and conceals himself within it. He possesses few of the modern devices of war that are easy to detect, such as fixed bases, motorized equipment, communications facilities, and heavily travelled routes of supply.

Acquisition of useful intelligence was even more difficult for fire support than for maneuver. An infantry commander could commit his forces against an imperfectly located enemy. But the same level of information was not precise or timely enough to be used by a fire support coordinator for targeting. To be able to target a guerrilla force, its location must be known to within an area approximately the size of two football fields.[123] It must be found, fixed, targeted, and engaged with a fury of concentrated firepower, coordinated and timed to suprise and overwhelm the enemy before he breaks and flees. To do these things when an elusive enemy can be seen and engaged with direct fire is very difficult. It is extraordinarily difficult when he is distant and unseen—located only by instruments or vague intelligence reports.

Target intelligence in Vietnam was gathered using either human or electronic means. The eyes of forward and aerial observers continued to be the principal source of target intelligence. But restrictive terrain and the elusive nature of the enemy made observers less effective in Vietnam than in other wars. Technology aided the observer to some degree by extending his vision and allowing him to see at night. Starlight scopes were telescope-like devices that amplified ambient light from the moon and stars. They were first used in Vietnam to give an observer greatly improved night vision.[124] Artillerymen mounted early versions on firebase perimeters, aircraft, and other platforms to provide observation above the jungle canopy. In January 1966, a small Special Forces detachment first used starlight scopes successfully to discover and thwart an enemy attack on a firebase. In February 1966, the 1st Division placed them in helicopters. In that month, an aerial observer destroyed a large motorized junk on a nocturnal resupply mission with a single (and very lucky) round from a 175-mm gun firing 11 miles away.

Starlight scopes were used most effectively mounted on C–47 "Spooky" gunships. On 4 March 1966, a Spooky detected a force of 200 VC as they prepared to attack an isolated village. The enemy were accustomed to taking cover only when gunships began dropping flares, so they continued the assault unconcerned until tens of thousands of bullets began falling among them. Before the enemy could withdraw, a quarter of their number were dead.[125]

A debate continued throughout the war over the worth of small, highly trained long-range patrols used as eyes for artillery and air strikes. Proponents of this method of target acquisition argued that small patrols would be able to call in fire support with much less chance of detection than large regular infantry formations. Long-range patrols could push the target acquisition process into the enemy's back yard and away from major base camps with little risk of increased friendly casualties. The Marines first used long-range patrols successfully for artillery observation with force reconnaissance companies operated in small groups ranging in size from four to twelve men. They were inserted into remote regions by helicopter to stay for several days, observing the enemy and avoiding direct engagement.

The effectiveness of long-range patrols as distant eyes for artillery and airpower is typified by the experience of one specially trained Marine unit, as told by Francis J. West in his *Small Unit Actions in Vietnam.* On 26 July 1966, a four-man team from the 1st Marine Force Recon Company, operating a few miles south of the border with North Vietnam, spotted a large collection of enemy encamped in a small, wooded grove. Sergeant Orest Bisko, the patrol leader, knew how to use artillery. Whenever he selected a concealed area from which to observe, Bisko fired in artillery at a set of known map coordinates so that fire could later be adjusted from that point to the target with speed and precision. The enemy company was resting and apparently in no hurry to move. Deliberately, Bisko whispered fire commands over his radio link to distant batteries. He ordered them to shift a short distance from the known target and fire for effect. Three minutes later a dozen shells crashed into the thicket. Bisko ordered continuous fire. At first, the enemy refused to scatter, assuming that the incoming rounds were only a few lucky harassing rounds fired blindly by the Americans. This gave the guns more time to work over the area. After half an hour, Bisko counted 50 enemy dead. His patrol escaped in the confusion.[126]

All major ground units in Vietnam eventually employed small patrols to destroy the enemy with long-range firepower. Special Forces "Delta" teams, consisting usually of eight US and native soldiers, became very adept at calling in air strikes on targets in distant corners of Vietnam and Laos. The Australians also favored the use of covert patrols, and often sent them far beyond close-support artillery range. Long-range patrolling ran up impressive kill ratios. The Australians claimed 14 to 1, the Marines, 36 to 1.[127] The 1st Brigade, 101st Airborne Division, achieved a 10 to 1 ratio by breaking platoons into smaller covert patrols, which continued to operate under the protective umbrella of light artillery. Once an enemy force was spotted or contact initiated by a patrol, the brigade used traditional "pile-on" tactics to reinforce the fight.[128]

Sergeant Bisko's surprise attack by fire was effective because he happened to have responsive artillery at his command. But most long-range patrols could be reached only by heavy guns and tactical airpower both of which responded too slowly to engage a fleeting enemy. Francis West, who told Sergeant Bisko's story, wrote,

> I worked outside Khe Sanh in five- to ten-man units, the basic unit. We could see thousands of them—but our indirect fire systems were not good enough to hurt them. If we had to use artillery, the probability was very high that we were going to miss the North Vietnamese, who moved rapidly in a single file.[129]

A covert patrol ran about an even chance of detection when it called in firepower on an unsuspecting enemy. For this reason, maneuver commanders were reluctant to use patrols for this purpose unless the nature of the target and the circumstances of its engagement were ideal. It was safer and perhaps in the long run wiser for the patrol to remain undetected and shadow the enemy for as long as possible.[130] Only very well-trained and self-reliant soldiers could hide themselves for extended periods in the enemy's back yard and handle the complex task of calling for and coordinating distant fires. Most regular line infantry simply did not have the depth of leadership and talent to divide into fully effective, autonomous, squad-sized patrols able to operate far from home. Until the end of the war, covert patrolling remained the purview of a few elite units.[131]

In keeping with tradition, the Army used technology to provide much of its target intelligence. Much of the equipment first brought to Vietnam for this purpose was either too old or inappropriate for a war in the Third World. The AN/TPQ–4 counter-mortar radar detected a shell in flight and determined its point of origin by automatically back-plotting along its trajectory. With a little luck, a skilled operator could zero in on an enemy mortar to an accuracy of about 50 meters. But the machine had only a very narrow sector of scan and operators easily grew tired of staring at a flickering screen 24 hours a day. The enemy soon learned to place his mortars where the radar wasn't looking and to fire them when operators were least likely to be alert.[132] The AN/TPS–25 ground surveillance radar was a more modern and somewhat more effective piece of gear. A radar that worked on the doppler principle, it could detect moving vehicles and troops out to a distance of about six miles. But the machine was intended for use in a conventional European war and often did not prove sensitive enough to pick up small, slow-moving bands of enemy in thick foliage.[133]

Radars were most often emplaced to protect fixed base camps from surprise attack. The 9th Infantry Division Artillery in the Delta region of Vietnam placed radars on top of mobile, 50-foot towers to protect its base camps. The flat, open terrain of the Delta proved particularly favorable for the use of surveillance radars. As many as 40 to 80 sightings were made on some nights. Almost half were engaged with artillery fire. Although the effect of these fires will never be known for certain, some fragmentary evidence gleaned from captured soldiers and documents revealed that occasionally casualties were inflicted if the artillery could respond quickly. No evidence exists that ground surveillance radars had any more than a nuisance effect on the enemy.[134] Yet radar contacts were certainly a more profitable source of target intelligence for unobserved fires than the usual "harassing and interdiction" programs fired at stream-beds or trail intersections plucked randomly from a map.

The search for target-quality detection systems received a boost when unattended ground sensors became available for tactical use. These small, battery-powered devices, emplaced by hand or delivered by air and artillery, could locate the enemy with great accuracy and timeliness. Sensors were activated by seismic, magnetic, and acoustic stimuli and were senstive enough to detect very small units, even individuals. Army sensors were linked by radio to artillery fire direction centers or other remote stations equipped with a readout monitor (or portatale).[135]

The first four sensors to arrive in Vietnam for Army use were given to the 25th Infantry Division to assist in detecting enemy movement toward Saigon. Major General Williamson, the division commander, ordered the sensors emplaced north of Tay Ninh along the Cambodian border and alongside the traditional attack routes of the 9th VC Division. He located the portatale at French Fort, an American firebase of four 175-mm long-range guns a few miles to the east of the sensor field. At

11:00 p.m. on 24 September 1968, the device detected movement along a trail intersection. The 175-mm guns opened up slightly north of the sensors. Six light howitzers fired blocking fires south of the sensors while two light mortars fired directly at the trail junction. At first light the next morning a patrol dispatched to the area found seven enemy dead and an additional thirty trails strewn with blood leading from the area.[136]

In spite of these and similar successes, additional sensors arrived slowly. Not until late 1969 were enough on hand to be used with any significant effect. The 25th and 1st Divisions emplaced large numbers of sensors to thicken the coverage around Saigon. Most were placed along traditional infiltration routes; some along main roads to detect and spoil ambushes. The remainder were scattered in hills around major base camps in areas likely to be used as rocket and mortar firing sites.[137]

Accurate artillery coverage of sensor fields was possible only if the sensors were located precisely. Since most were dropped by slow-flying aircraft or hovering helicopters, precise locations were difficult to pinpoint. Artillery units tried various means to improve emplacement accuracy. Aerial emplacement teams in the 1st Division tied smoke grenades to the sensors and photographed the smoke from the air.[138] The photo was then compared to a larger aerial photo map of the entire area to plot a precise location. Division artillery also fired guns into a sensor field immediately after it was implanted. The guns were adjusted until the exploding shells activated seismic sensors. Fire direction centers kept on file the firing computations used to hit the sensor field for use when the sensors were activated by enemy movement.[139]

The enemy did learn, over time, to "spoof" sensors or to avoid them whenever possible. Sensors were completely reliable only when used in concert with other systems such as patrols, radars, scout dogs, and aerial sightings. Yet, to the end of the war, sensors were the only target acquisition devices that provided the precision, responsiveness, and consistency necessary for effective engagement by indirect fire.

Khe Sanh

The first three years of American combat in Vietnam were characterized by fairly consistent success in attrition-style warfare. Enemy casualties rose and fell in a cyclical pattern roughly corresponding to the number of days of good campaign weather in each corps region. Often, enemy main force units would be badly mauled by American firepower in big battles fought for the control of strategic cities or large base camps. These fights would evolve in a pattern similar to the French success at Vin Yenh and inevitably would result in enormous loss of life to American firepower.[140] Large, costly face-to-face confrontations of this sort seem to belie the image of a patient, stoic enemy who chose to fight only when the advantage was clearly his. Some experts on the war ascribe these tactical anomalies to General Giap's impatient search for a second Dien Bien Phu—a chance to score a major political and propaganda victory by knocking the Americans out of the war as surely and decisively as he had the French. For the first three years of war with the Americans, past success clouded Giap's grand strategy and made him as obsessed as the French had once been with fighting the "Big Battle."

Some time late in 1967, Giap personally visited the area around the Marine base at Khe Sanh.[141] To Giap the base must have appeared strikingly similar to Dien Bien Phu. Like Dien Bien Phu, Khe Sanh sat astride the infiltration routes through Laos and across the border with North Vietnam. Giap believed that its location made it important enough for the Americans to stand and defend it at all costs. Khe Sanh appeared to Giap even more vulnerable than Dien Bien Phu to ground attack. It was located on a plateau surrounded by high mountains, and could be easily isolated and surrounded by cutting the ground life line to the Marine main bases at Con Thien and the "Rock Pile" farther to the east. North Vietnamese lines of supply were much shorter and far better developed than in 1954. The base was smaller and defended by a garrison only half as large as Dien Bien Phu with less than half the complement of artillery. As late as December 1967, the Marine defenders seemed even less enthusiastic about entrenching themselves than the French had been. The air strip at Khe Sanh was more vulnerable than Dien

Bien Phu's, and the Marines had only half the tanks possessed by the French.[142]

Similarities between Dien Bien Phu and Khe Sanh were by no means overlooked by the Americans. Both bases were occupied initially to extend allied influence into enemy regions and block infiltration. As the enemy's determination to attack became evident, both bases became points of strategic focus intended to act as lures to entice the enemy into a firepower trap. Once joined, the significance of both battles transcended mere tactical importance and became media symbols of one nation's tenacity versus another's technological and materiel superiority.[143] (See p. 124 for comparisons and contrasts.)

The battle for Khe Sanh lasted 77 days—roughly three weeks longer than Dien Bien Phu. Khe Sanh never fell. Although fighting was intense at times, the enemy was never able to mass in large enough numbers to threaten seriously the survival of the base. The French suffered almost 3,000 dead, the Marines one-tenth that number. Enemy casualties will never be known precisely, but they surely paid for defeat at Khe Sanh in the tens of thousands.

There were many reasons for such marked differences in outcome between the two battles. Giap was never able to shut down the aerial life-line to Khe Sanh. Supplies and aerial fire support continued to arrive uninterrupted throughout the siege. Although enemy artillery pieces were concealed as effectively as they had been at Dien Bien Phu, they were emplaced a safer distance away to avoid American airpower and were thus less accurate and responsive. Although the French suffered a barrage averaging 2,000 rounds daily, the Marines were subjected to only one-tenth that number of rounds. The worst single day's shelling at Khe Sanh fell 700 rounds short of the daily average at Dien Bien Phu.[144] The enemy was never able to capture several key Marine outposts on hills surrounding the main base, even though these positions were lightly held. One, on hill 950, was defended by only a reinforced platoon.[145]

The survival of Khe Sanh finally hinged on two factors. First was the traditional tenacity and steadfastness of the Marine 26th Regiment, which defended the base and its surrounding outposts. Second was the appearance of an effective firepower

Aerial view of Khe Sanh.

system that fused together, for the first time in warfare, both the electronic and firepower battlefields. This process of fusion occurred only when the heat and light of military necessity brought together a collection of elements from all services into a single functioning system for precise targeting and mass destruction.

The Air Force provided the first segment of the system when General Momyer, commander of the 7th Air Force in Vietnam, was given the task of locating enemy units converging on Khe Sanh. The tight geographical focus provided by the siege permitted the Air Force to go about its intelligence gathering and targeting in the most efficient and comprehensive manner. Momyer went so far as to solicit the help of French survivors of Dien Bien Phu to spell out in detail where they went wrong in their attempts to locate the enemy. He set up a targeting cell in Saigon that tied together traditional means of collection, such as air and ground reconnaissance, interrogation of captured enemy soldiers, and examination of captured documents, with more exotic technology—never before used as effectively in war—such as radio intercepts and ground surveillance radar.[146]

Most revolutionary, and ultimately most decisive, was the use of an elaborate sensor field emplaced around Khe Sanh by the Air Force immediately after the battle was joined. In four days, 250 seismic and acoustic sensors were emplaced by helicopter to cover trails and avenues of approach.[147] The Air Force system was similar to the Army's in concept, but more sophisticated. An orbiting C–121 aircraft picked up sensor activations and retransmitted them to an infiltration surveillance center in Nakhon Phanom, Thailand, equipped with two IBM 360–65 computers. The center collated and analyzed all sensor activations and transmitted information on enemy movements to the US command in Saigon only hours after enemy movement was detected.[148]

The striking power available to the garrison at Khe Sanh was without precedent. The small collection of artillery within the base was augmented by four batteries of Army 175-mm heavy, long-range guns located 10 miles to the east. All artillery possessed ammunition in abundance and expended it lavishly,

Dien Bien Phu and Khe Sanh compared and contrasted

Factors	Dien Bien Phu	Khe Sanh
Air lines of communication	170 miles to Hanoi	Helicopters, 35 miles; TAC air, 90 miles
Enemy lines of communication	From China; long, difficult	From North Vietnam; short
Terrain	Fishbowl; favored enemy	Plateau; favored enemy
Defenders	13,000	6,000
Attackers	50,000	20,000
Key outposts	Fell early	Held to end
Fortifications	Fair	Poor
Defending artillery	24 light guns	18 light howitzers, 6 medium howitzers, 24 heavy guns (at Camp Carroll, Rock Pile)
Attacking artillery	200 light and medium guns, emplaced close-in; multiple rocket launchers	Total unknown; included 100-, 122-, 130-, 152-mm guns and howitzers; 122-, 140-mm rockets emplaced at more distant ranges
Average daily incoming artillery	2,000+ rounds	150 rounds
TAC air	Less than 200 aircraft available; 30-40 daily sorties	2,000 airplanes, 3,300 helicopters available; average of 377 daily sorties (incl. B–52s)
Total ordnance	Less than 2,000 tons	110,000 tons
Defender's casualties	2,700 killed; 4,400 wounded	205 killed; 1,668 wounded (816 minor)
Attacker's casualties	7,900 killed; 15,000 wounded	10,000-15,000 killed (estimate)

Source: BDM Corporation, *A Study of Strategic Lessons Learned in Vietnam*, pp. 3–102.

firing whole batteries in multiple salvos without restriction. In 77 days, artillery of all calibers fired nearly 200,000 rounds close by Khe Sanh.[149]

The siege also provided the impetus to turn the B–52 from a strategic to a tactical weapon. Previously, the big bombers were prohibited from bombing any closer than three kilometers from friendly positions. It soon became evident that the enemy capitalized on this prohibition and pushed major ammunition and supply points to within 1,000 meters of Khe Sanh. General Westmoreland expressed dissatisfaction with the existing restrictions and requested that the Air Force and Marines agree on reducing the safety zone to 1,000 meters.[150] Both services were reluctant but agreed to a partial test at Khe Sanh on 26 February 1968. Two skyspot stations were used for control. Otherwise the mission was identical to any other routine "arc light." The results proved the wisdom of close support heavy bombing:

> All bombs fell within the target boxes, and though the detonations shook the earth at Khe Sanh, there was neither injury to the defenders nor damage to bunkers. The spectacle of hundreds of bombs exploding almost simultaneously brought some of the Marines out of their shelters to cheer the B–52s.[151]

The strikes detonated a string of ammunition points that the enemy had carefully built up and camouflaged after weeks of effort. Some points continued to burn two hours after the raid. By March, B–52 close support strikes became common. Before the siege ended, B–52s flew 2,548 sorties and dropped 59,542 tons of bombs.[152] Fighter aircraft from three services and two nations contributed flexible, heavy firepower. During the height of the siege, 377 sorties were flown each day, almost two-thirds under radar control.[153] Total fighter firepower equalled that of the heavy bombers—a total of 110,000 tons was dropped, nearly twice what the Army Air Force delivered in the Pacific during 1942 and 1943.[154]

Target intelligence, provided by sensors and other means, and firepower from all services were brought together under the Fire Support Coordination Center (FSCC) headed by Lieutenant Colonel John A. Hennelly, commander of the artillery at Khe Sanh. Fortunately, in the Marine Corps, tactical control of both air and artillery were clearly subordinate to the ground

Bombs explode in a B-52 ''arc-light'' being dropped on a suspected Viet Cong position 18 miles north of Saigon, December 1965.

commander. Colonel Hennelly had total charge of coordinating these two firepower means into a single striking arm through his subordinate fire direction center for artillery and the Direct Air Support Center for air-delivered ordnance.[155]

To ensure that he could maintain this control without question, Hennelly permitted only Marine aircraft to fly missions underneath the artillery umbrella surrounding Khe Sanh. Hennelly did not intend this as a disparagement of Air Force and Navy bombing skills, but he knew from experience that only the organic Marine air wings had the close and habitual association with other Marine fire support agencies to permit them to deliver firepower together in close proximity.[156] Targets outside of the umbrella were important, but targets inside were critical to the survival of the base. The Marines understood that they could not afford the inevitable friction and confusion caused by unfamiliar voices demanding that all artillery fires lift before making a bombing pass.[157]

Traditionally, information on the enemy first went to the intelligence officer (or S–2), who processed and analyzed it before sending it to subordinate maneuver and fire support units. At Khe Sanh, however, the process of targeting was so vital and immediate that the S–2 first engaged the most promising sightings with firepower before conducting any routine analysis. The intelligence and fire support functions thus became a single system at Khe Sanh; consequently, the time from acquisition to delivery, which might have taken days, was reduced to minutes. The remote location of the battle and isolation from friendly towns and villages further aided the process. The FSCC was the final authority for clearing all fires, and anything that moved outside the perimeter wire could be safely assumed hostile. The process, however, was inhibited to some degree by the assortment of services and contributing headquarters through which information and fire assets passed on their way to the Marine FSCC.[158]

During the most intense portions of the battle, the targeting officer in the FSCC would receive the sensor information passed from Thailand to 7th Air Force in Saigon. The sensors were imperfectly located because they had been emplaced in haste. But a long string of sightings indicated the general ebb and flow of major enemy units as they moved nearby.[159] The FSCC analyzed sensor "readouts" and collated them with other, less precise means to derive reliable target-quality sets of information. To exploit the sensors fully, Marine planners developed discrete "packages" of firepower tailored to the nature of the target indicated by the sensors and the relative accuracy of each sighting. Because the Marines had absolute control over both air and ground means, these "packages" were both flexible and immediately available. A "mini arc-light," so called because its effect was similar to a smaller version of a B–52 strike, combined Marine and Army artillery with Navy and Marine strike aircraft into a single time-on-target that saturated an area 500 by 1,000 meters.

Fire manipulations such as these required great dexterity and absolute control. The fire control center called in a flight of two or four aircraft for a radar bomb run. While the aircraft were en route, the center alerted batteries at Khe Sanh and Army 175-mm batteries far to the east. At this point, timing had to be perfect. Thirty seconds from bomb release the 175s began firing 60 rounds. Marine batteries began firing shortly thereafter and in the midst of the raining artillery the attack aircraft "pickled" their loads. The trajectories and flight times of all means of delivery were carefully computed and coordinated so that all projectiles landed at the same instant. More refined targets were engaged with "micro arc-lights" blanketing a 500-meter-square area. A mini arc-light took 45 minutes to execute, a micro arc-light only 10 minutes.[160]

Marine virtuosity in control of the firepower battle was best illustrated late in the siege when a single-company raid conducted by B Company, 26th Marines, was dispatched early on the morning of 30 March 1968 to attack a heavily fortified NVA bunker complex 850 meters south of the perimeter. The sweep was carefully coordinated with the FSCC so that the men moved toward their objective protected on three sides by two concentric firepower "boxes." The inner box was formed by Marine artillery and "marched" with the patrol, all the while maintaining its tempo using a time-sequence rolling barrage. The outer box consisted of radar controlled fighters dropping bombs in continuous waves and Army 175-mm heavy guns firing from distant

Camp J. J. Carroll. As the sweep drew near the enemy, the sides of the outer box were shifted inward and outward 500 meters at a time, accordion fashion. As the company advanced, the firepower boxes advanced. After two months of continuous bombardment, the enemy had experienced similar strafings before and were caught by surprise when the inner box of fire suddenly lifted and the Marines rushed the NVA bunkers with flame throwers and satchel charges, killing over 100 in less than two hours. As the Marines retired, the primary and secondary boxes closed back in around them. They returned to the safety of the base having suffered nine killed. During the eight hours of the operation, the Army and Marines expended 3,600 rounds of all types plus several tons of bombs. The total for one afternoon's work was fully one-fifth of all the artillery shells fired during the entire siege of Dien Bien Phu.[161]

Air traffic control became difficult over the very constricted airspace above Khe Sanh. An air strike was delivered every four minutes, around the clock. Four or more Marine, Navy, or Air Force FACs were on station constantly to vector in fighters in rare periods of good visibility. Aircraft "stacked" themselves neatly in spiral columns stretching as high as 35,000 feet above the battlefield as they awaited their turn to bomb. Veteran pilots recalled that the air around Khe Sanh was so thick with flying objects that they feared a mid-air collision far more than enemy ground fire. With so little time on station, ordnance was often delivered inefficiently. Most aircraft "pickled" everything at once before breaking off and heading for home. All too often the FACs fell behind and fighters, running low on fuel, were required to break off and dump their ordnance into the jungle or the sea. The system may have been wasteful at times, but constant practice in the confined space around Khe Sanh made it very effective.

The enemy waited nearly a month to conduct a serious ground assault against the Khe Sanh base. This wait proved fatal. The Marine firepower system had been shaken down and perfected. Air Force sensor analysts at Nakhon Phanom picked up heavy sensor readings early on the evening of 29 February that indicated a division-sized force moving toward the base from the east. Successive blocks of fire using "mini" and

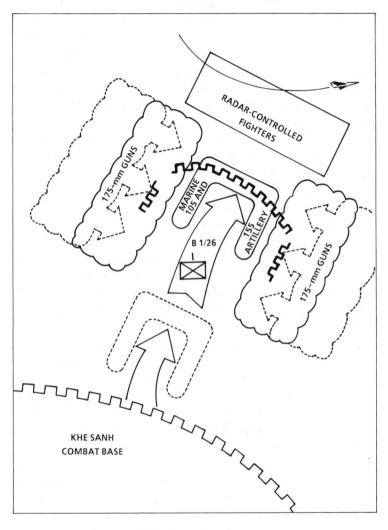

The firepower box,
30 March 1968

"micro" arc-lights were laid in their paths, killing the enemy by the hundreds. What was left of the enemy force tried three successive assaults during the early evening of 1 March, but too few soldiers were left alive and unwounded to penetrate close-in artillery and air strikes. Friendly trail watchers reported after the battle that the North Vietnamese had to stack the bodies of their dead by the hundreds along trails leading away from the battle. The main base was never threatened again.[162]

Much has been made since the battle about the concerted Air Force effort to control all of the air resources around Khe Sanh. General Momyer warned General Westmoreland in early February that the battle might be lost unless a single service controlled all strike and resupply missions into Khe Sanh.[163] Eventually Momyer's side prevailed. Fortunately the Marine Direct Air Support Center still reserved most close-in missions for Marine aircraft under Marine control. The controversy over who would be in charge clouded the real lesson of the campaign. In a battle like Khe Sanh, control of aircraft traffic was not as important as control of the firepower that the aircraft delivered. Throughout the campaign, the Marines maintained firm control of this function and managed to coordinate it closely with the targeting process and the ground commander's scheme of defense. Ultimately it was this ability to fuse all aspects of the targeting and fire support processes that proved so terribly destructive at Khe Sanh.

Giap Changes Strategy

Although Khe Sanh, and the greater Tet offensive of which it was a part, may have enhanced the political position of the North Vietnamese, the battles had been so terribly destructive that Giap could no longer afford to continue with this wasteful tactical method. The folly of standing up to American firepower had cost him almost half his available force in South Vietnam in less than six months of battle. In 1965 and 1966, the NVA soldiers had been well trained, well led, and highly professional. By 1968, General Peers noted, "We have seen the tables turn. The enemy has suffered heavy losses in men and weapons. Hardship, sickness, continued exposure to allied firepower ... have caused NVA morale and fighting spirit to plummet."[164]

Faced with these realities, Giap decided to adopt a new strategy of indirect approach. He realized that Tet had set the Americans on a path toward withdrawal. His strategy centered on expediting this process by continuing to kill Americans while rebuilding his tattered army so that it would be able to renew the general offensive once the Americans were gone. The directive issued by the North Vietnamese High Command for the post-Tet campaign summarized Giap's new campaign philosophy:

> What we should do: For each additional day's stay the US must sustain more casualties. For each additional day's stay they must spend more money and lose more equipment. Each additional day's stay the American people will adopt a stronger antiwar attitude while there is no hope to consolidate the puppet administration and the Army [of South Vietnam].[165]

The tactical dilemma for Giap was how to do this without suffering the unacceptable blood baths of the previous three years. He now understood that casualty rolls in the United States did not differentiate between first-line combat infantrymen and support troops. Therefore, the NVA were no longer to attack directly into the face of American infantry and their supporting firepower, but to attack less hazardous targets using more cautious and deliberate tactics. Rocket and mortar attacks against major bases were the cheapest and surest means of killing without suffering undue losses. Before the Tet offensive, the North Vietnamese trained 16 regular battalions of rocket and mortar troops and sent them south beginning in October 1965. The airbase at Danang was first to be hit by a rocket attack on 27 February 1967.[166] After Tet, Giap ordered a substantial increase in stand-off rocket and mortar attacks.

NVA artillery battalions began receiving the newest Soviet 122-mm rocket in large quantities. These weapons were ideal for the new NVA strategy. A firing tube, tripod, and aiming instruments could be carried by four or five men over great distances. Although not as accurate as artillery, the rockets were accurate enough to hit a large area target such as a major base camp, where crowded living facilities ensured some casualties among US support troops. The rockets had a maximum range greater than American light artillery, permitting them to stand off a safe distance to launch.

Contrary to popular opinion at the time, these were not crude home-made devices employed by untrained guerrillas. To fire their rockets the NVA used communications, survey, and sighting instruments every bit as sophisticated and precise as those used by American artillery.[167] Attacks were mounted using up to two battalions dug securely into firing positions. Normally the enemy placed 12.7-mm heavy machineguns on the flanks of a deployed battalion to shoot down any intruding aircraft. A normal volley consisted of 30–36 rounds, but larger attacks of up to 200 rounds were not uncommon.[168]

Giap's program of indirect rocket attack was more than just a harassment campaign, as the statistics clearly showed. US combat deaths from indirect attacks by fire doubled between 1967 and 1969. By then, rockets and mortars surpassed direct contact as the largest source of American casualties.[169] After Tet, the share of US combat casualties from enemy minings, booby traps, and other explosives increased sharply. In addition to killing and maiming soldiers, these cheap and greatly feared weapons affected morale and hampered speed and freedom of movement. The percentage of those wounded by indirect attacks of all sorts rose to 80 percent of all US casualties by 1970. A soldier in Vietnam was three times as likely to become a victim of these diabolical devices as in the past two wars. Such startling statistics show clearly the scope and the success of Giap's new strategy of attrition. To the end of the war, Americans continued to suffer from such attacks. They were never effectively countered.[170]

As an economy of force measure, Giap began after Tet to take greater precautions to protect his front-line troops from American firepower. Units badly mauled during the offensive were withdrawn from threatened base camps in the South to more secure sanctuary in Cambodia and Laos. Only small cadre units were kept in the South. These were carefully positioned in regions outside the American artillery umbrella. Experience had shown that such places were secure from intrusion not only by artillery but also infantry because the Americans rarely attempted to move against the NVA beyond the range of artillery.[171] Some cadre units remaining close to US bases confidently moved into nearby villages secure in the knowledge that

American rules of engagement prohibited the use of artillery and airpower near these areas.[172]

After he withdrew most of his main force units from direct combat, Giap maintained pressure on the ground by stepping up his use of highly trained assault troops, commonly called "sappers." These were elite units, each trained in North Vietnam for up to two years before being sent south. Sappers were masters at infiltrating strongly held base camps and, once inside, killing occupants with automatic rifles, rocket-propelled grenades, and small blocks of explosive.[173] Sappers were regular soldiers, not guerrillas, whose targets were selected carefully for the greatest political impact. The larger, more significant attacks were planned in Hanoi by the Central High Command.[174] In attacks against American installations, artillery firebases were a prime target. Often isolated and poorly defended, firebases offered the enemy a lucrative source of casualties and the added prospect of reducing the offensive effectiveness of US infantry by damaging their source of protective firepower.[175]

As Americans deployed more sophisticated devices for locating the enemy, the enemy developed, at a corresponding pace, equally sophisticated means for defeating them. He learned quickly that US soldiers relied too much on radios in the field and he established an effective network of clandestine listening stations to provide early warning of impending US operations. Likewise, he was able to "spoof" US aerial and ground-based radio intercept stations with a carefully planned program of deceptive transmissions. He built fires to fool infrared detection systems and constructed papier-mache trucks and phoney roads to divert aircraft from real infiltration routes. The enemy cleverly set off decoy explosions when trucks were attacked from the air to make pilots believe that trucks were destroyed.[176]

Many of the same methods proven in the first Indochina war, such as the use of submerged bridges, elaborate overhead coverings for major facilities, and entrenched, practically invisible artillery and mortar firing positions, were dusted off and applied successfully against the United States.[177] Some evidence from captured documents indicates that the North, beginning in late 1968, began to receive warnings of impending B–52 strikes. Because arc-lights took over a day to process and fly, the enemy had plenty of time to vacate a threatened area before the bombers arrived.[178] In the summer of 1969, the enemy began a campaign to shoot down as many helicopters as possible. The program was effective because of the increased availability of sophisticated anti-aircraft guns of heavier calibers, some of them radar controlled.[179] To Giap, destroyed American aircraft were a statistic as psychologically powerful as US soldiers killed in action.[180]

Whenever close attacks were necessary, the enemy became infinitely more cautious and deliberate. "Hugging tactics" were refined to the point that the enemy now launched his attacks from within the perimeter wire or, on occasion, from within the garrison itself to lessen the destructiveness of artillery and air strikes. The NVA went so far as to fortify themselves before offensive operations. After the bloody battle for Dak Seang in April 1970, the South Vietnamese were amazed to discover elaborate bomb-proof bunkers, complete with two feet of overhead cover, within a quarter-mile of the base camp's perimeter.[181]

The enemy quite literally went "back to school" to develop and teach a refined doctrine for breaking contact and withdrawing from a battle quickly to avoid being caught in the artillery killing zone. As part of his attack plan, an enemy battalion commander developed elaborate time schedules, withdrawal signals and routes, and reassembly points to minimize exposure. Whereas, before Tet, withdrawals might have been a few thousand meters, after Tet it was not uncommon for large NVA units to break down into small squad-sized elements and withdraw 10 to 15 kilometers to put themselves beyond the reach of allied artillery. Before Tet, an enemy battalion welcomed the arrival of an American unit into its base camp. After Tet, as a captured NVA major remarked,

> The battalion would first attempt not to engage an enemy force at all if it could be avoided. If contact could not be avoided, a platoon-sized element would attempt to lead the enemy away from the battalion defensive position ... ruses of this nature were used to keep the bulk of the battalion out of contact.[182]

The results of Giap's new strategy of "indirect approach" were both immediate and dramatic. In less than six months he reversed the terrible wastage of his first-line soldiers to allied firepower. While expenditures of American artillery and aerial ordnance continued to rise after Tet, the number of enemy killed in action declined precipitously. In the first quarter of 1969 the ratio of enemy to friendly casualties dropped by half, even by two-thirds in some regions.[183]

The US Response

Ground attacks against isolated firebases were not uncommon before the Tet offensive. After Tet, however, firebases became the object of a carefully directed, systematic program of attack. Giap's objective was to maintain the initiative by attacking vulnerable allied positions at the least cost. He had tried this tactic once before in 1950, when he sought to push back the French perimeter of outposts by attacking each one individually, in turn, with an overwhelming force. That campaign succeeded when the French abandoned control of the hinterland and withdrew behind the tighter and more easily defensible "de Lattre Line" surrounding the Red River Delta. The United States reacted differently, choosing instead to keep its artillery outposts in place and fortify them to withstand the heaviest assault. The Americans succeeded in this tactic where the French had failed, thanks to their ability to reinforce firebases quickly with overwhelming firepower. However, the added threat posed by sappers, rockets, and occasionally main force units of battalion size or larger led to a fundamental change in both the character and purpose of firebases.[184]

At the Ia Drang, forward artillery positions were nothing more than temporary laagers, briefly occupied and lightly defended. By 1968, even temporary firebases were carefully fortified and heavily defended. During its initial insertion by helicopter, a firing battery carried with it enough building material and defensive firepower to withstand a major assault. After a day in position, the gunners surrounded themselves with a protective berm of dirt-filled ammunition boxes or sandbags. Each fighting and sleeping position was bunkered and topped with at least two layers of protective sandbags for overhead cover. This required over 25,000 sandbags for a typical battery position.[185]

A fortified, static firebase in 1970. Contrast this base later in the war with the "Kinnard-style" 1st Cavalry Division artillery position in 1966 shown on p. 90.

An infantry platoon might have been sufficient to protect General Kinnard's batteries in the 1st Cavalry, but at least a company of infantry was considered essential later in the war. The smallest firebase became a major engineering effort. Helicopters delivered bulldozers in pieces on remote mountains. Engineers reassembled the dozers and went to work slicing off the mountain top to make room for the guns and underground bunkers. Helicopters lifted in huge foot-square timbers to form a skeleton for each bunker.[186] Gunners commonly put in service other unusual construction materials such as pierced steel planking, normally used for runway construction, and corrugated culvert for providing overhead protection. Even the smallest firebase would surround itself with row upon row of circular, accordion-like barbed wire entanglements. Artillery soldiers usually emplaced strings of command-detonated mines, trip flares, and barrels of jellied gasoline to defeat sappers in the wire. Most bases augmented themselves with additional firepower such as quad-mounted heavy machineguns, recoilless rifles, and tanks if the base could be reached by road.[187]

The artillery being expected to provide its own measure of self-defense, artillerymen developed elaborate means to engage the enemy with direct fire from the firebase. "Killer junior" was the name given to a 105-mm shell tipped with a time fuze pre-set with a very short delay. When threatened by ground attack, a battery firing killer junior could lay down a protective ring of deadly low-air bursts just outside the perimeter wire.[188] The enemy most feared the "beehive" round, a special 105-mm projectile filled with 7,000 tiny "flechettes," one-inch metal darts that could cut a deadly swath through an attacking enemy's ranks.[189]

Fire support from outside was essential, and bases were normally emplaced in pairs within artillery range of each other to provide mutual defense. Fires were planned carefully around the base, and artillery was expended lavishly once an attack began. During periods of heightened alert or low visibility, defenders would often fire a "mad minute," during which every rifle, machinegun, and howitzer would open fire around the perimeter to break up a possible assault.[190]

As firebases became objects of the enemy's attention, the US command began to employ them as a lure to draw an increasingly reluctant enemy into a firepower trap much as infantry platoons had been used during the "search and destroy" period of Vietnam combat. Fire Support Base Crook in the 25th Division area was built from the ground up for this purpose. It was established in April 1969, on a flat piece of ground nine miles northwest of Tay Ninh City, very near the Cambodian border and squarely in the midst of the enemy 9th Division base area. The US command hoped that Crook would be an irritant even the most reticent enemy could not ignore.[191]

The base was constructed in less than a day. Engineers began by marking a circle on the ground, 80 yards in diameter, to define the outer perimeter of the base. Bulldozers went to work pushing up a protective berm of earth around the circumference of the circle. The dozers also dug in a battery of light artillery and cut trenches for underground placement of the fire direction center, command post, and other key facilities. With geometric precision, the engineers spaced 24 protective bunkers evenly around the perimeter, each one quickly constructed by blowing a hole in the ground with a cratering charge. Infantrymen constructed a standard nine-foot bunker in each hole with sandbags and pierced steel planking.

Bulldozers continued clearing fields of fire outside the perimeter. They cut concentric circles of cleared area at 100–150 meters and 300 meters beyond the fighting positions to deny cover to enemy rocket and mortar gunners. From the air, Crook looked curiously like a gigantic bull's-eye. The circular contrasts between green trees and white sand radiating from the center of the firebase could be seen clearly from the air, aiding pilots and observers in locating and placing fires close-in to the perimeter.

Because it was intended to destroy the enemy and not just defend itself, the firebase defenders loaded Crook with electronic devices to detect the enemy at a distance. They mounted a ground surveillance radar in a 20-foot tower and placed large starlight scopes on the perimeter. Reconnaissance teams placed strings of "duffel bag" sensors close-in to the firebase and along all major infiltration routes from Cambodia.

Sensors detected the enemy's first attempt to take the base on 5 June. Alternately, sensors, starlight scopes, and radars detected the enemy's approach during the early morning hours of the next three nights. On every occasion, artillery, Air Force gunships, helicopters, and tactical airpower were employed simultaneously to turn back the enemy attack. On the second night the combined avalanche of firepower killed 323 enemy without loss to the Americans. The infantry arrived at daylight to make sweeps of the area and count the dead.

Success stories similar to Firebase Crook would be repeated several times by US forces. In the battle of the firebases, the United States came out the clear winner if one considers only the huge price in lives paid by the North Vietnamese for a much smaller loss to the Americans. But in another, more subtle sense, the campaign was as much a victory for Giap. As the US Army continued to erect more and more elaborate fortifications to protect its firepower, the number and intensity of strikes beyond the protective firepower umbrella began to decline. This was no conscious decision, to be sure. Yet, however unintentional, a military force that concentrates on protecting itself forfeits the tactical and strategic initiative to the enemy. As the US forces dug in, they also undermined their own offensive spirit.

Not coincidentally, Giap used his firebase offensive to rebuild his army in the South after the Tet offensive. As assaults by rocket fire and sapper attacks increased, sightings of enemy main force units declined, and with the decline came a corresponding decrease in confirmed enemy killed. It was soon apparent that enemy strength, once depleted below effective levels, was steadily on the increase. The days of combat for US soldiers were numbered. If the South Vietnamese were to stand a chance of survival when the United States withdrew, the repair of enemy units and his build-up of new forces in the South had to be stopped.

By 1969, public opinion in the United States made the destruction of main force enemy units by conventional infantry operations less acceptable than it had ever been before. The attempt by two battalions of the 3d Brigade, 101st Airborne Division, to assault Ap Bia Mountain in the A Shau Valley near the Laotian border in May 1969 served as a warning against other similar operations in the future. The so-called Hamburger

Hill fight developed because a North Vietnamese regiment stood and slugged it out in a six-day battle against overwhelming odds. The conduct of the battle on both sides was strikingly reminiscent of the Korean War. The NVA regiment was destroyed after enduring a bombardment by 1,200 tons of bombs and 513 tons of artillery. Any military advantage gained from the battle, however, was obscured by its political effect at home. A passionate outcry arose in the media and in Congress against the heavy loss of life for what seemed (at least in Washington) to be an insignificant military objective.[192] Far more soldiers were lost in 30 minutes at LZ Albany than during 10 days on Hamburger Hill. But the American public had grown tired and disillusioned from the mounting casualties and wanted no more costly battles.

Faced with such a discouraging climate at home, US commanders in the field had little choice but to increase even further their dependence on firepower to maintain the tactical upper hand over the enemy. But continuing increases in the levels of firepower applied in the South appeared to have reached a point of diminishing returns. To the end of the war, no field commander questioned the need for close support artillery and airpower when an infantry force was in contact or if there were good reason to believe that an untaken objective was likely to contain a sizeable enemy force or base camp. Protest arose over the growing tendency to expend huge quantities of ordnance fired in the name of "harassment" or "interdiction" at unobserved, imperfectly located targets. This classification of air and ground fire constituted the overwhelming majority of all ordnance expended in South Vietnam. For the artillery, "H&Is" variously accounted for 40 to 60 percent of rounds fired. For air operations over the South, the percentage of interdiction missions against intelligence targets was higher, averaging 65 percent of all sorties flown throughout the war.[193]

Some interdiction programs, however, were effective. Those tied to specific sensor activations seemed to achieve the intended purpose of interdicting enemy movements with sharp, precise fires delivered in a single 40- to 50-round time-on-target or an immediate radar-controlled air strike. But most H&Is were developed haphazardly by plotting targets based on day- or week-old sightings or by random map inspection. The artillery fired rounds throughout the night in ones or twos to "shake up" the enemy. Expenditures of 400 to 500 rounds per night in a brigade sector were not uncommon.

Brigadier General Kalergis, commander of II Field Force Artillery, during a periodic review of artillery effectiveness admonished one battery for firing over 90 percent of its missions on "interdiction" targets. He noted that the amount of ammunition spent on interdiction was most often inversely proportional to the level of enemy activity in the immediate area. He suggested, "The battery was firing ineffectively in that area (due to lack of targets, and inactivity of the enemy) and consideration should be given to moving the battery to a more lucrative area."[194]

During his first evening in command of the 4th Division in Vietnam, Major General "Ace" Collins was startled from his sleep by a night-long H&I barrage of over 700 rounds. He immediately cut this number in half the next night and to zero within a week. He asked his staff what impression such elaborate displays of nocturnal firepower gave to both allies and enemies alike. He explained that the South Vietnamese might assume that such fires indicated an enemy force all around the Americans. The NVA and VC might think the Americans were afraid of an attack on the divisional base camp. In fact, Collins welcomed such an attack as preferable to searching for the enemy in piecemeal packets in the jungle.[195]

Records of the war reveal little of the effects of the H&I effort on the enemy, partly because these were nocturnal missions, never observed directly. Artillery units made very little effort to assess their H&I programs by early morning surveillance or the dispatch of ground patrols to investigate an area recently engaged. Perhaps this failure serves as the greatest indicator of the confidence fire planners placed in the value of H&Is.

Although their effects on the enemy may never be known, H&Is clearly had an adverse effect on civilians. Much of the growing anti-American feeling in populated and re-settled areas in Vietnam stemmed from the nightly discomfort induced by endless explosions and the real danger that an error made by a gunner or airman might result in injury or death. As one observer noted, the Vietnamese understood the need for bombing and shelling in support of military operations and welcomed friendly fire when their villlage was threatened:

> But what they object to is the much more common thing of bombing in an area where someone thinks there may be VC, in the H&Is firing the 105 and 155 howitzers at night into rural areas which appears to them, and frankly to myself, an attempt to just keep things strirred up out there.[196]

A revolutionary war demands from those who fight it political sensitivity as well as military acumen. In the case of Vietnam, the soldier was faced with resolving two often diametrically opposed objectives. One was to kill the enemy in large numbers as part of the continuing strategy of attrition; the other was to maintain the support of the people, not an easy task when, increasingly, the only practical tool left to soldiers in the field was firepower. One brigade commander, speaking reflectively about the loss of life and damage to property that accompanied the use of overwhelming firepower in Vietnam, said, "You know, we haven't awarded any medals for military restraint, but perhaps we ought to."[197]

At the tactical level, some infantry commanders late in the war began to suggest that the firepower available to them had become too much of a good thing. There was a growing tendency to rely more and more on the brute force of airpower and artillery in order to save lives. This tendency was particularly apparent during the later stages of US involvement as units began to withdraw from combat. Brigadier General C. M. Hall, commander of the artillery in the Central Highlands region of Vietnam, reported that in the seven months from August 1969 to February 1970 his command fired 1,600,000 rounds— approximately 270,000 rounds per light and medium battalion. The total reported killed in action for the same period was 4,800, of which, optimistically, only one-third were killed by artillery. This would equate roughly to 1,000 rounds per kill.[198]

In his debriefing report, written after relinquishing command of the I Field Force in 1971, General "Ace" Collins reported a disturbing and pervasive tendency among his junior leaders to call for artillery, gunships, and air support in response to any contact, even some involving as few as two or three enemy. The result, he contended, was an immediate loss of the tactical tempo as troops waited around for the firepower to arrive and be coordinated. When the advance resumed, the enemy was gone. Collins suggested to his superiors that the infantry begin again to stress the importance of small unit tactics and the habitual use of rifles and grenade launchers. "When we have a large enemy unit, or when he is well dug in," he wrote, "we properly should use all the firepower available to get him out. But we routinely follow the overwhelming firepower route, regardless of enemy strength or size." [199]

Late in the war rigid instructions to use all available firepower became a tactical millstone around an infantry commander's neck. The "force feed fire support system," used by the 25th Infantry Division in 1969, illustrated the doctrinal rigidity that increasingly came to characterize the employment of firepower by units in contact. As soon as any unit in the field reported contact, the duty officer at division headquarters automatically dispatched a stream of firepower assets to the area, even before the unit's request. This firepower included all artillery within range, C–119 and C–47 Air Force gunships (Shadow and Spooky), three light gunship fire-teams, and two or three FACs for control of tactical air as well as helicopters loaded with tactical close support tear gas dispensers and a "flame bath" helicopter equipped with napalm. Thus, the battle was out of the battalion commander's hands before it began.

The commander's function immediately devolved into directing traffic and telling each delivery system where to orbit or where to fire regardless of whether a particular firepower system was appropriate or even necessary. [200] In defense of "force feeding," evidence clearly indicates that the system hastened the pace of firepower escalation and subsequently reduced the time for firepower, particularly aerial firepower, to arrive on the scene. Casualties suffered by units in contact went down as a result. But infantry commanders rightfully lamented their loss of flexibility and control. [201]

Friendly Fire

Round for round and sortie for sortie, all fire support agencies delivered ordnance in Vietnam with greater restraint and more concern for safety than in any previous American war. [202] As in all wars, incidents did occur in which errors made by gunners and airmen resulted in harm to friendly soldiers and civilians. Vietnam was different because these incidents were more visible and potentially more damaging to the allied cause. In a conventional conflict, an artillery round fired long or a bomb misdropped behind the lines was simply considered another shot at the enemy. In a war without fronts, however, any mistake was likely to cause casualties, particularly when made in or near populated areas.

Artillery firing incidents were more numerous but generally less serious than bombing incidents. ''Short rounds'' most commonly resulted from a computation error made by the fire direction center or mistakes by the gun crew when placing firing data on the gun or mortar. Occasionally, forward observers made mistakes at the other end, either by mis-plotting a position or by calling in rounds that exploded prematurely in the high jungle canopy above friendly troops.[203] The US command went to great lengths to reduce the frequency and severity of firing incidents. Regulations required that all firing operations be double-checked. An additional officer was added to each firing battery to permit round-the-clock supervision of the FDC and the firing line.[204] Higher headquarters investigated all reported firing incidents, and, when fault could be determined, punishments were often severe, ranging from relief from command to court-martial in some instances.[205]

Although fewer, close air support incidents tended to be more damaging and dramatic, therefore more visible to the public. Most were caused by mis-identification of target and friendly troop locations by the forward air controller or fighter pilot.[206] In one instance, during a firefight in the 1st Division area, a wayward can of napalm ricocheted off a tall tree and exploded near a group of ''Big Red One'' soldiers, causing great consternation, but no damage. General Momyer in Saigon was soon besieged by newsmen who had heard that 40 men died in the incident. As with many similar incidents, uninformed rumor put great pressure on the Air Force for explanations. To get the press off his back, Momyer asked General Depuy to explain the incident to the media. ''So, I went down the next night to Saigon—to what they called the Five O'Clock Follies,''

General Depuy later recalled, "and told them what had happened and said that the Air Force dropped their bombs and napalm exactly where we asked them to."[207]

Some incidents were more serious. On 19 November 1967, near Dak To, a single F–100 fighter flew in the wrong direction over a company of paratroopers and dropped two bombs into the command post, killing 42, wounding 45, and effectively halting the attempt by the company to take Hill 875. It so happened that 53 different news agencies and reporters were present in the 173d Brigade headquarters at the time, and word of the incident soon filled the newspapers and news reports.[208]

In spite of these and other incidents, cooperation between ground and air commanders remained close throughout the war. Incidents occurred infrequently, and when pressure from the top mounted to tighten controls or increase minimum safe distances to reduce the danger to friendly troops, ground commanders argued convincingly that tighter safety regulations would reduce the effectiveness of all fire support and ultimately cost more lives. Yet, even though safety regulations remained conducive to prompt delivery of fires, as the war progressed the responsiveness of all firepower agencies gradually declined. The principal cause of this decline was the increased concern among all members of the chain of command for reducing casualties from friendly fire. Caution and timidity crept inadvertently into the fire support system as liaison officers and FACs verified friendly locations more carefully, fire direction officers and supervisors on the gun line checked and double-checked the firing data, and pilots circled overhead a bit longer to ensure that they had the proper target in sight.[209]

From the viewpoint of a fire support coordinator, encirclement or cordon operations presented the greater risk of friendly casualties from friendly fires. Such operations were necessary in Vietnam to isolate and pick out local guerrillas who might be hiding in an isolated village or base camp. The encirclement usually began with multiple helicopter assaults to surround the target area. Normally troops would converge on the target immediately by forming a cordon with a radius of between 500 and 1,000 meters. A cordon any wider would be too porous or would require too many troops to ensure surprise. This left very little room to adjust artillery and air strikes. Even the smallest firing error in any direction would cause friendly casualties.

To reduce the chance of an incident, the direct support artillery commander took extraordinary precautions. Normally, he placed all available firepower under his direct control and kept all firing units and FACs on a single radio frequency. Distant guns were registered carefully and re-laid on the centerpoint of the encirclement. Once firing began, it was controlled, continuous, and deliberate. The initial rounds from all guns were white phosphorus, detonated high in the air over the target to further ensure against possible error. Ground observers along the circumference assisted each other by sensing and adjusting rounds controlled by other forward observers to ensure safety. An aerial observer, normally the artillery commander or an experienced officer of proven ability, orbited overhead constantly.[210]

Air and ground fires were separated by time alone in a cordon operation, since all agencies were delivering ordnance on practically the same spot. This procedure required that all artillery fire be suspended until an air strike was completed. Timing between air and ground fires became a very critical process. As the circle contracted, infantry units on the perimeter moved cautiously at a measured pace, their position indicated constantly by colored cloth panels, smoke, or flashing strobe lights at night. The enemy understood the reluctance of the Americans to pour firepower into an ever-shrinking circle and would often wait until the last moment to break from cover and attempt a counterattack. It was then that the artillery battalion commander orbiting above had to display flawless judgment under enormous pressure. Too little firepower within the cordon meant that the infantry would suffer from inadequate close support. Too much firepower carelessly delivered meant the loss of friendlies to their own fire.

If coordination was done well and surprise achieved, cordon operations could trap and destroy large enemy forces with little loss of friendly life. At the Battle of Phuoc Yen on 29 April 1968, the 2d Brigade of the 101st Airborne Division, supported by the 1st Battalion, 321st Artillery, successfully surrounded and annihilated an NVA battalion of 500 men, losing just 15 killed. This particular cordon remained effectively in place for several days, during which the artillery battalion commander coordinated all supporting fires including air strikes, naval gunfire, and 13,500 rounds of artillery into an ever-narrowing circle without incident.[211] Of all allied operations, without question the enemy most feared the cordon. He knew that, should he be trapped inside, the odds were great that he would be pulverized by firepower or flushed and captured by a closing ring of infantry.[212]

Firepower and Vietnamization

The American way of war is not suitable for all armies. It is particularly unsuitable for those unable to afford it. The failure of the United States to leave behind an armed force in the South capable of standing alone was the result of many factors, most of which were deeply rooted in the political and military structure of Vietnamese society. But some of the blame must be placed on an advisory effort that sought, to the end, to create a Vietnamese armed force in the American image. In the more narrow doctrinal scope of this work, the failure began during the earliest days of the American advisory effort.

From the beginning, the United States sought to augment and reinforce the ARVN with technology and firepower. As early as 1962, American helicopters ferried soldiers into combat and flew close support missions for soldiers in contact.[213] This support created a dependence that grew over the next decade. American advisors continuously complained about ARVN commanders' lack of aggressiveness and inability to maneuver decisively against the enemy. Yet the Vietnamese were merely following the example of their ally, who relied on helicopters to get to battle and on firepower to destroy the enemy. The United States was able to achieve decisive tactical results because of its many sophisticated weapons and a long-standing familiarity with their use. The South Vietnamese, even with continued US support, could not afford firepower on the same scale, and inexperienced ARVN commanders could never hope to duplicate American skill in orchestrating firepower.[214]

Once the commitment was made to "Vietnamize" the war in 1969, the US command spared no effort to wean the ARVN from their dependence on outside support. At the battles of Ben Het, Quang Duc, and Dak Seang, conducted almost continuously between April 1969 and May 1970 in the II Corps tactical zone, the advisory team attempted to improve the ability of the ARVN 22d Division to fight alone against NVA main force units. After a year of effort, the ARVN infantry commanders still refused to use fire and movement and to employ organic fire support, preferring instead to await the arrival of tactical airpower or supporting artillery. In spite of its dependence on external support, the division never developed even the most rudimentary air-ground or fire support coordination facility. A report written after a year of frustrating effort noted, "Artillery fire was halted for excessive periods to allow for Tac Air or gunships to support friendly troops and on several occasions all fire support was halted. This problem resulted from a failure of the commander to understand and appreciate the need to closely integrate the planning of maneuver elements and combat support."[215]

Repeatedly, US advisors had to intervene in these battles to coordinate and control the delivery of massive fire support to extricate ARVN units trapped by the North Vietnamese. The senior US advisor noted that in spite of overwhelming fire superiority, the division commander never brought the masses of troops and firepower at his command to concentrate on a single point to fix and destroy the enemy. He chose to fritter away his forces in a series of uncoordinated, often disastrous small unit defensive actions. The advisor concluded his report with the statement that the division failed because it lacked adequate staff planning, fire support planning, and coordination, and demonstrated a complete lack of command supervision at all levels.[216]

Lam Son 719 was the first full-scale effort to commit large South Vietnamese maneuver forces against the NVA in the enemy's home territory. Characteristically, although ARVN forces constituted all of the maneuver force, firepower and aerial support came mainly from the Americans.[217] The objective of the operation was to strike westward from Khe Sanh into northern Laos to cut off the last major NVA infiltration route into the South along the Ho Chi Minh trail. The ARVN would provide the planning staffs and major maneuver elements, the United States would add extensive troop-carrying and armed helicopter support. The plan, by US standards, was relatively simple. The ARVN 1st Armored Brigade was to make an armored thrust along Highway 9 into Laos using tactics reminiscent of the French mobile group operations in the first Indochina War. Rangers, marines, and airborne infantry formations would cover the flanks of the armored thrust by seizing, with successive airmobile assaults, key mountain tops overlooking the highway.[218]

The operation began with great optimism on 8 February 1970. The advance reached as far west as Tchepon, Laos, before the North Vietnamese pushed the ARVN completely out of the trail area by mid-March. The results of the battle, particularly who "won or lost," were debated heatedly in the Army and the public media for months after Lam Son 719 was over. Images of panicked soldiers hanging onto the skids of American helicopters further soured the American public on the war and brought into serious question the progress toward Vietnamization made to that point. To be fair, it seems clear now that the enemy knew of the plan months in advance and took extraordinary efforts to defeat allied airmobile operations by entrenching machineguns and registering heavy artillery on hill tops and other prospective landing zones. The enemy used precisely the same tactic of flank attack and ambush proven against the French to slow and then turn back ARVN armored thrusts.

American advisors were prohibited by the US command from accompanying maneuver forces into Laos.[219] Long accustomed to relying on outside help to plan and coordinate fire support, ARVN commanders badly handled supporting fires when sole responsibility suddenly became theirs. The enemy, on the other hand, retaliated with entrenched and carefully registered artillery and mortars, including 122-mm howitzers and 130-mm heavy, long-range guns. The result was a battle in which the firepower tables were turned. By mid-February 1971, the enemy outnumbered the ARVN two to one in maneuver forces, and maintained the tactical initiative throughout the campaign.[220]

It seems likely that the enemy might have been successful in defeating the Laotian incursion in detail had it not been for the brave defensive efforts of the Vietnamese Rangers and 1st Division, and the last-minute infusion of massive firepower delivered and controlled by US forces. Total disaster was averted thanks to concerted effort by American helicopters to lift out remnants of stranded units and a massive program of helicopter and fighter strikes to cover the withdrawal.

Lam Son 719 clearly demonstrated that the Vietnamese had yet to absorb the complexities of the American way of war. The campaign failed in large measure because the South Vietnamese, long since used to operating in semi-autonomous regimental units, had not developed the ability to plan and execute multi-divisional operations. Many smaller units, battalions and below, fought with great tenacity and courage. But conventional campaigns are won by larger aggregations. Higher-level commanders and staffs were never able to overcome a fragmented command and control structure. The ARVN commanders were inexperienced and incompetent in the use of modern firepower.[221]

Perhaps the ARVN would have been overwhelmed by a superior force from the North regardless of the most prudent and farsighted policies of the United States. It seems evident from the sad history of the later stages of the conflict, however, that the US allies would have fared better had Americans taught them to fight effectively with less material support. Critical professional skills were lost by the ARVN during the days of firebases, airmobile operations, and massive fire support. After ten years of neglect, ARVN leaders forgot the art of maneuver warfare. They rarely employed any form of maneuver other than frontal assault—a deadly business if not fully supported by firepower. They gave little thought to envelopment or flanking maneuvers. The principles of fire and movement using organic infantry weapons were also in eclipse. Seldom did young leaders establish a base of fire with rifles and machineguns while a maneuver element moved against the enemy. Battalions appeared to be completely dependent on outside fire support—a dependence that became tragic once massive outside support disappeared.

This prevailing sense of dependence not only caused an atrophy of martial skill but, in a real fashion, also drained the

fighting spirit and aggressiveness of Vietnamese ground soldiers. One district advisor, after observing an almost total lack
of aggressiveness on the part of the ARVN 22d Division,
blamed the presence of outside fire support for eroding the
national pride of the Vietnamese:

> This support sapped their pride and their will to combat their
> "brothers from the North" on equal terms. The enemy enjoys a
> tremendous moral and psychological advantage because he fights
> with relatively no outside assistance.... Continued massive com-
> bat support and a perpetual advisory presence erodes the national
> pride of our allies. A crippling dichotomy sets in: They are afraid
> to do without us, and, at the same time, are ashamed of receiving
> so much.[222]

In Retrospect

The American use of firepower in Vietnam followed a tradition
of flexibility, technological innovation, and copious application
long established in previous wars. Certainly, no other army in
the world at that time would have been able to duplicate such a
polished and complex mechanism. By war's end, all manner of
ground and aerial systems, strategic as well as tactical, could be
called up quickly and simultaneously to provide close support to
combat troops. With the introduction of troop-carrying and
attack helicopters, the US Army developed a new dimension in
warfare and gave it credence and respectability. The electronic
and firepower battlefields were combined for the first time to
create an effective system for instantaneous acquisition and
engagement of unseen targets. New munitions and streamlined
systems of delivery ensured that any target found and fixed by
ground forces could be dispatched with surety and precision.

Although still imperfect in many ways, US forces in Vietnam came closer than any other army in any other war to creating a system that integrated into a single striking hand the
destructiveness of all firepower, whether delivered by ground,
sea, or air. In the right circumstances the application of this system could be enormously destructive. Although the total casualties suffered by the enemy will never be known, there is little
doubt that the price of facing American firepower in open
combat was practically a generation of first-class soldiers.

With all of these tactical and technological successes, a continuing escalation in the destructiveness of firepower never produced the decisive results achieved by lesser efforts in earlier wars. If a single lesson is to be learned from the example of Vietnam it is that a finite limit exists to what modern firepower can achieve in limited war, no matter how sophisticated the ordnance or how intelligently it is applied.

Overwhelming firepower cannot compensate for bad strategy. A war of attrition is a test of political will and national resolve. Early policymakers decided to prosecute attrition warfare based in part on unrealistic expectations of the persuasiveness of American firepower. When escalating doses of destructiveness failed to crack the enemy's will, the United States had little strategic alternative but to pull out of the war in unfavorable circumstances or to increase the level of destructiveness seemingly without end. Ho Chi Minh's admonishment to the French returned full circle to haunt the United States, for it was indeed the Americans who eventually grew tired of escalations.

At the tactical level, firepower killed enemy soldiers in hugely disproportionate numbers. But terrain, a tenacious enemy, and the very nature of a revolutionary war made the firepower system far less destructive than a similar system would have been in a conventional war. The enemy rarely assembled in lucrative aggregations; he did so only in the safety of his sanctuary or under the protective cover of the jungle. As Americans became more adept at finding the enemy, the enemy became all the more skilled at avoiding destruction by fire. The need to maintain the allegiance of the local population placed a practical limit on the degree of destruction that could be unleashed on the more thickly settled and cultivated regions of Vietnam. In the end, exigencies imposed by political clearances, bad maps, miserable weather and terrain, unreliable allies, and interservice friction all limited to varying degrees the speed, reliability, and precision of American firepower.

By the time of American withdrawal, an unprecedented weight of bombs and shells had failed to break the will of the enemy to fight on. In fact, in 1971 the Army of North Vietnam was in a stronger position than it had ever been in, with over

350 heavy guns and 400 tanks set to invade and defeat the Southern armies. Yet, no matter how adept the enemy became at countering allied firepower, or how powerful his own firepower became, the stereotype still remained of the American "Goliath" pounding the helpless "David" into the ground. I hope this study has shown a different view. In the end, 6 million tons of bombs and 20 million rounds of artillery told very little about the eventual outcome of the war in Vietnam.

4
The Afghanistan Intervention

Mujahideen Commander Haji arranged ambushes on a grand scale. His own group of 150 followers waited, shivering in the early morning chill, for the main body of a mile-long convoy to work its way cautiously into the narrow pass. Several miles farther down the Sasi Valley, near the Soviet fort at Ali Khel, more of Haji's warriors sat patiently at two additional ambush sites with rifles and grenades poised to further punish the approaching infidels.

At first light, Haji ducked low as three armored personnel carriers of the advanced guard roared quickly by, their machineguns blazing away ineffectively at both sides of the road. The ugly, menacing shapes of six Mi–24 attack helicopters suddenly popped above the valley wall, swept over the personnel carriers and continued at breathtaking speed down the narrow valley. This was good news to Haji. The convoy must be Soviet. Afghan Army convoys merited only two helicopters for air cover.

Not until mid-morning did the main body of the convoy draw within sight. At that moment Haji heard the distinct sound of gunfire and explosions as the three APC's of the advanced guard were destroyed by an ambush force farther down the valley. Like angry bees, the Mi–24 gunships appeared again in the distance, diving low, firing rockets and machineguns into the ambush. After a few moments, black smoke drifted above the

mountains to the south, indicating to Haji that another ambush
had drawn first blood. Toward noon the distant firing stopped.

The main convoy crept maddenly close to Haji's ambush
but halted at the last moment, refusing to enter the killing zone.
For five hours the vehicles remained absolutely stationary. No
one fired. Tanks were buttoned up, and Haji could see clearly
the enemy soldiers peering nervously out of their vehicles.

Just before dark the convoy suddenly came alive and
vehicles began cautiously to move forward. Now every Soviet
soldier in the convoy was firing. Rocks and dirt flew around
Haji from the detonation of a tank shell just yards away. Haji
ordered his men to hold fire until he exploded a large mine bur-
ied in the road. One of the lead vehicles suddenly halted; an
alert group of Soviets discovered the mine and began to dig it
up. At that moment Haji ignited the mine and the soldiers disappeared in smoke and dust. The partisans opened fire. Immediately, two tanks swerved from the road and caught Haji's men
in a cross-fire. Under cover of a sheet of firepower, Soviet
infantrymen dismounted from vehicles and began to fight their
way toward the Mujahideen. Again, the ubiquitous, ugly helicopters appeared, this time circling above, apparently unable to
intervene for fear of hitting their own troops.

The Mujahideen were clearly horrified as they huddled,
trembling, under the onslaught of Soviet firepower. Most of
them were illiterate farmers, poorly trained and armed. They
possessed only a few anti-tank rockets. Haji knew that survival
of his band now depended on the daring of two trusted anti-tank
gunners. With great care and courage, the two gunners fired
rocket-propelled grenades and two tanks lurched to a halt,
momentarily immobilized. Two more rockets fired and both
tanks erupted in flame. Only now did the helicopters swoop low
to intervene, diving and firing at the dust kicked up by back-
blast from the rocket launchers. One of the gunners was hit in
the throat by a cannon shell and collapsed with a cry. No one
could help him, and he quickly bled to death in his foxhole.

The burning tanks served to break the spell of fear among
the Mujahideen. Shouting "Allah Akbar," they broke from hiding and poured fire into the convoy. Haji spotted a jeep blaring
its horn and weaving between the destroyed vehicles to reach

the head of the convoy. A concentrated burst of machinegun fire exploded the vehicle and killed what must have been the convoy commander.

Suddenly the Soviets were in disarray. Above the din of combat Haji heard them cursing, shouting, and bellowing orders to each other. After two hours the firefight degenerated into a stalemate, with both sides exchanging shots but causing no damage. The guerrilla force could do little more now than waste precious ammunition, so Haji blew his whistle to sound retreat. As fire slackened, a bulldozer clanked around a narrow bend and began to push wrecked vehicles from the road. In a last act of defiance, Haji sent his best marksman back to the scene. A moment later, a shot rang out and the bulldozer driver slumped in his seat.

Haji's badly shaken warrior band continued its tortuous climb up the valley wall. They were not pursued, nor were they harassed by artillery or airpower. They knew that retribution would come, probably the next day after the Soviets prepared carefully to mount a deliberate strike on all of the villages near the ambush sites. But this moment belonged to Haji. By night-fall he could hear more fighting several miles down the valley road. His third ambush had found its prey. The holy man accompanying the column looked toward the distant flashes. "Today is payday for the infidel," he said as Haji and his men trudged doggedly toward home.[1]

Their experiences in Czechoslovakia and in other similar interventions in Eastern Europe gave promise to the Soviet High Command that the military takeover in Afghanistan would be swift and decisive. Indeed, the sudden infusion of five complete mechanized divisions in three days during December 1979 was no mean feat of arms; it reflected the traditional excellence of Soviet staff planning and military diversion and deception. The invasion also demonstrated a lack of political sophistication within the Soviet High Command. The presence of hundreds of tanks in the major cities of Czechoslovakia immediately led to unquestioned political domination.[2] A similar presence established in Afghanistan gained the Soviets very little but the enmity of Afghans like Haji who have fought against infidels and invaders for 30 generations. The consequence of this political misjudgment was an unexpected, protracted revolutionary war for which the Soviets were woefully unprepared.[3]

An Unimpressive Beginning

The Soviets first took the war to the countryside in Paktia Province early in 1980. They intended that the brunt of the fighting be done by the few Afghan Army troops who remained loyal to the new puppet regime under Babrak Kamal. The loyal Afghans were buttressed by a few thousand Soviet troops, many of them from Soviet Muslim regions just across the border. The entire effort was supported further with massive firepower, mainly fighter-bombers and a few combat helicopters. The operation went badly from the start. Once the shooting was over, the Soviets hastily withdrew to their main base at Bagram. This first offensive failed because Afghan and Soviet Muslim troops had little desire to fight their racial kin. Many of the Afghan soldiers deserted to the resistance en masse, taking their weapons with them. The Soviet 40th Army at Kabul hastily replaced Asian troops with Europeans during 1980.[4]

From a tactical and strategic perspective, the winter and spring offensive in 1980 presented a picture to the world of stumbling ineptitude by the Soviet Army. Most of the initial efforts to defeat the Mujahideen insurgency in the field were undertaken by armor-heavy flying columns sent outward from the major cities to conduct short, firepower-intensive raids against guerrilla-held villages. It seems in retrospect that during these early battles the Soviets still believed that such ostentatious displays of mechanized power would be sufficient to intimidate the Afghans in the countryside and coerce them into abandoning armed resistance. This strategy had proved successful against rural hold-outs in Hungary in 1956, but against the fearsome Mujahideen, the Soviets only found themselves out-maneuvered and out-fought in narrow mountain passes where armored tactics were virtually useless.[5]

The Mujahideen noted in these early battles that the Soviets pushed tank-heavy armored columns recklessly down unsecured roads with little regard to flank protection.[6] When ambushed,

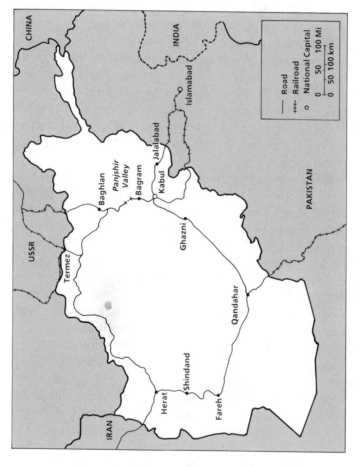

Afghanistan

the mechanized infantry rarely dismounted but chose to button up and race up and down the road firing ineffectively from vehicle turrets and firing ports.[7] The Soviet tactical love affair with the tank quickly went sour in Afghanistan. Soviet doctrine unequivocally directs that tank forces operate as part of a combined arms force with mechanized infantry, artillery, and engineers. Yet Afghans witnessed numerous examples of Soviet tank units being committed to battle in 1980 without the protection of mechanized infantry. When caught on the road by the Afghans, tank-heavy forces suffered severe losses. The Mujahideen learned to block convoy movements by knocking out the lead and trail tanks with mines or rocket-propelled grenades. In narrow valley defiles this tactic effectively blocked advance or retreat and left the convoy helpless to endure methodical tank-by-tank destruction.[8]

In steep terrain, the Soviets discovered that a main tank gun could not elevate to engage guerrillas entrenched in high mountain passes. Sometimes the long gun tubes could not be traversed without slamming into rock outcroppings that flanked many mountain roads. Tanks experienced difficulty firing accurately at long distances when positioned on slanting and uneven terrain.[9] Mountain roads also took their toll on clutches and transmissions. Engines overheated in the hot, thin air, and inexperienced drivers all too often snapped the tracks of their vehicles when trying to maneuver along rock-strewn trails.

Some of the early battles were disastrous for road-bound Soviet forces.[10] In June 1981, the Mujahideen ambushed a battalion of trucks at a choke point along the Salang Highway, which leads from the Soviet border to Kabul. According to the Mujahideen commander who led the ambush force, road blocks at both ends halted the convoy and prevented escape. The Soviets were obliged to blow up 120 trucks and evacuate their men by helicopter before any relief force could arrive.[11]

Early in the war, the Soviets seemed to be careless in their fieldcraft, almost to the point of indifference. During the Panjsher Valley offensive, armored units did not take up proper night positions, often leaving tanks parked in neat rows or pulled off to the shoulders of roads. Tank crews pitched tents, but did not post guards. This lack of care made it easy for alert

Afghans to infiltrate to within rocket-grenade and machinegun range.[12] One Western observer with experience in Vietnam found it incredible that Soviets guarding Bagram, the largest airbase in Afghanistan, would allow armed resistance groups to pass within a mile or so in broad daylight with neither side firing a shot.[13] The Soviets admitted candidly that troops attempting to maneuver in deeply cut, rugged mountainsides often lost contact with each other. Backpack radios could communicate with vehicles on the valley floor but could not reach nearby subunits just a short distance away tucked into rocky clefts.[14]

The Soviets were remarkably forthright in admitting the difficulties inherent in fighting an elusive enemy in the mountains. One official journal noted that terrain clearly favored the insurgent:

> You don't have to be a military man to understand that in the mountains it's much easier to set up a defense than to wage an offensive. After taking up an advantageous position, even a few men can hold off a company, or even a battalion.[15]

Reports of Soviet attempts at off-road maneuvers in these early battles elicited nothing but contempt from Mujahideen and Western observers. A former Afghan colonel turned freedom fighter noted that the Mujahideen forces under his command rarely encountered Soviet ambush patrols. The Soviets preferred instead the simpler and safer tactic of stationing two or three tanks or armored carriers as mobile road blocks.[16] Ahmed Shah Massoud, the accomplished leader of the guerrilla groups defending in the Panjsher Valley, stated reflectively, "Soviet soldiers are not trained very efficiently for mountainous countries." Often they charged off the roads laden with equipment and moving too slowly. "This is why we could kill them very easily," he concluded.[17] An American journalist with experience in other wars in the Third World was less generous when he called these early efforts "decidedly third rate."[18]

Although less seen or noted by Western observers, the Soviets found it equally difficult to practice their traditional methods for supporting maneuver forces with firepower. Soviet doctrine is firmly rooted in the principle that offensive action is only possible after the enemy has been crippled by a meticulously planned, deliberate bombardment by artillery and airpower. In Afghanistan, fire planners found no fixed targets worthy of large-scale bombardment. The Mujahideen moved too quickly to be countered with a set-piece plan. The Soviets found themselves trying to swat flies with a sledgehammer.

At first the Soviets attempted to support armored forays using artillery collected in relatively secure fixed bases located near major cities and key communications facilities. Fires from these rudimentary "firebases" were effective as long as tank columns remained in flat country nearby. But as soon as tanks disappeared into more distant mountain passes, batteries in fixed locations were unable to communicate easily by radio with forward elements or to fire over high mountain crests. Most tank formations interspersed towed artillery pieces throughout the march column to provide some basic fire support. Light and medium mortars pulled by trucks added more responsive firepower for convoy protection. The Soviets found to their dismay that often ambushes ended and the enemy withdrew before accompanying guns could be brought into action. On winding, twisting roads hewn into steep canyon walls, artillery crews found it difficult to pull off quickly and select suitable firing positions. Often the killing zone chosen by the Mujahideen was cleverly masked by rugged terrain and could not be reached by any supporting weapon except mortars.[19]

Observation was another serious problem. Soviet doctrine does not provide for artillery "eyes" well forward as in most Western armies. Soviet battery commanders are traditionally both observers and fire direction officers. They locate themselves in relatively fixed and formal "observation posts" located near the forward maneuver battalion headquarters. This system of fire control works very well when implementing a prepared plan of fire, but in Afghanistan armored columns could only be supported by a system that could keep pace and react quickly to the unexpected.[20]

From the beginning, the Mujahideen most feared attacks from the air, particularly from the deadly Mi–24 attack helicopter. Experienced guerrilla commanders sought to attack columns unprotected by air cover. Early in the war, response times for close air support to come to the rescue of a convoy under attack were usually measured in hours, giving the guerrillas enough time to strike and withdraw before the Soviets could bring overwhelming firepower to bear.[21]

Western observers and the Mujahideen reserved their most biting criticism for the apparent lack of initiative and imagination among Soviet soldiers. At the tactical level, junior officers and NCOs often seemed paralyzed when faced with the unexpected. They reacted under fire according to set patterns, not according to circumstances. Experienced Mujahideen commanders spoke with both pity and derision when describing young officers sending soldiers up a valley wall to their doom when it was obvious to friend and foe alike that such tactics were suicidal.[22]

Obsessive obedience to central authority permeated the higher reaches of Soviet command in Afghanistan. Before becoming a member of the resistance, Colonel A. A. Jalali was chief of the tactics wing of the Afghan Army Staff College in Kabul. Just before the outbreak of hostilities, a high Soviet military delegation headed by Colonel General Merimskiy, Deputy Chief of Staff for Training, visited Kabul, ostensibly to assist in developing training manuals for the Afghan Army. Jalali's assistant, a Soviet colonel who had been seconded to the Staff College as a tactics instructor, was told by his visitors to prepare a two-day map exercise that postulated the employment of Soviet forces in familiar Afghan terrain. He chose a Soviet mechanized regiment to attack through one of the narrow valleys surrounding Kabul. Faithfully following established doctrine, he placed a rectangular template, four by two kilometers, across the valley floor, and with geometric precision interspersed each sub-unit of tanks, mechanized infantry, self-propelled artillery, and rocket troops within the rectangle. Jalali mentioned tactfully that the flanks of the formation overlapped mountains ten thousand feet high. His Soviet counterpart recognized the incongruity but said with a shrug, "For the purposes of this exercise, we shall assume the mountains to be low hills."[23]

Soviet Tactical Reform 1980-1984

Early problems experienced by the Soviet Army in Afghanistan have been the subject of much telling and re-telling by the

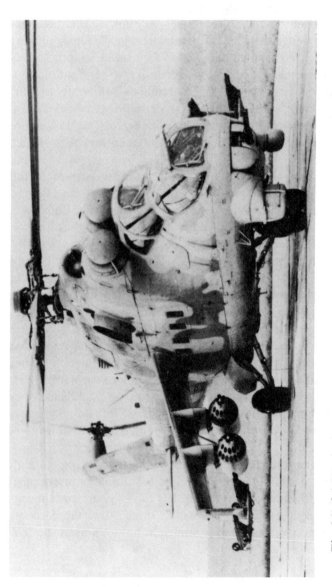

The Mi–24 Hind, the most effective firepower instrument in Afghanistan. Designed as a flying tank, the Hind can carry six passengers and can deliver free-flight rockets, wire-guided missiles, free-fall bombs, and automatic cannon fire.

Western press. In addition to tactical difficulties, stories have filtered back from the battlefront of low morale and drug abuse among the Soviet troops. Desertion, disobedience, and cowardice in combat have also been reported.[24] Unfortunately, though understandably, many of these early impressions remained long after the military situation shifted dramatically. One side of a global contest tends by nature to wish the worst of its adversary. Also, the war has been sold in the popular media as "Russia's Vietnam," so any fact that tends to validate that thesis receives more attention than perhaps it justifies. As a result, this one-sided reporting from the field has misrepresented many of the more significant lessons to be learned concerning the performance, both good and bad, of the Soviet Army in its first test by fire since World War II.

Afghanistan was not Vietnam, and other than the obvious fact that both were revolutionary wars fought by conventional armies, one holds very little resemblance to the other. In terms of frequency of battle, casualties to combatants, and numbers of participants, Afghanistan was less than one-fifth as destructive and intensive as Vietnam. US military strategy in Vietnam was driven by the overriding need to reach a favorable conclusion to the war before internal pressures at home forced a premature and unfavorable withdrawal. The Soviets assumed they had plenty of time. With a contiguous border to the combat area and practical isolation from the prying eyes of the outside world, the Soviets seemingly could afford a war that might last a generation. Like the United States in Vietnam, the Soviets faced a dedicated enemy inured to combat and hardships. But unlike the North Vietnamese, the Mujahideen possessed few modern weapons, with little hope of acquiring them in great quantity across a supply line so long that weeks were required to traverse it by camel and foot.

Substantial evidence indicates that the Soviet style of war underwent significant change after the first "horror stories" appeared in the Western press. If one sifts through the political hyperbole on both sides, a picture emerges of a modern mechanized army learning slowly, often painfully, the lessons of combat in the Third World. Certainly, many stories of ill-discipline and discontent are true.[25] But in the Soviet system of war and political control such individual glimpses of human imperfection are largely irrelevant. From a larger perspective, the Soviet Army progressed professionally through a logical process of assimilating combat experience and began, belatedly, to apply its experiences to tactical reform.

For much of his professional career, Colonel David Glantz has studied the Soviet art of war. Perhaps no serving US officer has written more on the subject. Glantz believes that the Soviet Army throughout its short history has developed its own unique method for modifying its fighting doctrine to keep pace with advances in technology and the military art. The process of reform within the Red Army has been difficult to follow in the West because the Soviet method of tactical change is substantially foreign to Western armies.[26]

Since the American Civil War, tactical innovation and change in the American Army has come from the bottom up. Young soldiers and leaders were the first to learn which peace-time doctrinal concepts did and did not prove valid in combat. At Antietam and Chancellorsville, geometric formations of infantry dissolved into indistinct skirmish lines as infantry on both sides sought to defeat the killing effect of the muzzle-loading rifle. As we have seen, rigid doctrine restricting the use of airpower in support of mobile troops in World War II was quickly forgotten within the fighting theater as ground and air commanders on the spot recognized that close air support was necessary to achieve a breakthrough on the battlefield. It has often been said that an army reflects the society it defends. So it comes as no surprise that a nation prizing ingenuity and individualism places in the field armies that can adapt quickly to the unexpected.

In contrast to the West, Colonel Glantz explains, the Soviet system of tactical change is reflected in the structured, autocratic, and hierarchical nature of Soviet society. Change comes more slowly—and it comes from the top down.[27] Lower-level commanders are driven by strict regulations and tactical "norms" dictating behavior in combat to a level of specificity unheard of in the West. The result is a rigid method of warfare that leaves little to chance or uncertainty. Tactical norms are directed by the Soviet General Staff or Stavka.

Norms are statistical and are derived within the Soviet staff system through empirical study of past conflicts. They accommodate a remarkable number of variables for operational planning, such as the defensive posture of the enemy, weather, terrain, the degree of destruction desired; and they often include an estimation of the enemy's psychological state. An artillery commander, for example, receives a specific number of cannon and shells to perform a mission. Using tabular norms, the commander plans with great care the time sequence and ammunition allocation for all targets within his designated area of responsibility. Once the battle begins, the artillery commander has no latitude to alter the firing sequence. He is to execute his plan, and his own performance in battle is determined by the precision of his execution, not necessarily by his contribution to the success or failure of the overall enterprise.

Colonel Glantz describes this aspect of personal liability as the important conceptual difference between wartime leadership among Eastern and Western armies. In a society where the cost of personal failure may be banishment, disgrace, or worse, a prudent commander excuses the possible failure of his unit by demonstrating fidelity to the planned concept of operation. The artillery fired its allocated number of rounds accurately and on time. The attack failed. Fault rests, therefore, with scientific calculations and norms that determined the original plan and resource allocation. There was scientific miscalculation, but no human failure. Technical errors could be corrected by calculating revised norms in light of new experiences and by applying them with exactitude in a renewed effort.

Responsibility for adjusting the norms rests with the general staff, not with the troops in the field. The Soviets reason that Stavka can remain detached from the chaos of the moment and analyze dispassionately what went wrong. The result is a formally revised doctrine with attendant norms refined to the finest detail, dictated by the general staff, and hammered into the tactical method of units in the field. In true Marxist-Leninist fashion, the process becomes dialectic in nature, a continuing cycle of experiment by fire, reasoned adjustment, and repeated experimentation until the winning formula is found. Glantz is careful to admit that the process is slow and often costly, but he also shows that the process fits comfortably the Soviet method of war—it is inexorable, it is politically acceptable, and it requires nothing more from those who execute it than mindless obedience.[28]

The Soviet battle for Afghanistan followed Colonel Glantz's model with striking fidelity. As we have seen, the Soviets first tried to intimidate the Mujahideen using massive doses of firepower and large tank-heavy formations, following the established tactical norms derived from experience in previous European wars. Beginning in the summer of 1980, first signs of the tactical dialectic appeared in the field. A much-touted "limited withdrawal" began at that time, and Western observers noted a steady removal of heavy equipment such as anti-aircraft weapons, chemical weapons, heavy cannon, and missiles back to the Soviet Union.[29] A lull occurred in the fighting in early 1981, which the Soviets credited to their efforts to seek a peaceful solution. But careful observers noted that the Soviets used the time to fortify their large military bases and to bring in equipment more suited to war against partisans.[30] During mid-1980, Soviet ground tactics changed. Large tank formations disappeared and were replaced by greater numbers of mechanized infantry carriers. The proportion of helicopters within the expeditionary force doubled the first year and continued to increase steadily each year thereafter.[31]

The second or "counterinsurgency" phase of the war began in late 1980, as loyal Afghan Army troops took on most of the responsibility for fighting their countrymen in the mountains. The Soviets contributed advisors and heavy doses of ground- and air-delivered fire support. Throughout 1981 the Soviets became increasingly frustrated as their Afghan allies, instead of mounting a successful counterguerrilla campaign, deserted en masse to become guerrillas themselves. By early 1982, it became clear that the Soviet Army would have to shoulder the burden for some time until a reliable Afghan Army could be rebuilt in the Soviet image.[32]

The Soviet High Command seemed to conclude in late 1980 that victory would not be quickly won. They resisted the temptation to infuse large numbers of soldiers into Afghanistan as the United States had done in Vietnam. They chose instead a more patient strategy centered on control of vital centers and the routes connecting them. This was a "low risk" option that promised to keep the Soviets in control without commitment of large numbers of troops. The tactical concept to support this strategy created, first, a garrison force supported by position artillery to protect vital centers and, later, a mobile striking force to take the war into the heartland of the Mujahideen.

Position Artillery

As in both Indochina wars, firepower played a key role in protecting Soviet facilities and lines of communications. "Position" artillery arrived with the invading force. By the spring of 1980, the Soviets had made their major installations relatively secure from outside attack by stringing enormously thick anti-personnel minefields around base areas near Bagram, Kabul, and other major cities. Each major Soviet base was commodious. There was no defensive perimeter as such. A few fighting vehicles, such as tanks, anti-aircraft guns, and light howitzers, were placed on the perimeter to cover avenues of approach. A Soviet infantry battalion normally protected each base. The entire battalion remained within the confines of the base year-round except for occasional tactical forays or for seasonal training in the immediate environs.[33] One seasoned Afghan veteran praised the Soviet use of mines. They were so thickly strewn around the major bases and so well concealed that the Mujahideen dared not attempt to penetrate by ground attack.[34]

By the late summer of 1980, the inevitable "firebase" began to appear as the Soviets and their few reliable Afghan allies sought to extend military presence farther afield. The Soviet version resembled more an armed camp or bivouac than a true firebase. At that time, the Mujahideen possessed few stand-off weapons capable of doing any harm. So the Soviets collected their artillery into battalion groupings. The guns were normally not dug in, but were emplaced in doctrinally correct firing lines with tubes elevated and trained on the nearest and most threatening avenue of approach. The gunners assembled their carriers and trucks into neat parks, each vehicle precisely aligned with and the prescribed distance from its neighbor.[35]

Later, the Soviets began to mix together different calibers of guns at the major bases. Long-range 130-mm guns, accurate to nearly 20 miles, and 122-mm multiple rocket launchers started to appear scattered about in six-gun (or six-launcher) formations, allowing the Soviets to maneuver farther from their fixed bases under the protective umbrella of these formidable weapons.[36]

The Soviets failed to solve completely the problem of convoy protection. Unlike in Vietnam, distances are so vast in Afghanistan that an interlocking, mutually supporting network of position artillery to cover the main supply routes was impossible. Very small, isolated firebases appeared near the most dangerous ambush spots, such as the Salang Tunnel and the mouth of the Panjsher Valley. These bases were occupied mainly by Afghan government troops manning individual batteries of obsolete 122-mm M–30 howitzers. One observer noted that the outposts were scattered like "a string of pearls" along critical routes.[37] The Soviets, however, concluded that these bases were more trouble than they were worth. At best, their occupiers took a "live and let live" attitude toward their rebel countrymen. They opened fire reluctantly and with little precision or enthusiasm, and only when ordered to do so by Soviet advisors. At worst, the bases became ammunition supply points for the Mujahideen and were occasionally surrounded and overrun during periods of limited visibility when helicopters were unlikely to attempt a rescue.[38]

Because roads could never be covered completely, supplies had to be moved either by air or by heavily defended ground convoy. Armed helicopters provided the only sure protection for convoys. During the early years, convoys without aircraft overhead were very vulnerable to ambush. After about 1983, however, the time for helicopters to arrive on the scene of an ambush was cut in some cases from hours to minutes. Western observers reported that the Soviet Air Force discovered the value of "strip alert." When a convoy was on the road, two pairs of Mi–24 Hind gunships were continuously armed and manned at the nearest air base, prepared for liftoff in less than five minutes.[39] The Air Force also improved its system of fire control for routine resupply convoys. Each came to have an Air

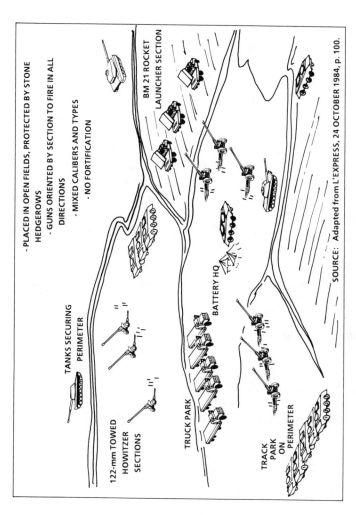

- PLACED IN OPEN FIELDS, PROTECTED BY STONE HEDGEROWS
- GUNS ORIENTED BY SECTION TO FIRE IN ALL DIRECTIONS
  - MIXED CALIBERS AND TYPES
  - NO FORTIFICATION

BM 21 ROCKET LAUNCHER SECTION

TANKS SECURING PERIMETER

122-mm TOWED HOWITZER SECTIONS

TRUCK PARK

BATTERY HQ

TRACK PARK ON PERIMETER

SOURCE: Adapted from L'EXPRESS, 24 OCTOBER 1984, p. 100.

A typical Soviet firebase in Afghanistan

Force "FAC" riding in the convoy with a radio tuned to the frequency of the air base.[40] A later refinement was the appearance of An–24 or An–26 twin-engined transports that routinely flew over major supply routes day and night. These aircraft served both to detect ambushes using some form of on-board sensor, and as forward air control aircraft to coordinate and vector in air strikes.[41]

Although the Mujahideen became less able to achieve dramatic successes against Soviet convoys, the threat of attack made the Soviets pay a high price in men, machines, and effort to supply their outposts. A convoy became a major tactical exercise, normally controlled at division level, and involved, at different times, dedication of effort from several divisions along the route. Some convoys were more than a mile in length and many took as long as a week to travel a complete circuit of outlying base camps. The expense of these efforts also served the Mujahideen by limiting the amount of fuel and ammunition an outlying garrison could expend on local combat operations and by tying up many troops in convoy protection duties who might otherwise have taken to the field in search and destroy operations.[42]

The Soviets understood the dangers of house-to-house fighting in urban areas and increased their use of position artillery and airpower to force Afghan civilians from more troublesome cities and villages. As long as "hearts and minds" are not considered, such bombardments act as an economy of force measure in the Soviet strategic scheme. The Soviets were able to empty whole sections of major cities by brutal bombardments.

In 1982, three battalion-sized artillery bases were constructed on the outskirts of Qandahar, one at the Qandahar Airport and one each near two former Afghan Army garrisons. The positions were protected by a company of mechanized infantry. Beginning in March 1984, the Soviets began firing into the southwestern quadrant of the city using 122-mm multiple rocket launchers supported by light and medium artillery.[43] What once was a thriving city of over 100,000 was reduced to less than one-tenth that population. Likewise, Herat felt the wrath of both artillery and concentrated aerial bombardment off and on for several years. The Soviets showed particular brutality in dealing with villages near major supply routes. Western observers reported that Soviet firepower created a *cordon sanitaire* virtually devoid of humanity for several kilometers on either side of the most vital roads.[44]

Maneuver Forces

By April 1980, two sobering facts became evident to General I. M. Tret'yak, Commander of the Far East Military District (VO), in overall charge of operations in Afghanistan. First, what had started as a war of intervention had become a war of attrition. Second, a major transformation in firepower and maneuver doctrine was necessary if the Red Army was to prosecute the war with any degree of tactical proficiency. Following Soviet custom, learned from Stalin himself in the Great Patriotic War, Tret'yak called a conference of many high-level general officers, at which the tactical lessons of the war were discussed and the first tentative correctives made to govern combat "in mountainous-taiga terrain." After Tret'yak outlined the general direction that tactical reform would take, he delegated further refinement to Colonel General Dimitriy Yazov, Commander of the Central Asian VO (who would become a Field Marshal and Soviet Minister of Defense).[45]

Yazov, a veteran of World War II, had special qualifications to direct the doctrinal reform effort in Afghanistan. While a Lieutenant Colonel, he spent six years as an instructor in the Vystrel Senior Officers Course conducted for battalion and regimental combat officers. The Vystrel is unique in that, in addition to teaching, instructors are involved in experimenting with new technological and doctrinal concepts. Yazov appears to have concentrated his study on small unit operations at night. He put theory into practice during the many years that he served in the Asian regions of the Soviet Union. According to Soviet literature, sub-units under his command established new standards of proficiency in operations involving night maneuvers by small units in mountainous and inhospitable terrain.[46]

Yazov began with the basics. The cumbersome, interconnected formations of divisions and armies that formed the building blocks of wars in Europe had no place in Afghanistan. His tactical problem was to streamline his combat forces, yet provide them with enough firepower to pulverize the enemy in traditional Soviet fashion. In keeping with the scientific nature of Soviet doctrinal development, Yazov and his peers turned to the Great Patriotic War for a conceptual model.

They chose the Manchurian Campaign fought at the end of the war against the Japanese as the closest approximation to the Afghan problem. In Manchuria, the Soviets overcame the challenges of inhospitable terrain and great distances by creating small "forward detachments" of battalions. Each battalion was provided with its own combined arms team, a battery each of artillery and mortars, and a company of tanks. This arrangement provided the battalion with a measure of flexible firepower without having to create an elaborate and delicate fire support infrastructure of liaison officers and observers necessary to call in outside, non-organic firepower. In combat against the Japanese, the Soviets found that forward detachments, once released from the restrictive bounds of higher and adjacent units, could paralyze the enemy by pushing quickly through to his rear area, destroying command facilities, and mopping up immobile Japanese infantry.[47]

Between July and September 1980, the Soviets introduced a modern version of the forward detachment in Afghanistan, with the appearance of the Combined Arms Reinforced Battalion as the core unit for the conduct of small-unit operations. The battalion was saturated with organic firepower, particularly artillery, tanks, and dedicated air support.[48] The use of artillery to support the reinforced battalion was particularly innovative. To ensure centralized control and employment in mass, conventional Soviet doctrine dictates that a battalion of 18 guns or rocket launchers is the smallest field artillery firing unit. But Mujahideen freedom fighters frequently encountered single batteries or even half-batteries accompanying a reinforced battalion. They saw, on occasion, BM–21 multiple rocket launcher sections detached and under the direct control of a reinforced battalion commander.[49] Such decentralization and tactical flexibility are extraordinary for any army, especially for the Soviets. To add more flexibility, and to assist movement of the battalion through mountainous terrain, one company within the battalion was trained and equipped to act as heliborne light infantry.[50]

The Soviets followed carefully the American experience with airmobility in Vietnam. By the mid-1970s they developed their own peculiar style of airmobile assault. Heliborne troops became an interdiction force intended to disrupt command and control and nuclear delivery units deep in the enemy's rear. In early 1976, in the course of the Kavkaz-76 exercise, helicopters were first used to transport troops into mountainous terrain.[51] By the late 1970s the Soviets had placed in the field a true air assault division complete with organic armored carriers, light trucks, and artillery.[52] Airborne and airmobile troops were the first to land on Afghan soil in December 1979 and formed the backbone of the Soviet mountain fighting force afterward.

Experience in Afghanistan taught the Soviets very quickly that the helicopter is the most important single weapon in a war against the guerrilla. They lifted infantry forces as large as a brigade by helicopter during major forays into Mujahideen mountain redoubts. Airmobile forces were deposited by helicopter in battalion strength on dominating heights and leap-frogged forward to protect the general advance of armored forces on lower ground.[53] Some knowledgeable writers, reflecting on the first four years of war, noted that without the mobility provided by the helicopter, the Soviets would have had absolutely no hope of subduing such a vast and inhospitable territory with less than 100,000 men.[54]

The Soviets learned from American experience in Vietnam that a counterguerrilla campaign relies most heavily on initiative and self-reliance among junior leaders. Yet these qualities were least likely to be found in the soldiers of a centrally controlled, autocratic state. Experience in Afghanistan seemed to indicate that these traits were indeed in short supply throughout the Red Army.[55] Following the traditional practice for military reform, in the spring of 1981 General Yazov chaired another major conference to determine a strategy for improving the decisionmaking attributes and flexibility of junior leaders in combat.[56] Promptly thereafter, training establishments in the Central Asian district began to emphasize small-unit training in mountainous terrain. The program exposed regular infantry to such tasks as the seizure of mountain passes, commanding heights, and road junctions. Weapons training concentrated on improving

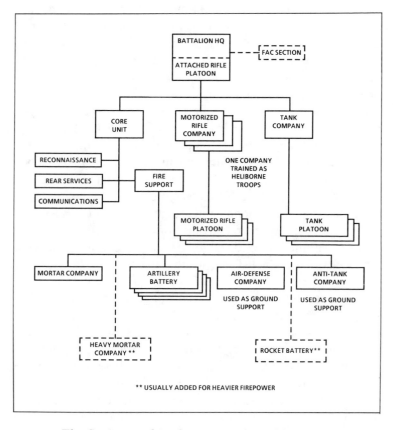

The Soviet combined arms reinforced battalion

shooting skills in alpine terrain and operating weapons and vehicles on lateral inclines and at night.[57]

The habits gained in three generations of strict obedience to central authority cannot be erased overnight. Nor was the Soviet leadership eager to develop a new generation of conscript soldier who learns too well to think for himself.[58] Therefore, the Red Army limited as much as possible the training for independent operations to carefully selected, politically reliable elite infantry. These soldiers are either airborne infantry or Spetsnaz, a corps of special operations troops roughly comparable to US Army Special Forces and Rangers.[59] The Soviets placed great reliance on these elite troops to provide the "quality edge" in Afghanistan. They conducted long-range reconnaissance patrols, assaulted isolated guerrilla hideouts, and acted as shock troops to lead the charge against heavily defended mountain redoubts.[60]

Mujahideen leaders still have little regard for the fighting qualities of Soviet mechanized infantrymen and little more than scorn for Afghan regular infantry.[61] They have more respect for special troops. Guerrilla leaders admit that Spetsnaz are good and the airborne seemed to get better.[62] They show aggressiveness and elan missing from more pedestrian Soviet conscripts, and are physically fit and at home in the mountains.[63] The airborne units in particular re-learned how to fight without armored carriers by introducing time-tested "fire and movement" tactics, with one section moving forward while another covers its advance by fire. This technique contrasts with traditional Soviet tactics, which rely on speed, heavy firepower, and rapid advance to overwhelm an opponent.[64]

Firepower In Support Of Maneuver

The Soviets applied the same deliberate, measured method of reform to produce a firepower doctrine suitable to support mobile forces in Afghanistan. They sought to add flexibility and responsiveness to the system while changing existing methods and equipment as little as possible. The Soviets were particularly fortunate in possessing firepower weapons well suited to war in the Third World. Tanks, long favorites of the Soviet war machine, proved useful for protecting convoys and fixed

The Soviet firepower team in action in Afghanistan.

bases.[65] A powerful main armament was capable of devastating guerrillas located near main roads. On flat terrain, tanks were fast and agile enough to keep up with mechanized infantry carriers and provide them with direct fire support. However, tanks in close terrain are more vulnerable to infantry equipped with hand-held anti-tank rockets.[66] On occasion, the Soviets were obliged to assign a motorized rifle squad to each tank to protect it against anti-tank weapons and mines, and to assist and guide it across obstructions and other obstacles.[67]

The Soviets experimented with various other means of adding more flexible firepower to convoys. One successful experiment was the placement of four-barreled 23-mm anti-aircraft guns in beds of trucks. Also, a light 30-mm automatic grenade launcher, the AGS–17, was mounted on BTR–60 and some BMP infantry carriers.[68] Unlike tank guns, these weapons could be elevated and trained quickly to engage fleeting targets and Mujahideen firing from extreme heights. Self-propelled artillery often accompanied convoys, and seemed to replace tanks in many direct-fire roles. Self-propelled guns possess the necessary characteristics of high mobility, armor protection, explosive firepower, and the ability to fire at higher elevations.

The most popular indirect-fire weapon for close support of maneuver forces in mountainous terrain was the mortar.[69] Mortars have long held a special place in the Soviet system of fire support, and are considered far more essential in the Soviet fire support system than in Western armies. Mortars are cheaper, simpler, and more reliable than cannon, yet the killing effect of a mortar shell is greater than a comparative cannon shell.[70] The Soviets found that high-arcing trajectories allowed mortars to fire over mountain tops and to drop shells into deep crevasses where neither artillery nor airpower could reach. Mortars could be emplaced quickly in response to an ambush and required very little space. This space requirement was important in narrow Afghan valleys where often only mortar sections were able to pull off the road and come into action.

The Red Army learned during World War II that mortars were the ideal weapon for providing close support for attacking troops.[71] Communication between the assault line and the mortar battery is direct and uncomplicated. The steeply plunging trajectory of mortars allows them to be fired within a few yards of attacking troops. In the relatively inflexible Soviet system of fire support, most fires come from outside the maneuver unit and are planned beforehand. Mortars frequently provide the only immediate support an infantry battalion commander can rely on to engage fleeting, unexpected targets.[72]

Many mortar types appeared in Afghanistan, from light, man-portable 82-mm to huge 240-mm behemoths firing 200-pound projectiles. Introduction of the "Vasilek" 82-mm automatic mortar in Afghanistan marked the first major technological advance in light mortar design since before the Second World War. The Vasilek uses an automatic feed device to fire 120 rounds per minute. It can be fired horizontally like a conventional gun using direct fire, or elevated to high angle and fired like a conventional mortar. The Soviets deployed it in towed and self-propelled versions and equipped each "reinforced" battalion with six of them.[73]

Although the Soviets favored the Vasilek as an area suppression weapon, the Mujahideen were generally ambivalent toward the effects of mortars and artillery alike. The typical pre-planned program of fire was often ineffective thanks to a thorough saturation of the Afghan Army with guerrilla informants who passed on information of impending operations well in advance. The Mujahideen commonly pulled out of an area to be strafed or burrowed deep into mountain tunnels and fortifications to escape the worst of the Soviet shelling. In fact, the Mujahideen suffered hardly at all from the best prepared and most precisely executed preparatory fires.[74] The Soviets relearned through practical experience the lesson learned by the Americans in Korea: that troops dug-in and defending mountainous terrain are almost impossible to dislodge with indirect firepower. A study done by the Operational Research Office of Johns Hopkins University shortly after the Korean War concluded that many thousands of rounds of artillery were necessary to kill a single enemy in such circumstances. There is no reason to believe that the Soviets were any more successful.[75]

Soviet efforts to achieve decisive effect using ground-delivered firepower were hindered to some degree by an obsolete and inflexible fire support doctrine. As with maneuver, fire support methods were slow to change as a result of experience in Afghanistan because they were so deeply ingrained in the Soviet way of war. Soviet firepower philosophy agrees with the American in that it seeks to achieve a breakthrough or to break an enemy's assault with overwhelming firepower. But the Soviets' method of execution is different.

US firepower doctrine is based on the principle that all guns, regardless of caliber, participate in both preparatory fires and fires in support of subsequent maneuver. Therefore, the fires of many guns attached to many different units and scattered widely across the front must be reoriented to concentrate on a specific point and must be controlled by a single hand. Such a system requires great flexibility to mass fires without massing guns. The American Army has traditionally fielded an elaborate system of communications and liaison and observer officers to make the firepower system work.

The Soviets prefer the less complex solution of massing fires by massing guns. Instead of an elaborate communications and liaison network, they use a well-developed staff planning system to shift large artillery formations across the front and line them up opposite the point of attack. In the Great Patriotic War, the Soviets fielded whole artillery armies and corps to mass enormous battering rams in the best medieval tradition. At the battle of Stalingrad, for example, the initial barrage was conducted by a concentration of guns as dense as 200 pieces per kilometer of front. Even in the modern era of nuclear warfare, the Russians prefer to cluster guns and rockets of various calibers together into concentrated regimental, divisional, or army artillery groups under the temporary control of a single artillery commander.[76]

Whereas the US Army provides separate liaison down to battalion and observers to platoon level, in the Soviet Army the battery commander himself acts as liaison officer to the maneuver battalion. Such a system works well when most fires are planned before an operation. But in a war without fronts or a clearly identified enemy, an infantry commander rarely knows what fire he requires beforehand and must find and fix the enemy before he can employ heavy firepower with effect. The failure of the artillery to develop such a system in Afghanistan cost the Soviets. Mujahideen commanders uniformly stated that Soviet artillery fired in response to an ambush or other unforeseen event was most often slow and inaccurate. On many occasions, Mujahideen commanders reported that they were able to strike a Soviet formation and withdraw without receiving artillery fire at all.[77] This failure may have been the result of a fire support system too inflexible and cumbersome to respond, but more likely its cause was a curious but all too common hesitation among ground commanders to call for ground or air support unless the support had been planned beforehand.[78]

"Victor Suvorov," a highly placed Soviet Army defector, explained the phenomenon again in terms of norms. The attacking commander's superiors, after careful scientific calculation, may have allocated specific firepower resources to seize a guerrilla position. For the commander on the spot to ask for more firepower or to request a shift of fire toward an unexpected threat would reflect distrust of his superiors or his own inability to do the task with the resources provided. In a discussion with Western officers, Suvorov was asked, "If a Soviet platoon or company commander, whose men are suffering heavy casualties, asks for artillery support, does he get it?" "He has no right to ask for it," replied Suvorov bluntly. Suvorov explained that if every platoon commander had the authority to call for fire support, the total offensive effort would be hopelessly diluted. Firepower in the Soviet system is reserved to support the main effort, not to save lives.[79]

The Soviet High Command realized early in the war that old habits and inappropriate doctrine would be difficult to change quickly. Just as the Soviets were reluctant to inculcate the spirit of initiative and self-reliance throughout the maneuver force, they also recognized early on that the creation of a suitably flexible and responsive fire support system to cope only with special conditions in Afghanistan would be both prohibitively expensive and inappropriate.

The solution to this tactical dilemma was both appropriate and typically Russian. As we have seen, firepower for road-bound forces was increased by breaking up larger aggregations of guns and rockets and attaching many of them down to the lowest tactical level, usually at reinforced battalions, sometimes even to separate companies. By doing this, the Soviets forfeited to some degree the ability to mass but gave the lower-level maneuver commander responsive and flexible firepower without the need to make fundamental changes in the firepower system.

The armed helicopter provided a second key ingredient in the new Soviet firepower doctrine tailored for Afghanistan. Early experience in the war taught that in the Hind the Soviets possessed a weapon capable of providing close and responsive firepower in support of troops in combat. It became the perfect instrument for shifting and massing fires without the need for detailed movement plans or an elaborate system for coordinating or controlling firepower from distant sources.[80]

The Soviets watched the US experience with attack helicopters in Vietnam closely and began to experiment with cargo helicopters variously modified for rockets, machineguns, and bombs. In 1967 these jury-rigged gunships were first observed in Operation ''Dnieper'' providing close air support to maneuver troops. Not until 1972 did rumors of a fully capable attack helicopter begin to circulate in the West.[81] Although slow to start, the Soviets caught up fast, and while debate raged heatedly in the United States over the worth of attack helicopters, the Mi–24 Hind became fully operational in the Soviet Union. By all accounts, the Hind is a superb aircraft. Designed essentially as a flying tank, it is heavier, faster, and more heavily armed than the American AH–1G Cobra. It can carry up to six passengers and its short, stubby wings can be loaded with an assortment of armament including 57-mm free-flight rockets, wire-guided missiles, and free-fall bombs. Later models pack a four-barrelled 12.7-mm Gatling gun mounted in a stabilized chin turret.[82]

Unlike Western helicopters, Soviet Hinds belong to Air Force Frontal Aviation. Before the conflict in Afghanistan, Hinds were collected into regiments of about 60 aircraft and were intended for use by the army commander as a mobile anti-tank force. After 1979, however, their role was expanded. Hinds became the sole means of providing very close air support to combat troops. They effectively supplanted artillery for most ''on call'' support of ground commanders. They completely replaced fixed-wing aircraft for all missions, planned and on call, near friendly troops.[83]

The Soviets consider the Hind much more than an aerial fire support platform. One Soviet Air Force officer, when describing its employment in "mountain-taiga terrain" (a euphemism for Afghanistan), listed for it a series of roles not seen in combat for a single aircraft since the Huey gunships in Vietnam. They were employed to support attacking sub-units, to perform reconnaissance, to observe artillery fire, to land tactical airborne forces, to move weapons and equipment across unpassable terrain sectors, and to deliver supplies and evacuate wounded.[84]

The coordination between helicopters and ground forces in Afghanistan was conducted by a frontal aviation staff that paralleled the army tactical staff from the 40th Army in Kabul down to maneuver battalion level. It was generally similar to the American system of close air support except that the army commander had somewhat greater control over fixed-wing aircraft such as fighter-bombers and reconnaissance aircraft and somewhat less control over helicopters than his American counterpart.[85] The Soviet ground commander dictated when close air support was required, what targets were to be struck, what level of destruction was desired, and what method would be used to coordinate the strike when close to friendlies. The air commander in Afghanistan controlled all aircraft inside the country and determined which aircaft to use and the size and type of munitions best suited to the target.[86]

In recognition of the increased numbers and importance of helicopters in the close support role, the Soviet Air Force steadily reinforced its frontal aviation liaison and control elements with forward units. In addition to the normal "air representative" (*Aviatsionnyye predstaviteli*) at division and regimental level, the Soviets apparently provided a forward air controller (*Avianavodchiki*) to each major convoy and battalion formation in the field.[87] Each convoy came to include an FAC armored vehicle equipped with radios linking the convoy to higher Air Force headquarters and the parent air field. Hind aircraft routinely escorted an airmobile force to the landing zone and remained on station to provide immediate fire support.[88] The Mujahideen noted that elite airmobile infantry could talk directly to the Hind aircraft orbiting above. When summoned, the response of the Hind was immediate and precise.[89]

The Soviet Air Force used airborne command and control during major operations. Mujahideen reported that large, multi-engined An–12, An–14, and An–26 transport aircraft often orbited for hours at high altitude over contested areas, apparently observing and controlling air strikes. The arrival of an An–12 overhead became so common during Soviet operations in the Panjsher Valley that the guerrillas called them "flying Kremlins." Their presence was a sure warning of an impending air strike and provided more than enough time for the guerrillas to move out of harm's way.[90]

Increased Soviet success with close air support was a result of growing efficiency of their heliborne forward air controllers.[91] FACs flew in modified Mi–8 cargo aircraft and occasionally in Hinds, and used control techniques very similar to those used by Americans in Vietnam.[92] Heliborne FACs shot smoke or white phosphorus rockets to mark a target. At first the Mujahideen recognized the mark and dispersed before the attack helicopter rolled in. In later offensives, FACs became practiced enough to mark only seconds before the aerial strike, giving the guerrillas little time to escape.[93]

Attack helicopters usually worked in pairs.[94] One aircraft circled very high, between 6,000 and 9,000 feet, to keep clear of heavy machinegun and surface-to-air missile fire. The second dove to the target and began firing its cannon and rockets at about 3,000 feet. After expending ordnance, the attacking aircraft became the observer, and his partner continued the attack. Although two aircraft were normally the limit for a single engagement, up to four pairs were observed providing air support during major division-level operations into the Panjsher Valley northeast of Kabul.[95]

The system for control and coordination of attack helicopters seems somewhat cumbersome by US standards.[96] Hinds were equipped with three separate radios, each used for a single function: one for directly contacting the air field, one for communicating with other helicopters, and the third for maintaining contact with troops on the ground.[97] Response times were quick for aircraft already in the air over a particular convoy or dedicated to airmobile infantry, but reinforcement aircraft tended to arrive very slowly, if at all. An Afghan Air Force

The Mi–8 troop-carrying helicopter was modified to fire rockets and machineguns, providing additional firepower for the Soviets.

defector stated that reaction times for an attack mission not previously briefed or cleared with 40th Army Headquarters in Kabul were at least 90 minutes. Curiously, almost a third of this time was spent in briefings and pre-operations checks.[98]

Although Hinds frequently worked with artillery and fixed-wing aircraft during preparations and other pre-planned missions, Mujahideen commanders uniformly stated that the attack helicopters engaged targets of opportunity only after other firepower means had been shut down or shifted away. Artillery would take up support after the helicopters departed. Until fairly late in the war, Hinds were not observed firing any closer than about 200 meters from Soviet troops.[99] The reason for this reluctance to fire any closer can only be surmised, but Hinds had begun to attack at higher speeds and altitudes than the American Cobras, perhaps making Soviet pilots more cautious.

Mujahideen feared the Hind. Artillery and fixed-wing fighters were effective as terror weapons against civilian populations, but only the Hind could effectively thwart guerrilla operations in the field. Its presence over convoys greatly diminished the effectiveness of ambushes. When employed properly in close cooperation with airmobile troops, it proved to be the only fire support system in Afghanistan capable of causing substantial casualties.[100] After observing the Hind in action against the Mujahideen, Phillip Jacobson, in a reminiscent analogy, wrote,

> It is also possible to draw a comparison between the stunning impact of the mobility and awesome firepower of the Hinds ... and the early success of US helicopters against guerrillas in Vietnam. One Mujahideen leader still trembles as he recalls six Hinds flying line abreast just above the ground, devastating everything before them.[101]

The Hind does have vulnerabilities. Some were shot down with "borrowed" Soviet SA–7 surface-to-air missiles.[102] One guerrilla leader even claimed success using an SA–7 against a Hind equipped with flare dispensers, which the Soviets strapped to aircraft to decoy heat-seeking missiles.[103] The Mujahideen became more successful against the Hind after they began receiving large numbers of US Stinger shoulder-fired heat-seeking missiles. In certain circumstances, heavy 12.7-mm machineguns downed attack helicopters. Mujahideen gunners preferred to fire down on their targets from high mountains, hoping to strike the vulnerable rotor head or the unarmored upper portion of the aircraft.[104] During the early years, Hinds swept through narrow valleys in pairs at very low level, much like World War II "fighter sweeps." Afghan gunners learned to let the first aircraft fly past and engage the second as it began to turn. The Soviets countered with their "high-low" technique, which reduced losses to ground fire but also lessened the accuracy of bombing and strafing attacks and made guerrillas harder to spot.[105] Although not many gunships were downed, missiles and machinegun fire seem to have had a noticeable deterrent effect in keeping both fixed-wing strike aircraft and helicopter gunships from pressing attacks too closely.[106]

The Soviets used fixed-wing aircraft solely for interdiction, armed reconnaissance, and terror bombing. Older fighter-bombers such as MiG–21s and Su–7s were reserved for large area targets far from troops, such as flanking mountain passes and villages thought to sympathize with the guerrillas.[107] These aircraft dropped 250- and 500-kilogram bombs from higher altitudes and smaller parachute retardant bombs on low-level passes. The guerrillas reported that cluster bombs were used commonly against populated areas and proved tragically destructive against unsuspecting villagers. The Soviet versions of these weapons contain both high-explosive and incendiary bomblets.[108]

Newer ground support aircraft such as the MiG–27 Flogger and Su–25 Frogfoot were employed for more precise work, striking fortified positions or engaging fleeting targets.[109] The Frogfoot was particularly respected because of its deadly 30-mm gun and its ability to loiter over an area for hours waiting for targets to appear. It can bomb with great precision.[110] Like the Hind, Su–25s operated in loose pairs, with one aircraft orbiting at approximately 9,000 feet to observe while the other dove on the target and released at about 3,000 feet. The Frogfoot can dive steeply, which made it often the only aircraft able to deliver ordnance into mountain gorges where the Mujahideen commonly retired to escape heavy bombardments.[111] In spite of the Frogfoot's success, the Soviet Air Force deployed only two squadrons of the plane to Afghanistan. Guerrilla leaders in some regions profess that they never saw the aircraft at all. This seems to indicate that the Soviets were still unsure of its value in conditions other than limited war.[112]

The Soviets had their own version of an "arc light." Beginning in 1981, heavy Tu–16 bombers stationed at Termez, just across the border in the Soviet Union, carried out heavy saturation attacks against Afghan settlements in the Andarab Valley, halfway between Kabul and the Soviet border.[113] In April 1981, the Soviets mounted a 200-bomber raid against villages in the Panjsher Valley as a precursor to a major ground offensive. The bombers attacked at high altitude, sometimes with no warning. Seven hundred civilians died in the Andarab bombing. Later, the Mujahideen were able to receive some forewarning of the larger attacks and casualties declined. Still, these terror attacks by heavy bombers depopulated and destroyed entire regions of rural Afghanistan and were principally responsible for expelling over 4 million rural villagers that still crowd refugee camps in Pakistan.[114]

In spite of major aerial campaigns, which during peak periods reached 100 sorties per day, Soviet interdiction does not appear to have been very successful in reducing the fighting strength of the Mujahideen.[115] This failure resulted partly from the nature of the war. As the United States learned in Indochina, a pre-planned and deliberate aerial campaign, though effective against regular armies, has little chance of success against a light, mobile, and thinly scattered guerrilla force. The Soviets found also that mountainous terrain inhibited the effectiveness of air-to-ground fire. Even the heaviest bombs do little harm to guerrillas secure in mountain caves or deep ravines.[116]

Soviet munitions were unreliable in the mountains. One former Afghan pilot contends that 30 percent of the bombs he dropped failed to detonate. Some bombs tended to split open on rock hillsides before detonating. Others were defuzed or otherwise incapacitated by Afghan Air Force ground crews secretly loyal to the insurgent cause.[117] Borrowing a page from the Viet Cong, the Mujahideen commonly made crude mines from undetonated bombs and returned the explosive to its rightful owner. Edward Girardet, a correspondent for the *Christian Science Monitor*, spent several months with the freedom fighters in 1982 and described one aerial attack in which 223 bombs were dropped on a large guerrilla settlement. One person was killed and another injured. Three houses were destroyed and a cow was killed. He described a Soviet bombing attack against a guerrilla heavy machinegun position overlooking the town of Bazarak. The attack lasted an entire afternoon. After repeated bombing and rocketing, "only one small tree was all that was left standing, but the gun was firing away the next day."[118]

Another reason for failure of the air interdiction campaign is strictly Soviet in character. Colonel Jalali recounts an afternoon in 1982 when he was speeding across a flat, arid region of Afghanistan in an open vehicle. Flying lazily above were two Hinds, each taking turns peeling off to attack a destroyed, obviously deserted village. The jeep was throwing up clouds of dust and surely must have been visible from the air. Nervously, Jalali asked the driver why the Hinds didn't attack. "Don't they know that we are Mujahideen," he asked? "Of course," replied the driver, "but they were ordered to bomb the village, not us."[119]

Such incidents were reported occasionally by Western observers in Afghanistan. Aircraft routinely flew over heavily armed guerrilla bands and ignored them. Soviet pilots ordered to attack a trenchline or open space obviously unoccupied would do so while ignoring hostile troops firing madly at the helicopters from nearby positions. After two years of war, the lack of initiative and self-reliance among aircrews began to appear in the Soviet military press. Articles praised pilots for thinking for themselves and acting independently during maneuvers. One article in *Aviatsiya I Kosmonavtika* "noted that problems concerning tactical training of aviators, the development of iniative and creativity in our air warriors ... are at the center of attention of commanders, staff officers, and political workers, and party and Komsomol organizations of the unit."[120] Such revelations in Soviet professional literature are rare and describe a problem not soon to be solved in any branch of the Soviet armed forces.

Soviet Firepower in Action

During the war, the Soviets conducted at least a dozen major combined arms offensives into Mujahideen strongholds. Not enough first-hand, unclassified information is available to provide a

The Mujahideen fought back doggedly and effectively against the most modern Soviet firepower systems.

detailed account of a specific operation, but enough information exists from several Soviet, Western, and Mujahideen sources to piece together a general description of how the Soviets coordinated firepower and maneuver in Afghanistan.[121]

Major operations were seasonal, usually conducted in the spring or fall. Because they had so few combat forces, the Soviets were careful not to waste effort on blind jabs into enemy territory. They collected information carefully and patiently over several months, relying mainly on paid informants or intelligence gained from the most brutal means by Khad, the Afghan version of the KGB.[122]

The Soviets normally devoted a stripped-down mechanized division and a composite airborne division to each full-scale foray. The divisional artillery moved forward first and established a divisional artillery group (DAG) within range of the valley to be attacked (see illustration, page 193). The DAG was composed of a large assortment of guns, usually 30 to 50 consisting of 122-mm medium guns for close-in support, 152-mm and 130-mm howitzers and guns for longer-range support, and 122-mm rockets for concentrated doses of firepower. Most of these guns and launchers belonged to the divisional artillery regiment; some were loaned for the operation from 40th Army fire support assets.[123]

The Soviets plan their fires in extreme detail.[124] Where a Western army might plan a single preparation phase, Soviet gunners take weeks to prepare a schedule of fire computed to the last round, for up to five continuous days of operation.[125] The initial softening up of the target would begin as maneuver troops moved out of their garrison and approached the mouth of the valley. Fixed-wing aircraft, helicopters, and heavy bombers would carpet the valley methodically with a huge volume of firepower laid down over several days. These fires were intended to terrorize the population, mainly wives and children of the freedom fighters, in the hope that the guerrillas would foresake fighting to take their families to safety. More distant fires were planned to seal off escape for those already in the valley and to prevent reinforcement or resupply.[126]

A few hours before troops would be committed, the Antonov command, control, and observation planes would

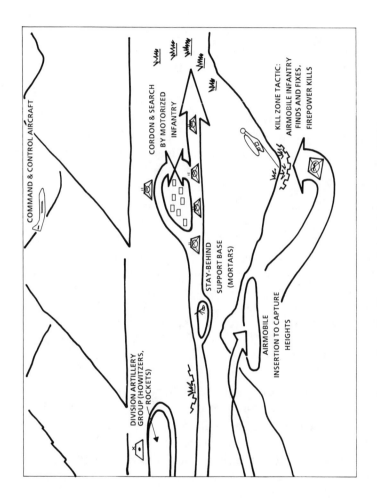

A set-piece Soviet attack in Afghanistan, 1984

arrive overhead.[127] Fires then would be shifted to specific air-mobile landing zones in the mountains and ground tactical objectives in the valley floor. Waves of fighter-bombers would attack first, for perhaps three hours, followed by an intensive artillery bombardment from all guns and rockets within range. Mi–24 Hinds and Mi–17 (an improved version of the Mi–8) rocket-firing transport helicopters would immediately precede the airmobile assault. The more vulnerable Mi–17s would stand off and fire free-flight rockets at the LZ from a distance; Hinds would close to within a few hundred yards with cannon and rockets and then take station overhead as the airborne soldiers arrived by helicopter.[128]

Once the heights were secure, mechanized forces would begin to move quickly up the valley floor under protective artillery fire.[129] Artillery would be placed on likely ambush sites and sniper locations. All fires were pre-planned. The tanks, mortars, and artillery with the column were expected to take care of unforeseen resistance.[130] The Soviets learned that the Mujahideen preferred to let combat elements of the convoy pass, waiting to attack vulnerable resupply vehicles that bring up ammunition and fuel in the evening. To protect communication with the rear, the mechanized force would drop off small contingents of artillery and mortars at suitable spots near the road. These small "firebases" were normally not larger than a battery of mortars with a platoon of infantry or tanks for local protection.[131]

As the armored force in the valley drew parallel, the airmobile force would leap-frog to more distant mountain tops in a succession of heliborne assaults preceded by the obligatory fighter-bomber and helicopter preparation.[132] Once firmly positioned in the insurgent's territory, Soviet troops would begin to hunt the Mujahideen using two tactical methods. Mechanized forces conducted "cordon and search" operations to surround and isolate a village and work methodically to sort out the guerrillas from other inhabitants.[133] Some cordons could be lengthy affairs. As the reinforced mechanized battalion maneuvered toward the target village, its own attached firepower would suppress or destroy isolated pockets of resistance. Self-propelled artillery and mortars were used for such very close work. The

Soviets preferred to employ artillery in the direct-fire mode if possible, particularly against buildings, bunkers, or other hard-to-hit point targets.[134] In January 1982, a large mechanized force surrounded the towns of Bagram, Kuhestan, and Koh Bani, trapping approximately 2,000 freedom fighters. The siege lasted ten days and resulted in a bloody battle in which nine Soviet tanks were destroyed.[135]

Lighter forces preferred the "kill zone" tactic. After consolidating landing zones, heliborne companies and battalions would attempt to push the guerrillas from peaks and valley walls into specific, pre-designated valleys and gorges. Once in position, the light forces would dig in or take cover and call in supporting firepower to pound the Mujahideen with carefully planned and coordinated attacks from the air.[136] Because troops were positioned so close to the kill zone, aircraft were unable to continue close support at night, giving the Mujahideen trapped inside the kill zone a welcome respite during which to escape or to dig in for a heavy fight at daybreak. To permit round-the-clock bombardment, the Soviets began lifting heavy mortars by cargo helicopters into surrounding valleys just before dark. Mortars would then pick up the fire support task once aircraft departed and would be lifted back to garrison in the morning when the Hinds returned

With each major advance into the contested Panjsher, the Soviets refined this technique. During incursions in early 1984, they conducted increasingly complex and sophisticated air operations, employing and coordinating diverse support means ranging from transports dropping sophisticated fuel-air and fragmentation bombs, Tu–16 and Su–24 heavies carpet-bombing close to airborne troops, and attack helicopters providing flexible and immediate close air support. It is significant that Soviet light troops were able on occasion to maneuver across difficult terrain and inflict decisive losses on the Mujahideen, all the while supported closely by aerial firepower and air-transported mortars.[137]

Insurgent leaders concur that Soviet control and coordination between firepower and maneuver steadily improved with each successive operation of this sort. Qari Taj Mohammad, general commanding 26 guerrilla elements in Ghazni and Zabol

Provinces, remarked that the Soviets perfected their ability to fire multiple rocket launchers in response to immediate requests from forward infantry. They also learned the intricacies of engaging larger targets, such as battalion base camps and full-scale ambushes, with aerial and artillery fires delivered simultaneously and in combination.[138] Qari Taj Mohammad noted that, during the course of the war, fire controlled by spotter aircraft and "C&C" ships came to be concentrated on his forces quickly, often within a few minutes of engagement. Fires routinely shifted among mortars, rockets, artillery, and bombs.[139]

An equally sinister development was the marked improvement in the precision of Soviet firepower. High mountain caves no longer provided absolute immunity from attack, as the Soviets became more adept at locating and striking cave entrances with rocket-firing helicopters and large-caliber artillery. Qari Taj Mohammad also noted the gradual improvement in the ability of Soviet soldiers, particularly elite infantry, to maneuver very close to Mujahideen bunkers while maintaining a continuous and accurate bombardment using mortars and artillery. Often Qari Taj Mohammad's men had only a few moments after the artillery fire lifted to return and counterattack before the Soviets closed to decisive small arms and rocket grenade range.[140]

The Soviets learned the art of war in the Third World slowly, with fits and starts, and at great expense, befitting a system that tolerates very little innovation from below. Yet careful inspection shows that their method, brutal though it may be, accommodates comfortably the traditional Soviet military virtues of obedience to authority and detailed staff planning, which have served them so well in previous wars. In a prophetic statement, Babrak Kamal, then puppet leader of Afghanistan, once boasted that his forces had the "firepower to melt the Afghan mountains." Although not able to displace mountains, the Soviets dedicated most of their firepower mechanism in Afghanistan to displacing the population from its mountain homes. Anthropologist Louis Dupree has rightfully labeled the brutal strategy as "migratory genocide."[141] The first four years of aerial and ground bombardments forced perhaps 20 percent of the entire Afghan population to flee its villages and farms and take refuge in Pakistan. No one knows how many died in this frightful application of firepower, but it surely must have been in the hundreds of thousands.[142]

From a tactical viewpoint, the Soviet application of firepower was as flexible as it could be under the circumstances of Soviet military tradition and the nature of the war in Afghanistan. Through the pervasive and clever use of attack helicopters, the Soviets added a measure of responsiveness without changing the fundamental structure of their fire support system. The Soviet High Command's degree of commitment to attack helicopters as fire support vehicles is evidenced by the curious lack of heliborne artillery so often a fixture of US airmobile operations in Vietnam.[143] Nor did the Soviets find it necessary to devise a system to permit augmentation of helicopter fires with artillery and close air support.

From a hesitant beginning, the attack helicopter became the sole success story and the centerpiece of the firepower system in Afghanistan. A Western journalist recalled an occasion early in the war when he waited with a convoy on the Kabul-Ghazni road and watched several Hind gunships pound possible ambush positions in scrub and rocks for almost an hour. He remarked to a Soviet officer waiting with him that it reminded him of "reconnaissance by fire," Vietnam style. "Perhaps so," the officer said, "but here the helicopters are going to win."[144]

It is a credit to the fighting quality and resolve of the Afghan freedom fighters that they endured and strengthened themselves while the foe grew more capable. But, then, war was nothing new to the Mujahideen, incredibly brave warriors like Commander Haji who fought the British Empire to a stand-still for over a century.

5
The Falklands Campaign

For *six hours Lieutenant Colonel "H" Jones fought his four* rifle companies of paratroopers southward toward the main Argentine positions protecting the settlement at Goose Green. Darkness and surprise had been his only allies. The early morning was bitterly cold, and in the disappearing darkness the paras could see that the terrain surrounding them was completely devoid of cover or concealment. As Jones feared, with daylight the attack began to stall. The Argentines could see the paras now, laying prone on the sodden, featureless terrain, exposed to increasingly accurate mortar and artillery fire. What was supposed to be a company or so of Argentines had become a reinforced battalion dug into hillsides in well-prepared bunkers and trenches.

Jones began his attack on Goose Green with meager fire support. By daylight he had practically none. The frigate HMS *Arrow* was to support the attack from off shore, but a mechanical failure in its single 4.5-inch gun forced the ship's withdrawal as soon as the attack began. Jones had less than one-third the artillery normally dedicated to support a deliberate attack by an infantry battalion. Three guns of 8 Commando Battery, Royal Artillery, had been lifted by four Sea King helicopters into a depression northeast of Camilla Creek House during the previous evening. A total of only 12 helicopter sorties were dedicated by the brigade to the artillery, so Lieutenant Mark

Waring, the battery gun position officer, could provide only one lift for his men, three for guns, and eight for ammunition. In all, 28 artillerymen and less than 1,000 rounds of ammunition were ready to support by the morning of the attack.

The early departure of HMS *Arrow* and the unexpected strength of the Argentine defense caused the artillery to fire many more rounds than expected. By daybreak, 8 Commando Battery was practically out of ammunition. Jones took two of his own light 81-mm mortars with him on his trek to Goose Green. But without transport, mortar shells had to be carried on the backs of his soldiers. What little ammunition the mortars could husband for the attack had been fired by morning.

Every moment of exposure in daylight meant more casualties. Jones' companies were now fragmented into small clusters, each struggling to win the upper hand in separate, scattered firefights. The greatest threat to the advance was a set of untouched Argentine machinegun nests on Darwin Hill. Without external fire support, small groups of paras were obliged to inch their way up the hill to within 50 meters or less of a trench while constantly under fire. Once in position, one man would fire a 66-mm shoulder-fired rocket at a machinegun embrasure, followed quickly by a mad rush by perhaps a dozen men firing rifles and throwing grenades.

Jones huddled with his headquarters group of a dozen men just north of Darwin Hill. He grew increasingly frustrated with the lack of support and the slow progress of the attack. Just above his head, a machinegun position was raking a large portion of his most forward company. Unable to call for more fire or to influence the scattered and confusing fighting around him, Jones decided to assault the machinegun using only the troops in his headquarters section. He divided his men into two small squads. Jones himself led one, his adjutant, Captain David Wood, led the other.

Wood tried to work his way south of the hill, to attack the machinegun from the right flank. The Argentines spotted the maneuver, opened fire, and killed Wood instantly. Jones led his force to the left of the enemy position. He threw several smoke grenades to cover the advance across a bare ridge-line leading to the machinegun nest. The smoke blew away quickly, exposing

Jones' party as it broke from cover. Captain Dent, the headquarters company commander, was killed. Jones quickly ran to cover, followed by Sergeant Norman from his section.

The enemy now was fully alert and firing furiously. By pressing himself close to the soggy ground, Jones managed to crawl within three feet of the nearest enemy position. Sergeant Norman, firing desperately to protect his leader, noticed a previously unseen trenchline to Jones' rear. He shouted a warning, but too late. Argentine troops hidden in that trench shot Jones in the neck and he died waiting in the cold morning for an evacuation helicopter to arrive.[1]

The death of Colonel Jones should have broken the back of the assault on Darwin Hill. Instead, within two hours the assault succeeded; the Argentines were pushed off the high ground surrounding Goose Green, and within a day the isolated garrison surrendered 1,300 men and 30 guns to the paras. The paras were successful for two reasons. Goose Green was the first conventional battle that the paras had fought since World War II, and the men on Darwin Hill were not about to lose it. As one young soldier commented after the battle, "We wanted to show the Regiment that we could fight too."[2] War was a new experience, and the paras were full of the exhilaration and elan that often accompanies elite troops new to combat. Junior leaders, officers as well as NCOs, took on the Argentine defenses doggedly and methodically in a series of isolated skirmishes. It turned into a very personal sort of combat, with little outside direction and very little outside support. But after so many years of preparing for this moment, every soldier in the regiment was determined that the attack would succeed.

The second reason for eventual success was the prudent use made by Colonel Jones' second in command of the limited fire support remaining to the battalion. After hearing of his leader's death, Major Chris Keeble moved quickly to the forward position. Two lead companies were still making slow progress, but needed fire support to break into and through the enemy defenses. Keeble ordered a fresh company forward to assist the two hard-pressed companies in heavy contact. He also ordered

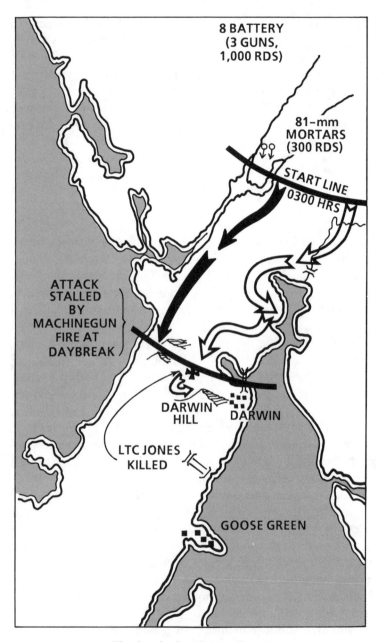

The battle for Goose Green
to the death of Lieutenant Colonel Jones

up the three 105-mm howitzers of 8 Commando Battery closer behind the forward companies.[3] Throughout the morning high winds had been blowing the shells off course. Keeble hoped that shortening the range would lessen the dispersion of the shells. He ordered up wire-guided MILAN anti-tank missiles to take out the hardened Argentines positions. The pinpoint accuracy of the MILAN quickly demoralized the Argentines and proved just enough to tip the scale of battle in favor of the attacker. By evening, the paras dominated the heights above Goose Green. The next day, the Argentines at Goose Green surrendered.[4]

The Attack on Goose Green

In the general sense that "all's well that ends well," the attack on Goose Green was a resounding success. At the relatively minor cost of 14 dead, 2 Para had single-handedly killed 250 Argentines, including some of the best marine troops in the Argentine armed forces.[5] A considerable stock of modern arms fell into British hands. Thanks to an effective sea blockade, every weapon captured was one less to be called into action against the next phase of the land campaign, the attack on the defenses of Port Stanley. Most important, the success at Goose Green served to dispel lingering clouds of failure and establish the psychological ascendancy of British arms that, for the rest of the campaign, would never be relinquished.

The shift in self-confidence swept through both sides immediately after the battle. British assurance of ultimate success became absolute. The only questions remaining were how long the campaign would last and how high would be the cost. Conversely, all manner of rumor and doubt began to pervade the Argentine side, particularly among the rank and file. Stories of British martial prowess and the power of British arms grew with the telling, as rumor merged with inflated fact in the dugouts and trenches of the defenses surrounding Port Stanley.

The British were quick to take concrete lessons of this first encounter to heart. It seemed to both leaders and troops in the field that the Argentines fought well initially, sometimes with enthusiasm, as long as they were not distracted by unexpected threats or heavy doses of firepower. But the Argentine defense lacked resiliency. After exploding shells had deflated much of their self-confidence, and British infantry began to close, the Argentine will to resist dissipated quickly. The British observed little attempt to reinforce or counterattack, and no imagination in maneuvering against an attacking force.[6] The timidity, confusion, and lack of tactical initiatives witnessed by the British seemed to be amplified at night. This condition was all the more remarkable because night usually favors the defender who occupies familiar ground in relatively static positions. Also, the Argentines were equipped with high-quality electronic night vision devices far superior to those carried by British troops.[7]

Argentine fire support at Goose Green exhibited many of the same shortcomings as the maneuver arms. Artillery and mortar fires were delivered on time and with workmanlike precision as long as the Argentines themselves were not under indirect fire. When they received fire, however, the efficiency of Argentine gunners dropped off precipitously, far out of proportion to the number of British shells or the relative damage inflicted.[8]

The British were uncertain of the reasons for the considerable Argentine tactical imperfections. Goose Green provided some clues. The men of 2 Para were struck by the small number of officers and NCOs killed or captured in the front lines. Others noted that while some soldiers, notably the marines, were tough and well indoctrinated, others seemed poorly trained and apathetic.[9]

Goose Green also taught some valuable tactical lessons. Colonel Jones had been correct in choosing to attack the Argentines at night. The paras and the Gurkhas in particular practiced night operations and were confident of their ability to beat the Argentines in nocturnal combat. Less wise was the decision to move on Goose Green silently without a heavy dose of firepower to precede the attack. The overwhelming consensus was that enemy strength had been badly underestimated before the attack and that two mortars, three howitzers, and a frigate were insufficient to support a battalion assault against fixed positions. After Goose Green, the British resolved that future attacks would be supported from the beginning by a carefully prepared and coordinated fire plan using as many guns and as much ammunition as the supply and transport system would allow.

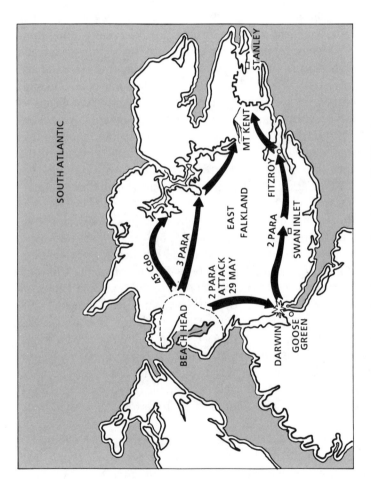

The British land campaign in the Falklands

With the fall of Goose Green, the British turned their attention toward major Argentine concentrations at Port Stanley, located at the opposite end of East Falkland Island and 50 air miles from the main British beachhead at San Carlos Water. The difficulties encountered in moving artillery and ammunition forward from San Carlos to the vicinity of Stanley would determine the pace and the timing of the remainder of the campaign.[10] The Argentine air threat against British shipping made forays to deliver supplies closer to the front from ships at sea extremely risky. Roads were little more than tracks able to support limited traffic. Helicopters provided the only sure means of resupply. Unfortunately, the British had underestimated the number of aircraft necessary to support the operation. The situation was made all the more precarious with the sinking of the container ship *Atlantic Conveyor*, which took with it to the bottom of San Carlos Water three of the four available large cargo-carrying CH–47 Chinook helicopters.

By 9 June, 68 helicopters were ashore. Of these, only 13 Sea Kings and the lone Chinook could carry artillery and ammunition. The British called on 23 smaller Wessex helicopters to haul lighter loads. The ordeal endured by the Chinook and its crew gives some indication of the extreme limits to which the British were forced to push their machines. In 28 days, it logged 150 hours in the air, carrying 1,500 troops and 600 tons of cargo. More than 80 troops were carried on single lifts, nearly twice the normal payload. Flying at extremely low level at night to avoid enemy fire, the Chinook once pancaked into a lake and bounced back into the air only to resume flying the next day after the outer skin of the bird was patched back together.[11]

The elements and the enemy did nothing to make aerial movement easier for British chopper crews. Most flying was restricted to daylight. Severe weather conditions reduced flying time even further. Air raid warnings frequently forced helicopter pilots to land, particularly after at least one of their number was shot down by marauding Argentine aircraft.[12] The shortage of cargo helicopters was exacerbated by an inadequate system of disposition and control that overworked some aircraft and crews while others waited idly for missions. In desperation, some units in the field with cargo to move "hijacked" helicopters and diverted them from their assigned tasks, often leaving units split or exposed in forward positions without adequate ammunition or support.

By far the greatest demand on helicopter flights was the task of moving forward guns and ammunition. Fully 85 percent of all sorties were used for this purpose. To move a single battery required 45 Sea King sorties. It took a Sea King at least one-and-a-quarter hours to fly 36 complete 105-mm rounds from San Carlos to the forward positions around Port Stanley. During the week before the final assault on Stanley, 29 Battery required three full days to move from San Carlos to Bluff Cove. On 1 June, 97 Battery was ordered to relocate, but the move was not complete until six days later.[13]

Although artillery drained away most of the expedition's airlift, it remained practically the only means of fire support proven effective in the campaign. The British could have used the pinpoint accuracy of attack helicopters to take out Argentine strong points at Goose Green, but neither the British Army nor the Royal Marines had in service a true attack helicopter. They took to the Falklands several light scout helicopters capable of firing machineguns and wire-guided missiles, but these aircraft were extremely vulnerable to Argentine ground fire and their services for scouting, observation, liaison, and medevac were considered far too important to risk the helicopters in dangerous maneuvers near heavily defended areas. In the coming attack, helicopters would fire a few air-to-ground missiles at Argentine positions, but none of them would achieve any significant result other than to blow up an Argentine police station at Stanley during the final days of the campaign.[14]

The experience at Goose Green seemed to show that close air support by the Royal Air Force would be limited. The entire expedition had fewer than 40 Harrier aircraft and needed them all (and more) to defend against fanatical Argentine air attacks.[15] Nonetheless, several close air support sorties were flown during the Goose Green operation to destroy the troublesome Argentine anti-aircraft guns, which were being used with effect to slow the ground advance by 2 Para. The paras reported that the strikes were effective. But before being silenced, the excellent radar-controlled guns succeeded in downing a single Harrier. Throughout the campaign, ground fire accounted for most Argentine and British aircraft losses. The early experience at Goose Green would make the RAF reluctant to further risk their valuable aircraft against ground targets until they first established unquestioned air superiority and some mastery over the troublesome Argentine anti-aircraft guns.[16]

The premature departure of the frigate HMS *Arrow* from its fire support duties at Goose Green was disappointing, but the British were still convinced that if the air and ground anti-ship threat could be contained, naval gunfire would provide an essential source of heavy firepower for the final assault. This confidence came in part from previous successes. Nearly a month before Goose Green, small teams of naval gunfire spotters from 148 Battery, 29 Commando, began landing by helicopter on East Falkland Island to direct harassing and interdiction missions against Argentine positions. The 148th was a gunner unit composed of men very carefully selected for their commando as well as spotting skills. Its composition and functions are very similar to American air and naval gunfire liaison companies. Perhaps no other unit was as well prepared to call for and adjust supporting fires. In addition to naval gunfire spotting, the officer observers of the 148th were equally skilled in artillery adjustment and the control of close air support. This latter skill proved particularly valuable at Goose Green when the regular RAF forward air controller was injured and replaced by a comparably qualified officer from the 148th.[17]

Before the Falklands War, the Royal Navy, like other Western navies, considered shore bombardment to be a dying and increasingly irrelevant "black art." Ironically, for that reason, 148 was just three months short of deactivation when dispatched to the Falklands. Perhaps partly because the British naval gunfire team had become so small and seemingly neglected, they were a tightly knit, cohesive group. Observers knew and worked continuously with helicopter pilots and ships' captains. Each knew the strengths and weaknesses of the other.

Long and intimate associations had led, over the years, to a working relationship that required little verbal communication or lengthy written instruction to work smoothly. One former

The British Navy's harassing and interdiction campaign was successful because it relied on direct observation of all fires.

member of the gunfire team described the routine of climbing into the back of naval helicopters that flitted around the fleet during the campaign. He needed only to read the name stenciled on the back of the pilot's flight helmet to know what instructions to give and what level of flying and spotting proficiency to expect. Likewise, from years of experience, the spotters knew how each ship could shoot and selected their targets accordingly.[18]

The naval gunfire H&I campaign, code-named Operation Tornado, was intended to keep the Argentines around Port Stanley busy and off balance while the main force landed far to the west. Bombardment followed an irregular pattern. Rounds were scarce; each "strafe" could not exceed 150 to 200 rounds per night. Instructions from Whitehall dictated that no buildings were to be damaged and not too much harm was to be done to enemy soldiers while some hope of a negotiated settlement still remained.[19]

The British understood what the Americans had learned in Vietnam. H&I fires were counterproductive unless they were observed and directed against worthwhile targets. For this reason, the Navy executed a complex firepower hit-and-run program that relied exclusively on direct observation of all fires. One or two frigates would steam in quickly toward the target area under cover of darkness to avoid Argentine air attack and drop off spotters from the 148th by helicopter. The frigates would then take up station along a "gun line," usually 10 miles off shore to avoid, as much as possible, Argentine return fire from Port Stanley.

When the air or ground spotter was in position, the ship would fire a short ranging round. The observer normally made only a single correction of a few hundred meters, and then the ship would follow with a five-round burst. The ship would continue firing under spotter control until just before daylight. At first, ship captains questioned the wisdom of risking their vessels for such an apparently futile effort, but after a few days of successful attacks they changed their attitude considerably. After three weeks, the ships were firing double the normal load, on some nights as many as 750 rounds, and the task for gunfire controllers changed from coercing fire support from their naval counterparts to reigning in overly enthusiastic ship captains who insisted on firing too much.[20]

The three weeks of Operation Tornado were a success, although the British had no way of knowing it at the time. One Argentine soldier recalled after the surrender,

> We were very demoralized at that time because we felt so helpless, we couldn't do anything. The English were firing at us from their frigates and we couldn't respond.[21]

Goose Green in fact only served to amplify the psychological ascendancy gained by the British through periodic nocturnal naval bombardments. Long before news of Goose Green reached Port Stanley, the Argentine soldiers began to lose heart when the ships appeared night after night:

> They began to say the English were going to wipe the floor with us. Until 1 May no one really believed we were going to have to fight. But when the (naval) attacks began everyone started getting more worried.[22]

Why, then, were H&Is so successful in the Falklands while, according to most evidence, they proved such a wasted effort in Vietnam? The answer lies in several factors: the nature of the war, the character of the enemy, and the manner in which the program of fire was conducted. The old saying, "familiarity breeds contempt," applies here. No matter how effective shell fire might be, in the course of a long war soldiers learn to accommodate and become accustomed to even the most fearsome bombardment, particularly when they realize that shelling often does little harm. But in a short and sharp conflict like the Falklands, the Argentines did not have time to become inured to H&Is. The novelty and terror was still present and had only begun to wane when the main attack against Port Stanley began:

> I gradually got used to the shelling, because from then on they bombarded us every night.... But there was a junior sergeant, a very nervy man who hardly slept; he was always very uptight.... He was always awake, smoking very nervously. In the morning when everyone woke up the sergeant would be totally wired up.[23]

The psychological impact of Operation Tornado was all the greater because it brought home to the amateur Argentine soldiers the hard fact that war with Britain was real. The shelling carried with it the implicit promise that worse punishment was to come. Few Argentine soldiers were harmed by the H&I program, but most of the shells were directed toward, and landed on or near, specific targets—bunkers, foxholes, and trenches clearly visible to SAS (Special Air Service—British Special Forces) patrols and gunners of 148 Battery hidden in the surrounding hills. This accuracy not only gave British firepower credibility, but it also led to a sense of frustration among an enemy helpless to respond. Such precision was in marked contrast to Vietnam, where H&Is were normally unobserved and shells were invariably scattered randomly about the countryside.

Since World War II, naval gunfire has carried with it a reputation among soldiers for being erratic and unreliable for precision work such as close support of friendly troops.[24] Experiences during Operation Tornado seemed to indicate that while this might have been true for routine shore bombardments in the past, modern technology and the presence of skilled observers had transformed the naval gun into a precise, if not altogether reliable, fire support weapon. Once bugs were worked out of the system, observers from 148 Battery found that a salvo of 25 rounds of 4.5-inch shells normally had a dispersion smaller than a tennis court.[25] This degree of accuracy is somewhat misleading. The initial rounds of a salvo may be far off the mark because of imprecise location of the ship as it moves continuously on the gun line off shore, or because of slight disparities in the oceanographic and geographic data used to plot positions. Often these errors are not large, but they can compound each other and lead to firing errors of several hundred meters. However, an experienced spotter can quickly adjust the errant initial rounds onto the target, and the analog or digital computation equipment aboard ship can be programmed to compensate for these errors in all subsequent missions.[26]

British 4.5-inch naval guns were of two types. The older versions fired a 55-pound shell 18,000 yards, one round every half-second, or one ton of firepower each minute from each ship. Newer ships such as the type 21 and 42 frigates were equipped with a digital fire control system and were much more accurate. These ships possessed a fully automated loading and firing system and could deliver 24 4.5-inch shells every minute out to a range of 24,000 yards.[27]

Goose Green taught the value of "carry-along" firepower to the infantrymen of 2 Para. Particularly prized were weapons of great precision such as the MILAN wire-guided missiles, which ultimately broke the back of the bunker defenses around Darwin. For lesser targets, engaged closer in, the infantry succeeded with light 66-mm anti-tank rockets and 40-mm grenade launchers, both American weapons.[28]

Conspicuously missing from the assault on Goose Green were any of the eight light armored vehicles dispatched to the Falklands to provide mobile, protected firepower. Before the attack on Goose Green, Colonel Jones had requested the attachment of four light tanks. However, a staff officer at brigade refused the request because of "mission priorities elsewhere" and a wrongful belief that the boggy Falklands terrain would not support off-road movement by tracked vehicles. Painful experience demonstrated that 2 Para could have used any form of direct or indirect fire support. The battalion would not attack without tank support again.[29]

The "Blues and Royals" tank regiment was equipped with two similar varieties of light tanks, differing only in their main armament. The best known of this "family" of vehicles was the Scorpion, a fast, agile vehicle of eight tons, armed with a 76-mm medium-velocity gun capable of shooting 5,000 meters. The Scimitar mounted a 30-mm Rarden automatic cannon. Without a serious Argentine armored threat, all of the light tanks provided fire support to the infantry. The heavier gun was used to destroy fortifications, the lighter cannon against troops and less well fortified positions. Since night attacks would continue to be the practice, the second-generation night sight in each tank would make them the only "carry-along" fire support capable of providing pinpoint accuracy in the dark.[30]

Mortars at Goose Green held great promise as fire support weapons, but proved somewhat disappointing in practice. Problems stemmed as much from the dearth of transport and the sodden terrain as from any shortcoming in the weapons or the manner in which they were employed. Without helicopter lift, mortar bombs had to be added to the already punishing loads of individual infantrymen. At best, each soldier could carry only two or three rounds, leaving the mortars at Goose Green with fewer than 300 rounds to support the entire assault.[31] Artillery- and mortarmen had great difficulty keeping recoiling weapons from sinking into soft ground. Unlike artillery, mortars dissi- pated recoil almost vertically into the ground, making them prone to sink into the soft soil after a few rounds. Throughout the evening of the attack at Goose Green, crews frantically dug mortar baseplates out of sodden, water-filled holes to set up on more solid ground, only to go through the process again and again until out of ammunition.[32]

The Attack on Port Stanley

By 1 June, the British land forces under Major General Jeremy Moore consisted of two brigades. First into action was 3 Com- mando Brigade, Royal Marines, composed of three Royal Marine commandos (battalions), 40, 42, and 45, supported by an organic artillery battalion, the 29 Commando Regiment, Royal Artillery; in addition, two battalions of the Parachute Regiment, the 2d and 3d, and an extra light gun battery were attached to 3 Commando Brigade. While 2 Para opened the match at Goose Green, 3 Para and 42 and 45 Commandos began an epic trek toward the hills to the northwest of Port Stanley. By 4 June, through pluck, audacity, and Argentine tactical inepti- tude, most of 3 Brigade had positioned itself in the vicinity of Mount Kent on the northern axis of advance toward Port Stanley without incident. As helicopters became available and weather permitted, the three batteries of 29 Commando Regiment joined up with their supported units. The light guns could just range Port Stanley from battery positions to the west of Mount Kent.[33]

Later into the battle area came 5 Infantry Brigade. It was a smaller, less cohesive force than 3 Brigade, composed of 2d Battalion, Scots Guards, 1st Battalion, Welsh Guards, and 1st Battalion, 7 Gurkha Rifles. The Scots and Welsh Guards, hav- ing been on ceremony duty only a few months before, were somewhat unaccustomed to the light infantry style of dis- mounted combat. In addition, 5 Brigade was short a battery of artillery, having only two from 4th Field Regiment, Royal Artil- lery, to support three battalions.[34]

Before the move on Port Stanley, Argentine firepower gave the British gunners considerable concern. Artillery at Goose

Green had been well handled initially; in the hands of more aggressive and resourceful gunners, it might have caused considerable damage. The 29th Battery was shelled sporadically throughout the attack by two 155-mm medium guns at Goose Green using ground and air burst fuzes. The shells either missed by only a small margin or exploded high in the air. The battery suffered no casualties, but there was little doubt that had the Argentines fired all three of their available batteries in unison with variable-time fuzes, these near misses would have incapacitated perhaps three-quarters of 29 Battery.

The potential danger from Argentine guns was made all the more acute by the fact that camouflage and entrenchments were practically impossible in the East Falkland peat. The water table was so high that digging stopped at a spade's depth. One alternative was to bulldoze revetments for each gun. But scraping away the surface turf made massive scars, easy to spot from the air. Some crews provided limited protection by stacking around the guns empty ammunition boxes filled with turf and dirt. Effective protection only comes when soldiers can take cover underground, and to the end of the campaign exposed British guns and crews provided the Argentine artillery with a perfect opportunity to blunt the British attack with an effective counterbattery effort.[35]

The Argentine Air Force presented a formidable threat to British ground forces. The British soldiers had little to fear from high-performance jets flown from the mainland, which arrived too low on fuel and too intent on attacking lucrative naval targets to bother with ground troops. However, stationed on the island were a number of Pucaras, two-seat turbo-prop fighters similar to the OV–10 used by the US Marines in Vietnam. Pucaras flew low and slow enough to spot targets on the ground and possessed an imposing array of ground attack ordnance including rockets, bombs, napalm cannisters, and cannon. They had caused the British little damage during the Goose Green operation, but a few close calls with near misses from napalm and cannon served to remind the British that, boldly handled, the Pucaras could tilt the firepower balance if not countered with effective air defense.[36]

Somewhat to his chagrin, General Moore had the battle plan for his newly arrived brigade written for him by the audacity of 2 Para. Just three days after the surrender at Goose Green, Major Chris Keeble, on the advice of a local Falklander, had the presence of mind to telephone Fitzroy settlement, well to the east. He discovered from conversation with a local who answered the telephone that the southeastern approach to Port Stanley was devoid of enemy. Immediately, Keeble crammed most of one company into the expedition's worn but serviceable Chinook and landed at Fitzroy without incident—and without the slightest thought to reinforcement, resupply, or fire support.[37]

Moore now had little choice but to reinforce 2 Para with all of 5 Infantry Brigade or pull it back. Fortunately, he made the audacious choice and began immediately to move 5 Brigade by sea to Bluff Cove. The plan was good because it completed the encirclement of Port Stanley quickly and permitted a separate axis of advance from the southeast for 5 Brigade reinforced by 2 Para. But the sudden appearance of a force in the south made coordination between the two widely separated brigades particularly difficult.

The movement of 5 Brigade to Bluff Cove was completed just as the ammunition resupply problem was about to be solved. With the abominable weather beginning to take a toll on the exposed troops huddled in foxholes to the north, General Moore wanted to get on with the final push without delay. Brigadier Wilson, Commander of 5 Brigade, therefore had little time to sort out his force on landing and array them for attack. His problems were compounded by the tragic sinking of the landing ship *Sir Galahad* in Fitzroy harbor as it was disembarking the Welsh Guards. Sixty-four died in *Sir Galahad*, and much needed equipment, including precious communications gear and wheeled vehicles, went to the bottom.[38] Wilson passed most of the few days remaining to him ashore trying to shake down his inexperienced staff and push his green, badly shaken soldiers into position, leaving little time for a detailed reconnaissance of the southern approaches to Stanley. Unfortunately, most tactical planning for 5 Brigade's portion of the final assualt had to be done from a map.[39]

Wilson's task of coordinating the maneuver of 5 Brigade was made all the more difficult by a complex scheme of

The lone Chinook helicopter, here taking on troops for movement to new positions, was pushed to its limits hauling artillery and ammunition as well as carrying troops.

maneuver. General Moore intended that the attack would be continuous once begun. His plan called for a series of one-two punches, alternating attacks by each brigade, beginning with 3 Brigade on the night of 11–12 June to capture the outer ring of hill defenses at Mount Harriet, Two Sisters, and Mount Longdon. Next, 5 Brigade's punch would be against high ground closer to Stanley, including Wireless Ridge, Tumbledown Mountain, and Mount William. Then 3 Brigade would continue the attack until resistance ceased. All attacks would be at night.[40]

The fire plan to support the offensive differed little in principle from many that British staffs had prepared during countless exercises in Europe. But several aspects, in response to the imperatives of real war, were unique. The artillery would be massed in two groups, three batteries in the north supporting 3 Brigade and two in the south behind 5 Brigade.[41] Neither adequate communications nor time for coordination were available for the two artillery regimental commanders to form their units together into a force under the control of a single hand. The guns were positioned too far behind most objectives and were spread over too wide an area to permit all 30 to range a single target. Helicopter transport dictated tactics. Batteries could only stay and fire from where they had been dropped. Each battery had 3,000 rounds of ammunition uncrated and scattered about.[42] Any movement of a gun battery, even for a short distance by air, was impossible.

Although naval gunfire support ships had suffered serious loss at the hands of Argentine aircraft and missiles, Rear Admiral Woodward, commander of Falklands Task Group, allocated one frigate to each of the eight engaged infantry battalions for the forthcoming attack in the hope that ships' guns would provide the heavy mass of firepower normally available from heavier calibers of field artillery.[43] General Moore was convinced by his artillery staff that naval fires, to be effective and responsive, must be integrated into a single fire plan with the artillery. From a staff planning perspective, this was no simple task.

When not on gun duty, ships remained 150 miles—or six steaming hours—away from the shoreline to ensure safety from

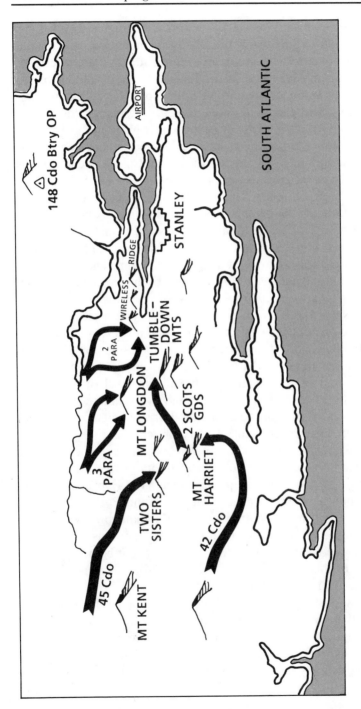

The battle for Stanley

hostile air attack. Some ships performed anti-aircraft picket duty and might well be many miles farther from the land action. During the planning phase for an evening attack, the artillery battery commander (who in the British Army is responsible for planning and coordinating all fire support for an infantry battalion) would receive his commander's fire request for the evening's activities. He would then have only a short time to extract those targets most suitable for engagement from the sea and transmit them by radio to Lieutenant Colonel Keith Eve, the artillery naval gunfire liaison officer aboard HMS *Fearless*.[44] Eve relied on a secure satellite link to request specific ships and ammunition allotments for the coming fight. Admiral Woodward's staff made the final decisions and dispatched the gunships just in time to make the often fearsome journey through gale-force seas to arrive at the gun line on time and properly fitted out to provide heavy fire support. Each ship came on station fully loaded with 1,000 to 1,500 4.5-inch shells.[45]

Naval spotter teams assigned to support specific battalions located themselves with artillery forward observing officers normally attached to those battalions.[46] To ensure complete flexibility, spotters carried two high-frequency radios capable of morse and voice transmission to call for naval fire, one VHF radio tuned to RAF frequencies, and two standard Army VHF sets, one to monitor the supported infantry battalion command net and one on a common artillery fire channel.[47]

Each brigade attack was given a small number of close air support sorties, usually no more than four or five. Moore knew that air support would be problematical. The Harrier was a fair-weather bomber, and the weather around Port Stanley was living up to its reputation for being abominable. Moore also realized that first priority for the Harriers was to keep the Argentine Air Force at bay. All aircraft might be needed at any time for this essential task. Wisely, the British planned around the availability of air strikes. If they appeared, so much the better. But just in case, General Moore's staff placed enough additional heavy naval firepower on each target to ensure its engagement whether or not the aircraft were available.[48]

The best way to ensure that a complex program of firepower delivery is executed efficiently is to make its execution at the lowest level as simple as possible. Although many hundreds of target numbers and sequences were plotted on firing charts, each spotter and observer memorized only five or six key targets. Likewise, junior leaders in the infantry battalion were given targets, designated by simple key words and indentified by prominent rock outcroppings and hill tops clearly visible to all troops at the jump-off point.[49] The commander of 29 Commando also decentralized the control of his guns for the forthcoming attack by dedicating the fires from a single artillery battery to support of each attacking infantry battalion.[50]

The concept behind the various fire plans was simple. Friendly lives would be saved and the enemy's will to fight broken quickly if the attack was preceded by an overwhelming, continuous wall of firepower. A traditional artillery and naval gunfire prep would begin the fight. Argentine strong points exposed by the attack would then be engaged by light tank fire from Scorpions and Scimitars. MILAN would be called upon to place missiles into small point targets such as firing embrasures and command posts. Mortars and hand-held anti-tank rockets and grenades would be reserved for a last-minute crushing blast of firepower to precede the final assault.[51]

The final act began on 11 June with Colonel Nick Vaux's 42 Commando attacking the steep, rock-strewn crest of Mount Harriet. The normal confusion and mistakes that attend a unit first in combat delayed the start of the assault. Gunners to the rear and ships off shore waited patiently for the signal to open fire. In the morning, the signal came, and all firing units began a systematic pasting of the mountain with thousands of rounds of high explosives. Protected by the barrage, Vaux's men pushed within 100 meters of the summit before the Argentines opened fire. By then it was too late. After a brief but sharp fight, Mount Harriet was in British hands with only a single British life lost.

The attack on Twin Sisters by 45 Commando was also late, and the men of the battalion had a more difficult time of it than their Marine companions. After two-and-one-half hours of hard fighting, however, they pushed the Argentines off the summit of Twin Sisters and dug in at dawn. As if to emphasize the dangers

Close air support posed problems for the British, as the Harrier, a fair-weather bomber, had to fight the gale-force winds of the South Atlantic.

of naval gunfire support, HMS *Glamorgan*, supporting 45 Commando, was struck by a ground-fired Exocet missile shortly after finishing its duties on the gun line. Thirteen men were killed and many more wounded, but the sturdy ship quickly recovered and steamed out of harm's way at a brisk 24 knots.[52]

The costliest battle of the campaign was fought by 3 Para to capture the heights of Mount Longdon. The battalion was fortunate in that it had had a week before the assault to reconnoiter the objective. Audacious patrols crept within yards of the enemy positions, searching out the best routes of advance. Colonel Hew Pike divided Longdon into three separate company objectives and ordered his supporting forces to remain silent until the enemy discovered the approach. The battalion had moved to the foot of its objective when one soldier stepped on an anti-personnel mine. From that moment the fighting was continuous and intense.

Captain McCracken, the forward observer, began dropping artillery and naval gunfire into enemy positions. Platoons fought their way steadily upward in a series of individual and section battles against fearsome resistance from recoilless rifles and heavy machineguns. Some were forced to pull back. McCracken kept the artillery close and continuous, bringing the 105s to within 50 meters of the most hard-pressed units. By first light the Argentines had abandoned the rugged, boulder-strewn heights to the paras. The all-night assault and sporadic enemy artillery bombardment cost the paras 23 killed and 47 wounded.[53]

General Moore had hoped that 5 Brigade might deliver the second blow against Tumbledown Mountain without delay. But Brigadier Wilson pleaded that he had yet to see his objective and needed time, at least 24 hours, to do the job with some semblance of efficiency. Time permitted only a map reconnaissance.[54] Fortunately for the Scots Guards, the route chosen to Tumbledown was a good one, and at 9 p.m. on 13 June, the first company passed the start line and continued toward the objective without serious opposition.[55] The initial move was aided by a particularly effective artillery preparation that continued until advancing troops were within 250 meters of the planned targets. Later investigation revealed that 11 out of 14 machinegun positions in the Guardsmen's path were destroyed by the preparation. A second company moved farther ahead toward the heights of Tumbledown and was met immediately with fearsome enemy machinegun fire.[56]

Artillery support for the Guardsmen became difficult at this point. Because the attack was hurried, the naval gunfire plan was not as well integrated as it should have been. The naval gunfire spotter did not arrive at the Guards' command post until after dark and had no time to see the objective first-hand. Confusion concerning troop locations and targets was exacerbated by gale-force winds that scattered the naval shells about dangerously as the spotter attempted to bring them in close to the infantry. To ensure the safety of the Guardsmen, the artillery battery commander shifted the naval fire from Tumbledown to nearby Sapper Hill and ordered his own guns to increase their rate of fire.[57]

After midnight, as the Guardsmen began to push toward the summit of Tumbledown, they came under increasingly more accurate and deadly mortar and artillery fire. Carry-along firepower such as hand-held rockets and grenades did not seem to be as effective against these enemy strong points as they had been in other actions. The situation grew more confusing as companies converged near the summit. Artillery support from the 4th Regiment guns to the rear began to slacken. High winds blew the shells about and made the fire appear erratic.

At that critical moment, the battery commander lost radio contact with his observers, and one infantry platoon leader, becoming disoriented, called in artillery fire too close to his position. Calm intercession by the infantry battalion commander and his artillery counterpart sorted out most of the difficulties. Artillery rounds were again landing accurately in front of the stalled forward platoons. The shock of this firepower broke the deadlock, and the attack continued up the hill with trenches and bunkers taken at bayonet point.[58]

The problems encountered at Tumbledown were little different from those that occurred in both brigades during the rapid-fire assaults between 11 and 14 June. From the moment 45 Commando crossed the start point, guns from all five batteries were in continuous service, and gunners were hard-pressed to keep up with the enormous volume of fire required of them by the infantry. Batteries expended in minutes what would have been a year's worth of service practice ammuntion on Salisbury Plain. Six thousand rounds were poured into the Stanley defenses in the first 24 hours, and before the battle ended, 17,000 artillery and 8,000 naval shells would be expended.[59]

Young, inexperienced gun position officers worked their men frantically to tear open boxes and containers and prepare the shells for firing. Cooks, air defensemen, and stray on-lookers were pressed into service as ammo handlers to satisfy the appetites of the hungry guns. Frantic efforts by resupply helicopters kept enough ammunition forward with the guns so that firing was never interrupted. But for some batteries heavily engaged, it was often a close run between expenditure and replenishment. Some guns were down to as few as 20 rounds at times.[60] Cold weather and boggy terrain made service of the guns all the more difficult.[61] Stiff, numb hands made simple acts like screwing on fuzes or setting firing data on gunsights difficult and slow. Equipment rarely failed; much of the credit for this success rested with detachment commanders who often slept with firing boxes and other sensitive gear in their sleeping bags as a precaution to keep them warm and dry.[62]

The 105-mm "light gun" was the only artillery piece used by the British. Although firing ammunition similar to the American version used in Vietnam, it was a much more modern and capable piece with a range advantage of nearly three miles over the US M–102 and six miles beyond that of the Argentine gun. After a few days of firing, the commander of 29 Commando Regiment RA ordered his guns to fire at the highest charges only when necessary, for fear that the excessive pounding would eventually cause delicate gunsights to fail. There were few spares—and no repair shops—8,000 miles from home.[63] Yet it is a remarkable credit to the light gun that it fired so many rounds in such a short time without a major breakdown.[64]

In their haste to move equipment to the front, batteries were seldom placed on terrain suited to sustained bombardment. Once in position, gunners had to make the best of many spongy firing positions because helicopters could not be spared for movement of the pieces to more advantageous ground. Once firing began in earnest, the guns began to sink into the bog. Firing at maximum charge, one gun of 97th Battery jumped back 15 feet on slippery ground.[65] After firing 20 or 30 rounds, a gun had to be pulled out of the mire, repositioned, and reaimed. Five of six guns could be kept in action by passing a tracked vehicle up and down the gun line, continuously winching out one gun at a time.[66]

Artillery was affected throughout the assault on Stanley by a lack of technical aids. To conserve ship space, the artillery left behind any means for measuring meteorological conditions in the battle area. In a temperate climate, this decision might have had slight effect on the precision of fire. But in the Falklands, gale-force winds were the norm during the South Atlantic winter.[67] A proper crosswind might blow a shell fired at great range as much as a kilometer or more off course. Without the means to predict and compensate for atmospheric conditions of this sort, firing close to friendly troops became very hazardous indeed.

To ensure safety, every target had to be adjusted in every time. Shifts from those targets to others nearby were made with great care and deliberation. No rounds were repeated unless every one could be spotted and marked by an observer. All modern gear to make this task easier, such as laser rangefinders and digital fire direction computers, was left behind at San Carlos. The return to basic "steam gunnery" worked well enough for providing close support, but at the cost of long delays between missions and a complete loss of the ability to deliver surprise or massed fires.[68]

Darkness, cold, confusion, and fear combined to make more difficult the formidable task of controlling and coordinating fires at the front. Firing close to or across the boundary between 5 and 3 Brigades was the most persistent problem. On several occasions, forward observers were frustrated when targets in adjacent brigades could be seen clearly but not engaged because clearance to fire came too slowly or did not come at all from the other brigade's tactical headquarters. Part of the problem rested with the difficulty in locating the exact position of friendly units in the darkness and confusion. There was no continuous "front" as such. Boundaries were also indistinct in the flat, featureless terrain, and some junior leaders never completely pin-pointed neighboring positions.[69]

Success under such difficult circumstances was a result largely of the flexibility and coolness displayed by artillery leaders under pressure. Battery commanders were far enough forward to gain a first-hand appreciation of the battle, and yet not so far forward as to become embroiled in the confusion and face-to-face terror of combat. Often in the heat of combat, the demands made on the firepower system were greater than the system could deliver comfortably. In peacetime exercises, a battery commander received simulated calls for fire from his supported infantry with measured regularity. But in combat, commanders were overwhelmed by a flood of requests, all of which would have qualified in peacetime for immediate and sustained engagement.

Battery commanders were obliged to make tough decisions. Supported units rarely received all the attention they requested, and never was the process as neat and precise as one would expect at practice camp. It was these men who quickly scrapped fire plans as the situation grew indistinct and improvised on the spot. It was they who filtered frantic calls for fire and determined which missions would be fired and in what priority. Battery commanders sorted out confusion and on at least one occasion intervened to prevent an air strike from being called on friendly troops.[70]

Observer officers attempted to be well forward with their infantry commanders, able to observe the firefight in progress first-hand.[71] But in the darkness within the cuts and crags of Longdon, Harriet, and Tumbledown, they were not always in the proper spot to observe and call for fire, so a young enlisted bombardier would be called upon by the infantry to perform this role. In 45 Commando, bombardiers did three-quarters of all shooting.[72] All forward observers had difficulty in the unfamiliar, featureless terrain. Usually a target was nothing more than a momentary muzzle flash in the dark. One young observer, when told to observe an exploding round to his front, exclaimed over the radio, "I don't even know which way 'forward' is!"[73]

Observers from the 148 Naval Gunfire Observation Battery secretly hid themselves in observation posts well behind Argentine defenses before the attack. From their exceptional vantage points, they could see most objectives and much of the enemy defenses. From the opening round, 148 Battery added considerable skill to the adjustment of artillery into the Argentine rear area. This observation proved particularly valuable because the British, unable to bring forward any technical means of locating enemy batteries, had to rely on small patrols and distant observation teams. On 9 June, Captain Hugh McManners from the 148th occupied a covert observation post on Beagle Ridge with a clear though distant view of Port Stanley. Although never able to destroy the Argentine guns, he did manage to overturn an occasional heavy gun, set fire to ammunition and vehicles, and chase enemy gunners into cover for long periods using both artillery and naval guns. The considerable damage done to British infantry on Wireless Ridge and Mount Harriet by Argentine artillery might have been much worse without such effective, if technologically unsophisticated, counterfire.[74]

British reports after the battle continually remarked that artillery fire seemed to have very poor killing effect. As we have seen in earlier examples, this has been a common observation in all modern wars. Artillery and mortar fire failed to kill in the Falklands because the large marshy fields of peat served as a sponge to absorb the steel splinters from exploding shells. One observer noted that rounds frequently landed as close as four yards from exposed Argentine soldiers without causing harm. The boggy terrain occasionally served the British by permitting artillery to be fired very close without causing serious injury to friendlies. The killing effect of artillery was greatly enhanced by using variable-time proximity fuzes, which detonated shells in the air only a few meters above the ground. Unfortunately, though 16,000 proximity fuzes were actually sent to the Falklands, many were misplaced among the cargo ships and most of those found were expended before the final battle for Stanley began.[75]

No skill was less practiced by artillerymen before the campaign, nor more in demand by the infantry during the campaign, than the ability to shoot very close. In the long and costly battle

for Mount Longdon, the enemy positions were captured only by
a process of calling for fire within 50 meters of troops pinned
down, followed immediately by systematic engagement of
enemy bunkers using anti-tank rockets and grenades.[76] On Tumbledown, progress could be maintained only when fire was
brought in very close. One participant lamented, however, that
close combat at night is not the time to learn such a skill:

> Peacetime training's inherent emphasis on safety takes away the
> sense of realism. Most of the troops had no idea what a 105-mm
> shell sounded like at 50 metres, let alone its effect. While they
> were getting used to it, the enemy had the upper hand.[77]

It was only fitting that the final act that broke the back of
Argentine resistance should come from the veterans of Goose
Green. The mission for 2 Para was to seize Wireless Ridge,
located on the extreme northern flank of 3 Brigade astride the
most direct route into Stanley. If the paras learned no other
lesson from Goose Green, they certainly learned the absolute
need for overwhelming firepower. Colonel David Chaundler,
the new battalion commander, gathered about him all the varied
sorts of fire support he could find, including two batteries of
light guns with plentiful ammunition (broken out and prepared
to send down range), a frigate for naval gunfire support, and a
troop of Scorpions and Scimitars. To ensure that his companies
would not again run short of firepower at the critical moment,
Chaundler detached 35 additional soldiers to carry forward
machinegun and mortar ammunition and extra anti-tank rockets.

This was anything but a silent attack. From the moment the
first company crossed the start line, Wireless Ridge erupted in a
volcano of detonating shells. What few Argentine guns dared
brave the bombardment to return fire were immediately
smothered by tank and artillery fire. Six thousand rounds of all
types eventually landed on or near the ridge. Compared to
Goose Green, Wireless Ridge was a cake walk.[78]

At dawn the paras stood on the objective and saw more
clearly the ground around them that once belonged to the
Argentines. They were struck immediately by the strength of the
position. The hasty fortifications at Goose Green were not
nearly as well prepared or as cleverly sited as those on Wireless
Ridge. They expected to see more evidence of destruction

caused by the many tons of ordnance fired into such a small spot. Shallow craters littered the landscape, but few positions were actually destroyed, and very little evidence remained of enemy casualties. Fewer than a dozen dead Argentines could be found on Wireless Ridge. Yet there was no doubt that the enemy left in haste. Rifles, tentage, and other flotsam abandoned by the Argentines covered the position. One command post dug into the hillside was left intact with radios switched on. A few souls were rooted out of bunkers. Some were discovered cowering, zipped up in their sleeping bags, oblivious to the presence of a foe fully capable of killing them.[79]

The will of the Argentines on Wireless Ridge had been broken largely by the psychological effects of firepower. Often, while in pursuit of modern statistical means for measuring the physical destructiveness of weapons, fire planners tend to overlook less tangible effects. The example of the Falklands has helped in some degree to bring attention again to the psychological or "moral" impact of modern firepower. Dr. Richard Holmes, professor at the Royal Military College at Sandhurst, published a paper on the psychological effects of artillery based on a series of confidential interviews conducted with nearly half of all 2 Para veterans six months after returning from the Falklands. Holmes documented and stated with scholarly precision a thesis long known inituitively to professional soldiers since the Napoleonic Wars.[80] Firepower, concludes Holmes, steels the soldiers it supports.

To infantrymen about to risk their collective skins in an advance across open territory, the sight of shells landing in the enemy's midst tells them that they are not alone, that indeed they are part of a larger, massively competent organization whose collective power is clearly superior to the opposition. To soldiers on the receiving end, firepower creates a sense of stress and alarm made all the more fearsome because of its impersonal and anonymous nature. Holmes quotes a corporal in 2 Para who put it rather succinctly:

> If it's a sniper or machinegunner it's just another man, and your training tells you what to do. But what do you do about some fucker four miles away?[81]

As the quotation suggests, shelling is an intensely personal experience. A soldier cowering in the bottom of his foxhole can find himself alone and isolated from his buddies only a short distance away. This feeling of isolation leads inevitably to vague imaginings and apprehensions, not only of dying, but of helpless inaction and the intense fear of being left to die alone. An Argentine soldier on Wireless Ridge described the sensation:

> We were just targets for their artillery: lots of times I felt like a duck on a lake, being shot at from all sides. I felt terribly helpless. We didn't feel like soldiers, we didn't want to make war, so we felt like prisoners.... I felt I was on the Island of Alcatraz.[82]

Holmes isolates two reactions of men under shellfire. Both were distinctly evident on Wireless Ridge. One is "palliation," or the process of psychological denial by which a soldier under extreme stress seeks to regress mentally into better times. The childish reaction of pulling bedcovers over our heads when frightened was evident among the Argentines, who in the midst of a hellish bombardment retired to their sleeping bags to dream the battle away.[83] A second reaction is simply to run, and this the Argentines did nearly to a man on Wireless Ridge. The impulse to flee is more complex than just a coward's reaction to fear. S. L. A. Marshall noted in his studies of men under fire in World War II and Korea that the impulse to run away spreads quickly through entire units composed, one must assume, of individuals variously inclined (or disinclined) to stand and fight. Marshall noted that flight began with a sense of hopelessness—the battle is obviously lost, so why should I stay and die when one more rifle can't make a difference?

Firepower creates this sense of hopelessness by demonstrating to a defender the overwhelming superiority of the opposition's combat power. A bombardment may harm only a few physically. But if firepower can persuade an enemy to quit his position before close combat begins, it serves a practical purpose far out of proportion to the physical damage it inflicts.[84]

One may ask why comparable if not greater doses of firepower failed to have a similar effect against the NVA in Vietnam. The first answer is that on many occasions the psychological effect of sudden bombardment did induce some North Vietnamese to flee. But in a war without fronts, a fleeing soldier, however demoralized, most often could retreat, recover, and fight another day, whereas the Argentines had no option after flight but surrender. Yet the option to flee answers only part of the question. The battles for Goose Green and Stanley demonstrated that poor units, badly led, with low morale, are infinitely better candidates for firepower shock than the tight, cohesive, veteran units that the United States confronted in Southeast Asia. In contrast to the almost super-human ability of North Vietnamese regulars to maintain themselves under shell fire, one young soldier after Wireless Ridge explained accurately the Argentine predilection to flee:

> They only had to shell us for a few hours for many to beat it, *starting with the officers and NCOs.* Later when some soldiers found themselves alone in the middle of the night in pitch darkness and looked for support from their superiors they didn't find it.... "If they, the professionals are going back, what are we supposed to do?" we asked ourselves, "If he's going, we're going too."[85]

David Chaundler, the new para commander, when deliberating his method of attack, considered first the psychological weakness of his opposition. "We decided to make this a noisy attack rather than a silent one," he said, "because second-rate troops do not like being shelled."[86]

Once the Argentine retreat began on Wireless Ridge it grew unchecked until all the forward defenses had broken. Standing on the vacant ridge, the men of 2 Para could observe masses of men running without arms or equipment toward Stanley. Some were killed by the artillery that pursued them, but mindless flight simply increased in tempo as fear gripped and overwhelmed the Argentines.[87] The war was over.

The limited duration and intensity of the Falklands campaign belies its importance as a laboratory for observing firepower and maneuver applied in a contemporary limited war. To an American observer, the events at Goose Green and the hills around Stanley are strikingly reminiscent of early battles in the second Indochina war. In both conflicts, leaders were obliged to contend with inexperience, unfamiliarity with combat, and the pre-battle jitters that invariably accompany soldiers first in combat. In the American example, dense jungle and a savvy, skilled enemy complicated the process of acclimating an army to war. For the British, however, early mistakes and false starts were aggravated by equally hostile climate and terrain, by the need to fight at night, and by the uncertainties inherent in supporting the battle across a tenuous line of communication. As in Vietnam, the cumulative effect of these frictions of war often slowed the pace of fire support considerably from what one would expect at practice camp. No matter how well trained, soldiers new to combat must, to some degree, learn to fight by fighting. This process carries with it an obligatory element of risk. The British fully accepted the axiom that hesitation to use firepower would, in the end, cause more casualties than it would prevent.

The orchestration of firepower requires close cooperation between land, sea, and air services to be successful. The US Army discovered in Vietnam that the task of wielding aerial firepower to support ground forces was particularly difficult and never completely efficient. The British were equally challenged to support the land campaign using firepower from the sea. They discovered that the complete integration of naval gunfire with the tactical scheme of maneuver requires a great deal of mutual training, familiarity, and trust between both services.

The British learned other lessons common to recent limited wars. Chief among these was the unparalled value of aerial support, including helicopters to move soldiers and equipment and to provide permanent high ground for observation and aerial fire support. They understood and clearly demonstrated that elite and fit infantry require less firepower to be effective, and they capitalized brilliantly on the long-held belief that poor soldiers can be intimidated by the psychological effects of massive shell fire. Indeed, it was firepower that broke the back of Argentine resistance around Stanley and, in the process, saved the lives of many infantry soldiers who were obliged to take far fewer bunkers and machinegun nests than they would have been without the guns and ships behind them.

6
The Gulf War

Lieutenant Saif ad-Din had spent months moving his artillery platoon in and out of a series of increasingly rocky, barren, and inhospitable firing positions.[1] The work of his cannoneers was harsh and unrelenting. With each westward relocation, his guns had to be sited south toward the Saudi berm and then laboriously entrenched. At first bulldozers and commercial backhoes were available to crack through the rocky crust of the desert floor. But with each displacement, mechanized digging increasingly gave way to picks and shovels. Ominously, once the allied air campaign began, the heavy trucks that provided mobility and sustenance to his battery were immediately withdrawn and sent northward to replace the trucks of resupply convoys destroyed by marauding allied fighter-bombers.

Day after day, Saif watched the tiny specks of allied aircraft wing northward with growing dread as fewer and fewer of his trucks returned with food, water, or spare parts. His battery was too far west to be connected by telephone to the outside world, and fear of allied intercept kept the division radio nets silent. Yet, in spite of growing hunger and isolation, his battery held up well. Saif's battalion commander had insisted that all guns be deeply entrenched. To fool allied intelligence, cannoneers scratched out dummy gun parapets several kilometers away from the main positions and created phantom guns with bits of scrap metal and pipe. The decoys looked remarkably real from three miles up. In the third week of the air war, the allies began to concentrate on frontline Iraqi units. For some reason artillery seemed to curry special favor. After dozens of attacks a few guns were destroyed. Saif's battalion lost three, but his battery remained untouched. In a desperate but effective effort to get the aircraft off their backs, Saif's cannoneers placed burning tires next to the guns to make enemy airmen believe that the entire battalion had been destroyed.

After six weeks of nerves worn bare, signs appeared indicating that the ground war was about to begin. Division reconnaissance elements posted near the Saudi berm reported the movement of allied armor. Air attacks intensified, although most were directed closer to the front. In the early morning of 24 February, Saif watched in detached fascination as American A-10 Warthog fighter-bombers swooped daringly low, dropping bombs and firing cannon into the trenchlines and bunkers occupied by his hapless infantry colleagues.

As darkness began to transform late afternoon into night, Saif's battery finally was called to fire in support of the hard-pressed infantry. Relief mixed with trepidation caused adrenalin to rush through the veins of Saif's middle-aged cannoneers as they went mechanically through the process of traversing and elevating the guns toward the unseen enemy. Gunners punched home projectiles and pushed brass propellant casings into breeches. Saif looked across the gun line for six raised hands to indicate the battery was prepared to shoot. His command to fire was followed quickly by a succession of sharp cracks. A waist-high mist of brown dust mixed with smoke danced momentarily into the air as the battery's first, and last, volley arced southward toward the infidel.

By his own recollection, the details of what happened next were blurred and confused. Only two or three minutes after the volley was gone, Saif and a few of his soldiers glanced up momentarily and saw a distant series of white, pencil-thin threads of light begin to arc toward their position from some distant point far across the dark horizon. He and his crews had seen so many demonstrations of aerial pyrotechnics lately that the innocuous streaks were unintimidating. Yet everyone halted for a moment to watch. Saif recalls hearing a series of sequential popping sounds in the air, perhaps two or three seconds apart, followed by a few seconds of ominous quiet. Then the image of Hell itself descended on the battery as a horrifying blanket of explosions, caused by the eruption of thousands of tiny silver metal cylinders dropped like hail all about them. The pattern of the bomblet barrage was so dense and deadly that each explosive cylinder seemed to search out every fuel tank, stack of stored powder, shell, bunker, and foxhole. In the following minutes, patterns of bomblets continued to descend one after another. Each left a shroud of dust hanging in the air. Between barrages, Saif raised his head briefly and saw ammunition burning and exploding all about him. With each new wave of explosions more of his men crawled about, wounded and in shock, seeking vainly to hide from the merciless metallic deluge.

After twenty minutes the pattern of steel rain shifted to the east, seeking another hapless battery with equal precision and horror. From a distance the exploding bomblets sounded like firecrackers set alight to celebrate some macabre festival. Most of Saif's battery was destroyed. Only two guns survived undamaged. His soldiers were too shocked and demoralized to carry on. With no trucks available for transport, his unwounded comrades rummaged through the flotsam of the battery to claim bits of clothing and other belongings, and, as if by some unsaid command, began to walk listlessly northward into the desert toward home.

The artillery of Lieutenant Saif's division, the 48th, began the war with 100 guns. Twenty-eight were lost to airpower during 41 days of aerial bombardment. In less than six hours on 24 February, all but seven were destroyed by incoming rocket artillery fire from the US 1st Infantry Division, VII Corps Artillery, and the 1st British Armored Division. Before the war much was made of Saddam Hussein's artillery arm in the popular press. The concern seemed justified at the time. Saddam had borrowed the best long-range artillery technology in the world and had spent billions purchasing the very best cannons available from Austria, South Africa, Brazil, and the Soviet Union.[2] Yet like Saif's battery, most of Saddam's artillery fell victim to allied counterfire. Why, among all the arms, had the Iraqis derived so little effect from such a huge and enormously expensive investment?

In short, Saddam's artillery had failed because Saddam's artillerymen failed adequately to comprehend the implications of a precision revolution that had occurred virtually under their noses during the previous 20 years. The precision revolution in weapons effectiveness matured after Vietnam and took two distinct forms: the first for direct fire weaponry such as tanks and anti-tank missiles, and the second for aerial and ground-delivered indirect firepower systems, principally fighter-bombers and artillery. The October 1973 Arab-Israeli war demonstrated dramatically that range finders, ballistic computers, and improvements in tank main gun ammunition had made armored warfare tremendously more lethal. A World War II tank required an average of 17 rounds to kill another tank at a maximum range of approximately 700 meters. During ferocious tank-on-tank engagements between Egyptian, Arab, and Israeli tanks, only two rounds were needed to kill at 1,800 meters or more. Both the Israelis and the Egyptians possessed precision guided anti-tank missiles: the relatively primitive Soviet Sagger, available in large numbers to the Egyptians, and the American TOW, used by the Israelis to kill with a 90 percent probability out to a range of 3,000 meters. To tank or infantry commanders, the realities of the first precision revolution when applied to the direct firefight meant, in soldier parlance, "What can be seen can be hit, and what can be hit can be killed."[3]

The second, or indirect fire, precision revolution actually predated the October War with the appearance of laser-guided bombs first used by the US Air Force to drop bridges over North Vietnam. Bridges that for years had stubbornly resisted thousands of unguided gravity or "dumb" bombs succumbed to a few weapons guided by laser energy to within a meter of the point of aim. Precise delivery of dumb munitions was first made possible toward the end of the Vietnam War with the appearance of the Air Force A-7 Corsair fighter-bomber. Onboard computers and sensors finally lifted the science of air-to-ground gunnery out of the iron sight age and permitted a quantum increase in bombing accuracy. Equally significant progress had been made at the end of the Vietnam conflict in adding precision and lethality to surface delivered artillery fires. However, because products of the air and artillery precision revolution did not appear on the Arab-Israeli battlefield in 1973, the damage that precision indirect fires could do remained substantially a mystery to all but the most observant armies for almost 20 years.

During the decade and a half between the October War and Desert Storm, second and third generation precision guided weapons were first refined, then proliferated in all the services in the United States. While earlier laser delivery systems required two aircraft to deliver a weapon—one to drop it and another to "designate" the target with a laser—later systems, such as the F-111, equipped with the Pave Tack designation system, and the Army's Apache helicopter, firing Hellfire missiles, allowed one aircraft to both carry the weapon and designate the target.[4] The development of laser-guided surface-to-surface munitions had to wait more than a decade after Vietnam until a laser seeker could be developed to withstand the 25,000 g force exerted on an artillery projectile inside the tube. The Copperhead laser artillery projectile arrived in US units in the early 1980s. Fired through a cannon like a traditional artillery round, the projectile contained a seeker and steering vanes that corrected its trajectory by homing on the laser energy reflected from handheld or vehicular- or helicopter-mounted designators.[5]

Equally important to this story was the further refinement of aerial platforms capable of delivering dumb projectiles with great precision. During Desert Storm, the F-16 Fighting Falcon fighter-bomber became the delivery means of choice for precise daylight delivery of dumb bombs. The fighter's onboard fire-control computer automatically compensates for all variables that affect the flight of a bomb from release point to target—to include atmospherics, such as wind and temperature, and the weapon's ballistic freefall characteristics. As Desert Storm later proved, the resulting improvement in bombing accuracy was remarkable.[6] Between World War II and Vietnam the accuracy of freefall bombs varied from several miles to several hundred meters depending on release altitude, the skill of the pilot, and the relative

Smart aircraft dropping dumb bombs provided most of the close air support to ground forces. Here, an F-16 fighter-bomber heads for its target with a payload that includes two CBU-87 cluster bombs.

sophistication of the bomb delivery system. The F-16 and similarly "smart" aircraft, such as the F-15E Strike Eagle and the Navy's F/A-18 Hornet, can deliver a freefall bomb to within 5 meters of a target.[7] The actual precision in combat during Desert Storm was greatly dependent upon a pilot's ability to hold the "pipper" of his heads-up display steadily on the target while flying an evasive pattern, and by the altitude of release.

The least known component of the precision revolution was the development of surface delivery systems capable of achieving equal precision at great ranges with conventional artillery projectiles. The surface-to-surface precision revolution was not well recognized because it occurred over a long period and because precision was achieved by an eclectic assortment of different instruments and weapons. A few key elements formed the basis for the precision revolution in artillery. First, adaptation of inertia navigation technology from aircraft and missiles to ground vehicles permitted artillery pieces to locate themselves quickly and accurately. Desert Storm also witnessed the combat application of the global positioning system (GPS), a small handheld device that gives a precise location by triangulating from a series of orbiting satellites. Thanks to GPS, gun and rocket batteries could move hundreds of kilometers across featureless desert and still retain the capability to halt and fire with speed and precision. Inaccurate targeting has traditionally been the greatest source of artillery error. In Desert Storm, the ground forward observer's traditional tools for target location, the map and compass, were augmented with laser rangefinders, GPS, and position-seeking gyroscopes.

Aerial observers have traditionally acted as the eyes for the "over-the-hill" targeting essential for long-range fires. The technique of placing light aircraft in continuous orbit over enemy territory used successfully in both Indochina wars would prove too dangerous in Desert Storm with so many Iraqi anti-aircraft guns arrayed below. Unmanned aerial drones provided a cheaper and safer solution. Only a tiny, unobtrusive, and expendable aircraft such as a drone (remotely piloted vehicle or RPV) could maintain uninterrupted surveillance of the enemy's positions without risking pilot or aircraft. When the Gulf War started, the Army had only one experimental platoon of five Pioneer RPVs at Fort

Huachuca, Arizona. With a 100-mile range, day and night capability, multiple-hour endurance, and near-real-time data link, the Pioneer showed great promise as a safe substitute for live aerial observers. The Army's single platoon did not arrive until after the air campaign began and even then was capable of supporting only one corps.[8] But the single Pioneer platoon more than proved the value of a platform that provided an unblinking set of eyes over the enemy.

The demise of Lieutenant Saif's battery was guaranteed by counterbattery radars. The use of radar to acquire artillery dates from World War II, when the US Army accidentally discovered that radars intended for acquiring enemy aircraft could also detect much smaller objects such as artillery shells in flight. The Vietnam era AN/TPQ-4 radar was designed specifically to acquire mortar fire. But the fleeting nature of enemy mortar and rocket attacks and the limited capability of the AN/TPQ-4 to acquire precise locations limited the ability of countermortar radar to perform reliably in Vietnam. The newer Firefinder radars developed after the war by the Hughes Corporation provided a precise location almost instantaneously. Modern counterbattery radars proved so effective that, as in the case of Lieutenant Saif's battery, a target could be acquired, its location transmitted to a rocket battery, and rockets fired with great precision often before the enemy's initial volley reached its target.[9]

Just as the F-16's fire-control computer took the guesswork out of bombing, similar devices served to reduce the radius of error of artillery projectiles. In the two decades after Vietnam, digital computers replaced slide rules for computing firing data. Automated meteorological stations were also developed to predict precisely and quickly the effects of weather on a projectile in flight. When the data needed to calculate all the variables were accurately applied, an artillery projectile could be expected reliably to fall within 50 meters or less of its predicted point of impact.[10]

As precision technology reduced the radius of error for aerial and ground delivered munitions, breakthroughs in the science of terminal ballistics created tremendously more lethal and effective bombs and projectiles. A quantum jump in lethality was made possible by the development of bomblet munitions. Explosive bomblets packed inside a carrying shell or bomb (so-called cluster munitions), were first used by both Germany and the United States in World War II. Aerial delivered cluster bombs were widely employed by the Air Force in Vietnam. The Army released artillery delivered submunitions for general use after the Tet Offensive in February 1968. Continued research and experimentation with bomblet munitions in the 1970s increased the number of munitions carried in each bomb and shell and greatly increased the lethal area of individual bomblets. The aerial delivered CBU-87 Combined Effects Munition and the Dual Purpose Improved Conventional Munitions (DPICM) for cannon and rockets, can lay down a wide pattern of destruction equally lethal against soft and armored targets.[11]

Just as Egyptian and Syrian tank crewmen discovered the terrible consequences of the first precision revolution during the 1973 October War, Lieutenant Saif and his battery witnessed firsthand the terrible effects of the second precision revolution in Desert Storm. With today's technology, the lethal area of explosive munitions delivered from a great distance is greater than the delivering system's radius of error. This means that, for the first time in history, distant, unseen predators can kill with the first round. Saif and his men discovered that in late twentieth century warfare a soldier no longer has to be seen to be killed.

The Road to Desert Storm

Saddam Hussein's invasion of Kuwait on 3 August 1990 was as massive as it was unexpected. With impressive speed, his elite Republican Guard rushed one armored and one mechanized division to the outskirts of Kuwait City. Saddam sealed the back door by assaulting three special forces brigades by helicopter, effectively encircling the city. The American response was quick but, for the first month at least, lacked sufficient mass and firepower to prevent Saddam from continuing his aggression into Saudi Arabia, thereby threatening the enormous Saudi oil fields, refineries, and port facilities at Al Jabayl and Ad Damman. Luckily, Saddam chose not to exploit the opportunity. His sudden bout of strategic cold feet was the first of many mistakes the allies would exploit to assemble an effective blocking force in Saudi Arabia during the early days of the buildup. The months of August and September were absorbed with a massive footrace that pitted Saddam's ability to move the remainder of his ground forces into southern Kuwait against American efforts to transport a credible deterrent force into northern Saudi Arabia to block him. By the end of September the Iraqis had pushed 22 divisions—13 light and 9 heavy—into forward positions along the border berm with Saudi Arabia. To oppose this force, General Norman Schwartzkopf began construction of a global air and sea bridge across which moved elements of the 82d Airborne and 101st Air Assault Divisions from Fort Bragg, North Carolina, and Fort Campbell, Kentucky. They were followed in late September by the 24th Mechanized Infantry Division from Fort Stewart, Georgia.[12] By October, Schwartzkopf had enough firepower available to blunt, if not substantially halt, any further Iraqi incursion to the south. His plan of defense was intended to trade Saudi space for the opportunity to engage Iraqi armor with a well-orchestrated program of attrition by fire. Ninety-three long-range attack helicopters from the 101st would catch Iraqi tanks as they crossed the border. Air Force A-10s and F-16s would join in to kill enemy armor as it moved along the limited and tightly constricted road network leading from Nuayriyah in the north to Al Jabayl in the south. Once Iraqi forces were slowed, demoralized, and worn down to size, the battle would be handed off to the direct fire armored forces of the 24th. The plan was risky. Central Command war games conducted prior to the buildup indicated that a firepower-based defense would result in high allied casualties should the Iraqis penetrate the aerial and artillery firepower screen with sufficient combat power to engage Marines and airborne forces dug in around major oil fields, ports, and cities.[13]

By late fall Schwartzkopf realized that, while the Saudi theater was stable, Saddam was giving no indication of withdrawing from Kuwait without a fight. On 10 November 1990 President George Bush approved a plan to put sufficient ground forces into the theater to eject Saddam from Kuwait by offensive action. By January the United States had assembled its largest expeditionary force since the Vietnam era. The XVIII Airborne Corps, which had initially checkmated Saddam's advance, was joined by the heavy VII Corps from Europe. Together, US forces consisted of five armored or mechanized divisions, one airborne division, and one air assault division, with 1,200 first-rate Abrams tanks, 1,000 Bradley Infantry Fighting Vehicles, 1,000 cannon and rocket launchers, and 500 helicopters—of which 200 were armed with tank-killing missiles. The Air Force armada was equally powerful. Virtually every apron and taxiway in Saudi Arabia, the United Arab Emirates, and Turkey was crowded to capacity with over 1,800 combat aircraft from 12 countries. Of these, over 700 were Air Force tactical fighters capable of executing ground attacks.[14]

Schwartzkopf intended to employ this massive force against the Iraqis using a doctrinal method unique to the American style of war. AirLand Battle doctrine had its roots in Vietnam. It was there that soldiers of Schwartzkopf's generation witnessed the futility and waste of close, jungle-shrouded firefights. Thousands of artillery projectiles and bombs delivered into an enemy position were all too often followed by a costly frontal attack against a still unshaken foe. Practical experience in Vietnam convinced these men that the traditional American fixation on attrition by fire as a means to win in combat was fundamentally bankrupt. What was needed, they claimed, was a shift from a firepower-attrition to a maneuver centered tactical and operational method. Firepower, principally in the form of aerial-delivered ordnance, would be employed to create the opportunity for decisive maneuver. If possible, a maneuver force would seek the indirect approach by attempting to avoid enemy strength in order to get behind him. Firepower would facilitate maneuver by momentarily stunning the enemy, to confuse and fix him in place long enough for a maneuver force to isolate him. The essential aim of this maneuver was psychological, not physical: to so confuse and demoralize the enemy that his will to fight would be broken by the uncertainty and isolation brought about by the presence of an enemy force to his rear. Firepower was also seen as an essential means to impede the enemy, as a source of friction to slow the enemy's response to offensive action. Friendly fire must hold the enemy in place. Enemy firepower must be negated so that untrammeled maneuver was guaranteed. If a maneuver force was to attack deep, then firepower had to be delivered deeper. The concept of a "deep battle" sought to extend the killing zone from the

few thousand meters commonly accepted as sufficient in Vietnam
to several hundred kilometers for an AirLand Battle scenario postulated to occur on the plains of central Europe.[15]

The Eurocentric focus of AirLand Battle doctrine essentially
determined its application in practice. A Soviet ground force invading central Europe was expected to appear in waves or echelons composed of corps or armies consisting of thousands of
tanks and tens of thousands of soldiers. The cumulative combat
power of all echelons was far too great to be defeated by direct
fire systems, principally tanks and armored fighting vehicles, defending along the German frontier. If left unimpeded, successive
echelons would eventually break through. AirLand Battle doctrine sought to employ deep fires to interrupt the ordered approach of successive echelons. Firepower would "shape" the
deep battle by creating spaces, measured in time and distance,
between echelons. The hope was that a counteroffensive could
be launched between the spaces created by firepower so that following echelons could be destroyed decisively by deep maneuver
forces before they reached the main defensive line. Unfortunately, nothing in the Army's arsenal at the time could reach far
enough with sufficient killing power to slow Soviet follow-on
echelons. That task fell almost exclusively to the Air Force. During the early 1980s the air in AirLand Battle was principally
defined by the functions of Battlefield Air Interdiction (BAI),
essentially a middle ground between close air support delivered
in immediate proximity to friendly troops, and Air Interdiction
(AI), very deep strikes intended to isolate the Soviet Army within
the greater European theater of operations. To be successful,
strikes devoted to BAI had to be linked in some way to an army
corps, which was the level of command responsible for conducting
decisive deep maneuver.[16]

To Schwartzkopf, the battlefield situation in January 1991
seemed well suited to an AirLand Battle campaign. He had at his
command a capable maneuver force in the form of the US VII
Corps, fresh from Europe and already acclimated to the tenets of
the doctrine as it applied to the European battlefield. Iraq and
Kuwait were physically much different from Europe to be sure,
but the flat, featureless terrain was, if anything, even better suited

to unfettered deep maneuver by heavy armored forces. The Iraqis appeared to array themselves into three distinct defensive echelons in accordance with the Soviet model. The first echelon consisted of 15 infantry divisions stretched shoulder-to-shoulder from the Persian Gulf coast, south into the boot of Kuwait, and then directly west to form an unbroken line 200 kilometers into the desert. Schwartzkopf and his staff recognized that these divisions consisted of very poor quality soldiers. Mostly overage and poorly disciplined, led, and equipped—if anything, they were thought to be more of a liability than an asset. But even poor quality soldiers required succor. By pushing so many so far into such a hostile environment, Saddam seemed to have exceeded his ability to supply them. A supply system so tautly stretched was vulnerable to being cut by allied air interdiction.[17]

The second echelon consisted of six regular armored divisions. Of better quality and more mobile, they were equipped with second-line Soviet T-62 tanks and armored personnel carriers. These divisions were arrayed behind the frontline infantry and were well positioned to conduct division-level counterattacks against any allied penetration. Most likely, Saddam's general headquarters (GHQ) would wait to discover the allied main attack before launching the regulars to destroy it. The US Central Command (CENTCOM) leadership believed that any movement by the second echelon could quickly be detected in the flat desert terrain and destroyed by deep counterattacks using air and mechanized forces according to the established tenets of AirLand Battle.

The greatest threat (and the greatest opportunity for allied victory) was the Republican Guard. Originally created as a palace guard of only two brigades, by 1990 the Guard had grown to a separate corps with 28 combat brigades arrayed within 8 divisions. The Guard was the heaviest and most modern of Saddam's forces. A Guard armored division possessed 312 T-72M1 tanks, the most modern Soviet tank then available. In addition, Saddam equipped his Guard with the longest ranging artillery in the world and some of the most modern field communications available. Unlike other echelons, the Guard would fight. Saddam ensured its reliability by paying the men well and by granting special

privileges to officers and soldiers alike. The Guard was positioned well to the north, where it could either be employed as a
strategic counterattack force or, should the first two echelons
fail to stop the allied ground attack, withdrawn quickly back into
Iraq. Schwartzkopf recognized that the Guard represented political legitimacy for Saddam. As such, it was Iraq's political
and military center of gravity. If the Guard could be held in place
long enough by allied firepower, a powerful, deep attack by
the entire VII Corps could destroy it in a single cataclysmic armored battle.[18]

Schwartzkopf's final plan, therefore, had as its main objective the destruction of the Republican Guard. To reach it quickly
at minimum cost, he planned to pass two entire American corps
entirely around the main Iraqi line in an enormous turning movement. Execution of the plan would resemble the swinging of a
gate 80 kilometers wide turning clockwise with the hinge fixed
on the westernmost portion of the Iraqi line. Four armored divisions from the VII Corps formed the length of the gate nearest
the hinge. They would swing from an initial east-west orientation
along the Saudi-Iraqi border through a 90-degree turn until oriented north-south, and then collide as a single mass into the Republican Guard. XVIII Airborne Corps, farthest out on the gate,
would send the 24th Mechanized Infantry Division on a broad
end run to cut Highway 8, the main escape route for the Guard.
The 101st Airborne Division would proceed with a preemptive
heliborne operation to block the highway temporarily until relieved by the 24th. At the extreme outside of the gate, the 82d
Airborne Division and the French 6th Light Armored Division
would screen the far left flank to prevent a counterattack by Iraqi
reserves positioned around Baghdad. The plan for Schwartzkopf's "Great Wheel" maneuver was a page extracted in its pur-
est form from AirLand Battle doctrine. On paper at least, the firepower scheme seemed equally doctrinaire. A brief air campaign,
lasting perhaps two weeks, would freeze all three Iraqi echelons
in place. Prior to the maneuver phase, air strikes would shape the
battlefield by helping to create a breach of the westernmost Iraqi
frontline divisions. Fires would also seal the shoulders of the
breach by destroying second echelon forces and by blocking

adjacent deep armored units that might move to threaten the penetration and subsequent northward movement of VII Corps.[19]

The firepower plan, however, would not be executed completely in the spirit or the letter of AirLand Battle. The air and ground phases of the war would take on the character of a firepower-attrition operation. There were several practical reasons for this. First and foremost was the growing realization that the war would have to be prosecuted with absolutely the lowest cost in human life. No single imperative carried more weight with the chain of command in CENTCOM or among the American people for whom, even after 20 years, the memory of Vietnam was still disturbing and fresh. While the battle was still intended to end with a single direct fire clash between VII Corps and the Republican Guard, an increasing reluctance grew among air and ground leaders to allow any direct fire engagement, no matter how masterfully executed, until everything had been done to soften the enemy and break his will to fight. Subliminally, the long-standing American impulse to trade firepower for manpower worked its way back into the doctrinal equation. This impulse was further magnified by several factors. The first was bred by the completeness and the promise of the precision revolution in long-range fires. In previous wars a practical limit existed to the salutary effects of firepower. Old style iron bombs and shells did little physical damage. Lethality often decreased over time as a forewarned enemy dug in or dispersed. His psychological will to resist, in fact, often increased as he became mentally inured to the firepower assault.[20] But in Desert Storm, modern precision weapons, whether dumb or smart, killed far more efficiently and continued to kill and wear down the enemy's will to resist with little diminution over time. Second, thanks to Iraqi inactivity, the maneuver battle was not held captive to a firepower timetable. The Iraqis lay dormant while the allies methodically dropped thousands of tons of explosive firepower on them. Without a serious threat from Iraq's maneuver forces there was simply no hurry to get on with the close battle.[21] Third, concern arose early among ground and air commanders concerning the danger of fratricide caused by friendly fires applied very close to green, inexperienced troops. Better to kill as many of the enemy as far away from friendlies as possible, so the logic went, to reduce the likelihood of Americans killing other Americans. Fourth, during the months that preceded the war, Air Force planners postulated that the war might be won by airpower alone. Favorable circumstances, such as a flat, featureless theater of war combined with an exposed and moribund enemy, seemed to offer the perfect opportunity to prove that a strategic air campaign could break the will of the Iraqi Army without having to resort to costly maneuver by ground forces.[22]

The Air Campaign

The harmony that allowed doctrinal agreements between the Air Force and the Army to be hammered out during the previous decade began to fray somewhat as both services prepared for the practicalities of real war. The debate that ensued during Desert Shield over how airpower would be applied was not the result of any loss of faith or ill will on either side. More than anything else, it reflected a sincere difference of opinion brought on by inherent divergencies in the respective operational environments that separated them. Air Force doctrine and thinking rests on the principle of centralized control and decentralized execution. Such operational flexibility is possible in an uncluttered aerial environment when employing only a few superbly flexible fighting machines. The Army's operational environment, on the other hand, consists of hundreds of thousands of individual soldiers and units widely scattered and tucked into the folds and foliage of uneven terrain. Soldiers thus require the certainty of a fixed plan carefully agreed on beforehand, then rehearsed and implemented with fidelity, in order to offset the inherent uncertainty of their own environment.[23] Well before the air campaign began, Lieutenant General Frederick Franks, whose VII Corps led the main attack through the densest forward defenses and subsequently against the Republican Guard, made it clear that he expected the Air Force to order enough BAI missions within his area of interest to permit a quick breakthrough and rapid movement to the Guard. Equally essential, he expected the Guard to be battered, cut off from higher headquarters, and fixed in place before he collided with it.[24] Lieutenant General Gary Luck, commander of the XVIII Airborne Corps, had similar expectations. However, his demands for extensive preliminary BAI missions were fewer because the march of his units to Highway 8 and the Euphrates River would sidestep any significant enemy force. The issue for both commanders thus was not how much of the total air effort was devoted to shaping the battlefield with BAI. They recognized that competing priorities such as gaining and maintaining air superiority and deep air interdiction would draw away most sorties. But they both wanted to influence when and where the aircraft flying within their respective zones of action would strike.

Initially, Schwartzkopf's air commander, Lieutenant General Charles Horner, planned to execute a sequential air campaign. First, his air armada would gain absolute air supremacy over Kuwait and air superiority throughout the entire theater principally by shutting down the extensive Iraqi air defense system. Once able to fly freely, he would concentrate on strategic targets such as national communications and the electrical grid. Saddam's extensive chemical and burgeoning nuclear industry would also absorb a great many sorties throughout the campaign.[25]

By 27 January the Air Force controlled the skies. After the lights went out in Baghdad approximately two weeks into the air campaign, Horner turned in earnest to the task of dropping ordnance to support the pending ground campaign. To ensure success with the least possible cost, Schwartzkopf was committed to whittling away the huge mass of Iraqi war materiel as much as possible before the deadly business of ground fighting began. Within the Kuwaiti theater he wanted at least 50 percent of Iraqi tanks, APCs, and guns destroyed. He was particularly concerned with the threat of artillery delivered chemical weapons and directed that, if possible, 90 percent of Iraqi guns and rockets be destroyed in the vicinity of the allied breach. Finally, because the Republican Guard was both the greatest threat and the political and military center of gravity, Schwartzkopf singled out Guard divisions for special attention.

Initially, attacks against pinpoint ground targets did not proceed as efficiently as expected. While anti-radiation missiles had effectively taken down radar controlled anti-aircraft systems, the

Iraqis still possessed and actively employed tens of thousands of anti-aircraft guns and heat-seeking, shoulder-fired missiles. To keep above this threat, Horner initially instructed his pilots to bomb from between 10,000 and 15,000 feet. Survivability was enhanced, but accuracy, particularly the accuracy of dumb bombs, suffered proportionally. Weather also was a problem at higher altitudes. High cloud cover over the battlefield was more than a nuisance. Half of the attack sorties flown into the Kuwaiti theater were diverted or canceled because of weather.[26] Focus on support of the ground offensive was diffused even more by pressure to hunt and kill long-range Iraqi Scud missile launchers. Scuds were so wildly inaccurate that they caused no damage of any military significance. But even a missile as primitive and inaccurate as the Scud could still strike a city as large as Tel Aviv, and pressure to end the sporadic rain of rockets on Israel eventually diverted almost 40 percent of air-to-ground attack sorties to this rather fruitless endeavor.[27]

Another problem was the sheer magnitude of the task at hand. Never before had an air force been expected to destroy such a huge mountain of metal scattered across such a large area. To be sure, the Iraqi mechanized war machine was fairly easy to locate. The featureless terrain offered the Iraqis few places to hide. From the air, even at 15,000 feet, pilots could clearly see the outline of trenches, bunkers, and parapets scratched out of the desert soil. Iraqi inactivity was also helpful. While intelligence agencies often spotted targets at a maddeningly slow pace, once located, targets rarely moved.

But the Iraqis were not completely passive. As the air campaign began to bite, better units become more adept at hiding equipment or at disguising good equipment as destroyed. Iraqi efforts at camouflage and deception exacerbated the problem of assessing the effectiveness of the air campaign. Battle Damage Assessment (BDA) provided a daily indicator of how the destruction of the Iraqi war machine was progressing. The issue of assessment was particularly important because Schwartzkopf and his Army field commanders would not begin the ground assault until the 50 percent attrition mark had been reached. The process of BDA is more art than science. If the system worked perfectly, each air-to-ground attack wave would have been followed by a reconnaissance flyover to determine the effectiveness of the strikes. But there were far more attacking aircraft in the theater than reconnaissance aircraft, and with competing demands to assess the effectiveness of the strategic and Scud campaigns, demand on the system exceeded capacity by a wide margin. Under pressure from the top, the Army intelligence chief in the theater, Brigadier General John Stewart, developed a "back-of-the-envelope" formula for estimating BDA. Using armored vehicles and artillery as a baseline, he first counted only half of A-10 pilot claims as confirmed kills and the same percentage of F-111 and F-15E kills that were supported by gun video. While the Stewart methodology created both concern and resentment in Air Force and political circles, later events proved Stewart's damage estimates to be remarkably accurate.[28]

By early February the Army leadership, the two corps commanders in particular, began to express concern about the pace of the campaign to shape the battlefield by destroying Iraqi armor and artillery. Under growing pressure, General Horner made some key midcourse corrections to the tactics his airmen employed. The changes came just in time and served to transform a sluggish ground attack effort into a decisive one. To make attacks more precise, Horner decreased the attack altitude to between 4,000 and 7,000 feet and F-16s were directed to release bombs below 8,000 feet. Lower release altitudes resulted in greater destruction of area targets, such as ammunition and supply dumps, and point targets, such as trucks and command posts. Dumb bombs, however, even if delivered with great precision, were not terribly effective against hardened point targets such as armored vehicles and artillery pieces. Tanks, in particular, were hard to kill. A 500-pound bomb had to physically strike the armor plate of a tank to knock it out. A near miss would at best only strip off antennas, crack optics, or maybe break a track or damage the road wheels. Towed artillery was even more difficult to kill because it was such a small, easily hidden target with few vulnerable parts. A shredded tire or broken sight on an artillery piece could be quickly replaced. Only a direct hit would separate the gun tube from its carriage or dismember the hydraulic system and trails. To achieve pinpoint accuracy, Horner concentrated more aircraft capable of delivering laser-guided bombs against

The A-10 Warthog was particularly effective in support of ground operations because of its ability to linger over the battlefield and prodigious bomb-carrying capacity.

Iraqi armor and artillery. A hastily conducted experiment with F-111Fs indicated that infrared sensors aboard these aircraft, normally employed against deep strategic targets, could pick out the warm bodies of tanks against the cool sand of the desert at night. The tests were successful and Horner diverted similarly equipped aircraft, F-15Es and Navy A-6 Intruders, to attack armor with laser-guided 500-pound and 2,000-pound bombs. Immediately, this so-called tank plinking effort caused the count of destroyed tanks and artillery to rise dramatically.[29]

Horner countered the problem of identifying point targets from high speed aircraft by employing fast forward air controllers (fast FACs) a technique learned from his experience with close air support in Vietnam. Mounted in an A-10 rather than a slow, propeller-driven L-19 "Bird Dog," a fast FAC would loiter over a 30 square mile kill box, carefully observing his piece of the battlefield and handing off targets to successive pairs of attack aircraft that were rapidly funneled into his assigned area. Army planners and targeteers added more precision to the gridlike geometry of kill boxes by identifying which boxes contained the most lucrative or potentially most dangerous targets. While kill boxes increased the number of effective sorties, Army ground commanders expressed concern that the technique took target selection out of the hands of soldiers, who best knew how to shape the battlefield, and left it to squadron commanders. Only an Army targeteer, they argued, could discern from a 30 square mile field of targets which ones were the most threatening to ground forces. A group of mess vehicles and a regimental command post might give off identical heat signatures, but the latter was an infinitely more lucrative target. In addition, the kill boxes were based on geometric convenience rather than the corps commander's scheme of maneuver and thus were not necessarily concentrated on the most menacing Iraqi defenses.[30] The technique worked as well as it did only because the Iraqis rarely moved and there was plenty of time to be methodical. Tough decisions that required making trade-offs were often unnecessary. Enough sorties were available over time to patiently destroy everything of value in those kill boxes containing the most important targets.

As the ground war approached, the two corps commanders became increasingly uneasy about what targets, rather than how many targets, had been destroyed. Controversy between the Army and Air Force commanders centered around the degree of influence that Army commanders had in the production of the Air Tasking Order (ATO). The only means for orchestrating the dispatch of such an enormous air armada was to combine all target selection and sortie assignment into this single document. The ATO was prepared daily by Horner's staff. Army corps staffs submitted target lists intended to shape the battlefield to Horner's staff through Army Central Command (ARCENT) headquarters in Riyadh. A disappointing number of corps targets survived the ATO screening process. During the air war ARCENT identified 3,067 targets, most of them in the US corps zones. Of those, 1,241 were attacked. Another 1,582 targets were hit in response to requests submitted directly to Air Force flying wings. Most of those sorties were flown into kill boxes.[31]

Corps commanders were also concerned about the long lead time for processing the ATO. In Vietnam, the target planning cycle took a full day. In Desert Storm, the process took three days. Because it was so inclusive, the ATO was an enormously complex and lengthy document of over 300 pages. The ATO was complex because the process it controlled—the scheduling, briefing, arming, and sequencing of thousands of aircraft—was equally complex. Once inside the 72-hour execution phase of the ATO, any change was very difficult to make without causing delays and disruptions.

When pressured to do so, the Air Force could shape the battlefield with deadly precision and effectiveness. General Franks's first mission of the ground war would be to breach the Iraqi frontline units quickly. While he had sufficient artillery in the form of guns and rockets to crack through the Iraqi 28th Division immediately to his front, he was concerned that second echelon units, specifically the 52d Armored Division, might counterattack from deep assembly areas into the vulnerable flank of his penetration. The more quickly the 52d could be destroyed by airpower, the more quickly the follow-on element of VII Corps would be able to charge through on its way to the Republican Guard. Speaking to the targeteers in his deep battle cell on 16

January, Franks slapped the map where armor was closest to the breach and told them, "I want you to make that unit go away!"[32]

With this single gesture, the Iraqi 52d Armored Brigade, the westernmost unit of the 52d Armored Division, was doomed. The unit soon became known to Air Force and Army targeteers as the "go-away brigade." Midmorning on the first day of the air war A-10s appeared over the 52d and destroyed 13 trucks and killed 15 soldiers. Already operating at the extreme end of an over-stretched supply system, the loss of these few transports immobi-lized the unit's tracked vehicles for later destruction. Coalition air attacks were unrelenting. The brigade lost an average of three to four tanks every day. Crews, helpless and demoralized, stayed away from their vehicles to stay alive. The BMPs, Soviet-made armored personnel carriers, were the last category of vehicles to be struck in the final five days before the ground war. Iraqi at-tempts at decoying the attackers with burning tires failed to fool the fast FACs, who kept constant watch overhead. On 15 Febru-ary, division headquarters attempted to reinforce the beleaguered brigade with 20 BMPs and one T-55 tank replacement. Despite the brigade commander's attempts to hide them alongside burn-ing vehicles, three were smoking hulks at the end of the day. On the day the ground war began, none of the brigade's battalions had more than seven tanks operable. One battalion, the 75th, had only 3 of its original 22. Some 35 soldiers were killed in the re-lentless attacks and another 45 wounded. Perhaps as many as 300 dispirited survivors deserted. The brigade commander was dumb-founded by his plight. As he watched his unit disintegrate under the air attacks, he could not understand why the other two bri-gades of his division were left relatively untouched.

Only after his capture did he learn that his unit had fallen victim to General Franks's dexterity in shaping the battlefield with deep fires. The 52d Armored had become the "go-away bri-gade" in fact as well as name.[33]

The Iraqi Attack on Khafji

During the evening of 29 January, in the middle of the air war, Saddam ordered what appeared at the time to be a fruitless and foolish ground attack aimed principally at the Saudi town of

Khafji. Perhaps he intended to end the pain of the air war by pre-
cipitating the ground offensive. Possibly he was lured into attacking by the XVIII Airborne Corps's elaborate deception effort.
While the corps was actually in the process of moving westward
into attack positions, corps and divisional deception teams employed elaborate electronic and visual deception measures to make
the Iraqis think the corps was still sitting in vulnerable positions
just 30 kilometers south of Khafji. Whatever Saddam's intention,
the Khafji attack was a disaster. The Iraqi 5th Mechanized Division, supported by elements of the 1st Mechanized and 3d Armored Divisions, attempted to strike across the border undetected
in three places. A mechanized brigade reached Khafji, holding it
briefly before being driven out and crushed by Coalition ground
and air attacks. The operation was complicated, involving heavy
units from two corps in a night passage of lines—perhaps the
most difficult ground operation. Units frequently got lost, missing passage points and attacking at the wrong time and place.
Movements were slow and attacks were often delayed. Consequently, armored units found themselves trapped along roads at
daylight, easy prey for prowling Coalition aircraft.

On the other hand, the news from the Khafji operation was
not all good for the allied side. The Iraqis proved themselves
capable of mounting a multiple-division attack, however hesi-
tantly. The example induced Army planners to ascribe that same
capability to other second echelon regular forces. At a time when
many on the allied side believed the Iraqi Army was too demoralized to do anything but go to ground, the battle demonstrated that
at least the regular heavy forces would fight—and the Republican
Guard would, presumably, fight even more fiercely. As an example of a coordinated military operation, Khafji was not pretty
by Western standards, but the Iraqis did execute the mission under constant pounding by air, artillery, and even occasional naval
gunfire.

The Khafji battle also rekindled fears of fratricide, particularly from the air. Thirteen Marines and four Saudi soldiers were
killed in three incidents, two occurring during air-to-ground operations.[34] All of these incidents could be ascribed to the confusing nature of the war and the inexperience of both air and ground
forces in conducting ground attacks in close proximity to

friendlies. But the long-term effect of the fratricide incidents would prove substantial. Once the ground war began, ground commanders would be very reluctant to call on the Air Force for close air support, particularly at night, in bad weather, or in the constant fluidity and confusion of mechanized close combat.

First Use of Army Tactical Missiles

Almost unnoticed among the hundreds of thousands of sorties flown during the air campaign was a much smaller interdiction effort by Army precision guided missiles. On the day the air war began, Staff Sergeant Ronnie Wint and his two crewmates from A Battery, 1st Battalion, 27th Field Artillery, had spent more than six hours wedged three abreast inside the stiflingly hot 30-ton mass of their tracked Multiple-Launch Rocket System (MLRS) rocket launcher. The crew inched the vehicle along behind an endless line of stalled traffic on Tapline Road, just a few miles south of the Saudi-Iraqi border. None of them expected anything exciting to happen until they could edge themselves out of the interminable traffic and reach the first night's defensive position. The boredom of the moment was broken suddenly by a hurried radio call from the battery commander, Captain Jeff Lieb, who was stalled some distance in front of the convoy. To their surprise Lieb had a fire mission—not for the 12 MLRS rockets they were carrying, but for their alternate load, two of the new but untried Army Tactical Missile System (ATACMS) long-range precision missiles. The target was an Iraqi surface-to-surface missile site located 100 kilometers away. Boredom quickly turned into a flurry of activity. While Wint scribbled down the coded firing data coming over the radio, his driver, Private First Class Russell Sullivan, zigzagged his way out of the congested column and roared off cross-country at 20 miles per hour, throwing up a sand plume as the launcher charged into the desert. Lieb gave Wint the six digit location of A Battery's assembly area, where two prepositioned ATACMS rocket pods would be waiting for them. Wint's launcher careened into position next to the two pods close enough for the gunner, Sergeant Steve Harmark, to download the MLRS pods and snap two 5,500-pound ATACMS missiles into the launcher's boxlike rocket pod container.[35]

Wint maneuvered his ponderous machine back and forth until it was centered over a wooden survey stake. He needed just a moment to punch in the survey data. With the initial navigation system updated, the three soldiers clambered back aboard and moved the launcher a short distance to a firing position. Once set, Harmark punched the target data into his fire-control panel and completed his prelaunch sequence. Automatically the missile container popped loose from the bed of the launcher, skewed slightly to the right and elevated itself 45 degrees. His video screen flashed the "arm missile" prompt. Harmark lifted a red toggle switch and the prompt changed immediately to "fire missile."

As soon as the mission was sent to Sergeant Wint's crew, both the ARCENT deep battle cell and the Air Force began the unfamiliar and turgid process of clearing a path for the missile. The Air Force had never had to contend with an Army missile that could climb up in an 80,000-foot arc to reach a target more than 100 kilometers distant.[36] A clear corridor was finally opened after midnight. At 12:42 A.M. on 18 January, Harmark pushed the firing toggle upward and with a blast of white light and dark brown dust, the rocket lifted away. The first shot that VII Corps had fired in anger since World War II also became the first precision strike by an Army missile in history. Two minutes after launch, the missile disgorged a thousand baseball sized bomblets directly over the Iraqi missile site with catastrophic effect. The strike against the al-Abraq SA-2 missile sites was the first of 36 similar firings, 25 of them by VII Corps Artillery.

The ATACMS proved its value in the Gulf because of its ability to strike deep behind enemy lines quickly and with great precision. The three-day ATO process required to identify, verify, and schedule weapons and aircraft could, in theory at least, be reduced to minutes with ATACMS without all the elaborate preparation necessary to launch a fighter strike.[37] The chief shortcoming of ATACMS in the Gulf was the dearth of deep "eyes" capable of spotting a lucrative target with sufficient precision and timeliness to justify expending a missile. Satellite imagery and the high flying U-2 aircraft, or its more modern TR-1 variant, provided some useful images, but only to an accuracy of 400 meters at best. To be effective, ATACMS requires a location error not greater than 100 meters. Only a few devices were available in the desert capable of providing such accuracy.

Early in the air war, VII Corps placed long-ranging AN/TPQ-37 Firefinder radars close to the front and discovered that the flat desert terrain permitted precise location of Iraqi rockets and artillery firing at a depth of almost 85 kilometers. Later, aerial drones arrived in the theater to support VII Corps's efforts to identify deep targets that might threaten the breaching operation. The Pioneer RPVs were an instant hit and turned out to be the only reliable system capable of finding static, passive targets with precision. Before Desert Shield, the Army and the Air Force had been developing the Joint Surveillance Target Attack Radar System (JSTARS), principally as a means to help the corps commander identify deep targets. The JSTARS is a highly modified Boeing 707 aircraft equipped with a synthetic aperture radar. In its targeting mode, the radar can search a 4-by-5 kilometer area and provide very precise locations for moving vehicles.[38] As the air war progressed, both the Air Force and Army became more comfortable with the process of targeting and clearing ATACMS missions. On two occasions JSTARS operators detected extensive vehicle movements in and out of fixed points inside Iraq. Both points were adjacent to major highways. The corps's deep battle cell identified the targets as a logistics site and a fuel station and each was taken out by a single missile. Eight long-range free rocket (FROG) and multiple rocket batteries were also destroyed with ATACMS counterfire after the batteries were discovered and pinpointed by counterbattery radars.[39]

In spite of a few successful acquisitions and engagements, the value of ATACMS in the Gulf was more one of promise than performance. Few lucrative targets could be found deep inside Iraq. Additionally, so few ATACMS missiles were available that the corps reserved most of them for long-range counterfire during the ground war, which did not last long enough for many such targets to be identified and engaged.

The Army's Assessment of the Air War

At ARCENT, General Stewart began to feel the pressure to get on with the ground war. He was charged with determining when the magic 50 percent attrition figure had been reached. Stewart had learned from many years in the business that raw data depicting numbers of vehicles destroyed could not provide a realistic picture of the residual fighting strength of the Iraqi Army. Using BDA figures as a starting point, he factored into his subjective analysis such intangibles as leadership, command and control, discipline, and morale.[40] From his analysis he was able to paint a picture of three distinct levels of Iraqi competence. Baghdad's frontline infantry units had been the hardest hit. The air campaign had had a devastating effect on the two forward-deployed corps. The situation on the eve of the ground war was reminiscent, on a much grander scale, of the effect that a few thousand British artillery rounds had had on the poor quality Argentine soldiers at Port Stanley during the Falklands Campaign. Again, poor quality soldiers, neglected and badly led, easily fell victim to the psychological terror imposed by firepower. Faced with an unrelenting onslaught and pushed along by a diabolically clever and effective psychological campaign of leaflets and loudspeaker intimidation, many frontline soldiers simply left the trenches for home. Stewart judged the two infantry corps to be 58 percent and 42 percent effective. For those who remained in the trenches, a sense of helplessness and a pervasively listless atmosphere of defeat permeated throughout. Stewart rightly concluded that these units would put up little or no fight.[41]

The regular Iraqi heavy divisions were in somewhat better shape. The strongest division retained 90 percent of its fighting strength. The 52d Division, which contained the hapless "go-away brigade" was at half strength or less. The Jihad Corps, consisting of the 10th and 12th Armored Divisions, retained an average effectiveness of approximately 60 percent. Stewart believed this force was capable of only limited counterattacks. The Republican Guard was in ominously good shape. Better soldiers, well equipped and cared for, the Guardsmen were far less intimidated psychologically by allied airpower. In fact, the long, drawn out period of the air campaign allowed Guard soldiers time to inure themselves to the sights and sounds of aerial firepower. While the initial shock had been severe, the Guard recovered its psychological balance steadily and by 24 February most

Guardsmen were relieved to have survived what they assumed would be the worst that the allies could dish out. They were confident in their ability to deal with anything that might follow. To be sure, much of the Guard's equipment had been destroyed. The most heavily battered of the three Guard heavy divisions, the Tawakalna, was judged to be only 57 percent effective. The others were rated at 65 and 72 percent. The Guard infantry divisions were believed to be well above 60 percent.[42]

Stewart's general impression was that 41 days of air operations had battered and fixed the Iraqi Army, but its central corps of heavy units—especially the Republican Guard—had not been defeated, much less destroyed. General Franks's VII Corps would be able to ride roughshod over the frontline infantry units, but he still had a significant fight waiting for him deep in Iraq. The unbroken barrier of the Republican Guard would require another significant dose of firepower, this time delivered from the ground, before the bulk of his tanks and Bradleys would be able to achieve overwhelming superiority in the direct fire engagement.[43]

Firepower in Support of Ground Operations

Once the ground war began, most of the fire support provided to ground troops was in the form of artillery rather than airpower. Thousands of air interdiction sorties continued to pound static Iraqi forces throughout the Kuwaiti theater during the ground phase. But as mechanized forces began to converge on the killing zone and take down the Iraqi armor in wholesale lots, the damage done against ground targets by airpower decreased significantly.

As in Vietnam, close air support (CAS) continued to provide effective air-delivered fires in relatively close proximity to ground maneuver forces. But the Army in Desert Storm relied considerably less on CAS as a source of protective firepower than in previous conflicts. The lessened reliance on close support from the Air Force did not reflect any loss of confidence in the system by ground commanders. On the contrary, in contrast to the concern over battlefield air interdiction, the Army was pleased with Horner's close air support plan. He developed

an innovative system for CAS that capitalized on the unique circumstances of the Kuwaiti theater. With the number of aircraft at
his disposal, Horner saw that the most efficient method of employing sorties to support ground forces in contact was to push
small packets of two to four aircraft forward at regular intervals.
Pilots in these so-called flow CAS packages would already be
briefed on a prospective deep target before takeoff. As they approached the Iraqi border, the flight lead would check in with the
Airborne Command and Control Center (ABCCC)—the equivalent of a flying tactical command post for the Air Force—to see if
the Army corps in contact had any priority CAS targets. Air liaison officers at both VII and XVIII Airborne Corps would either
divert them to a subordinate division for final vector into a close-
in target or, if no target was immediately available, pass control
back to the ABCCC so the aircraft could continue on to deeper
targets. Because the stream of aircraft flying into Iraq was so
constant and its mix of aircraft and munitions so varied, ground
commanders in contact had at their immediate disposal a wide
menu of attack options to pick from when planning an immediate
strike. Horner's system made sense. Even before the ground war
began, ground commanders agreed that it would be inherently
more responsive and efficient than the Vietnam system of holding back aircraft and crews on strip alert. Response times varied
using the flow CAS technique, but rarely did it take more than
half an hour to issue a fragmentary order to a fighter-bomber in
flight and divert it to an immediate target. Most response times
were considerably less than half an hour.[44]

The Army turned to CAS less frequently in the Gulf for several reasons unrelated to the efficiency of General Horner's flow
CAS system. The Air Force relearned the long-standing lesson
that the most pervasive enemy of effective air support is weather.
State-of-the-art infrared targeting and radar mapping systems had
made modern fighter-bombers more effective in bad weather. But
poor ground visibility still greatly inhibited precise weapons delivery for even the most sophisticated attack aircraft. Just as VII
Corps began to collide with the main body of the Republican
Guard, one of the worst rain and wind storms to strike the region
in decades literally shut down all fixed-wing and most helicopter

sorties for almost half of the ground war. While high winds and rain were not necessarily a significant impediment to fixed-wing flight, low ceilings, at times down to zero, kept orbiting aircraft from gaining the necessary positive visual identity of the target— an absolute requirement when delivering ordnance close to friendly forces.

As previously mentioned, ground commanders were reluctant to employ CAS aggressively for fear of fratricide. The terrible incidents at Khafji dampened enthusiasm considerably for all close supporting fires whether delivered from the surface or the air. Abominable weather, featureless terrain, inexperienced troops, and the unexpectedly rapid pace of the advance created just enough confusion and uncertainty among ground and air commanders to cause them to refrain from calling for CAS except when absolutely necessary. Thanks to the effectiveness of preliminary air interdiction, many of the most lucrative ground targets had already been destroyed. There were also fewer occasions when CAS was the preferred option because artillery and attack helicopters offered a degree of precision equal to close support aircraft while retaining the flexibility to work much more closely with forward maneuver units. Finally, truly *close* close air support really wasn't necessary for the most part during the ground war. In Vietnam, great pilot skill was required to drop freefall bombs and napalm to within 100 meters or less of soldiers pinned to the ground by an NVA ambush. But in the Gulf, direct fire engagements were almost exclusively at long range, more than a mile for tank-on-tank battles, so that such very close applications of CAS were rarely necessary.

The flow CAS system was only one part of a continuously applied sequence of firepower strikes against the Iraqi Army. Deep CAS or BAI was followed by deep helicopter strikes. Then, in rapidly accelerating sequence, MLRS, close-in CAS, tube artillery, and, finally, tank and Bradley cannon fire, combined to create a seamless drumbeat of precise firepower that drove the enemy to ground from the moment he was discovered by long-range reconnaissance to the final moment of his death or surrender. The success of fire support during the ground war, therefore, was not dependent on any one weapon but rather on the collective effect of an entire medley of land- and air-launched systems applied in such a fashion that the collective whole was far more lethal than the sum of its individual parts.

Ground commanders concentrated firepower at two critical points during the ground war: at the breach to ensure a successful and low cost passage of mechanized forces through the elaborate barrier erected by Iraqi frontline forces, and on the Republican Guard to support its destruction by the armored forces of the VII and XVIII Airborne Corps.

Pre–G-Day Feints and Deception

The shooting war for the artillery actually began more than a fortnight before G-Day, principally in the VII Corps's area. General Franks deployed most of his corps artillery well forward along the berm that defined the border between Saudi Arabia and Iraq. The berm also provided a convenient line of departure for the breaching operation. On 7 February Franks began a complex series of artillery raids near the Wadi al Batin in the 1st Cavalry Division zone. The raids served three purposes. The Wadi al Batin was well east of the site selected for VII Corps's main breaching effort. By concentrating artillery fires there, Franks hoped to deceive the Iraqis and, if possible, to draw Iraqi artillery into that area for destruction by concentrations of MLRS rocket fire. Second, Franks was still concerned about the inexperience of his firepower team, and he intended the raids to be a live-fire shakeout that would provide the opportunity to exercise all available firepower systems and forge a smoothly functioning mechanism. Third, Franks was still very much concerned that the Iraqi artillery in range of the breaching site appeared to be relatively untouched by allied air strikes. It became clear to Franks shortly after the air campaign began that his goal of killing 90 percent of the tubes within range of the breach would be impossible to achieve without significant artillery reinforcement.[45]

To Franks, Iraqi artillery continued to be something of an enigma. The attack on Khafji demonstrated how well the Iraqi maneuver units would fight, but the Iraqi guns had been strangely silent there. Of all the Iraqi branches, the engineers and artillery carried with them the best reputation for professionalism and

An MLRS battery fills the night sky with "steel rain" during a counterbattery raid before the beginning of the ground war.

technical skill. He also knew that Iraqi medium guns outranged American guns by about 16 kilometers. Of the artillery pieces capable of reaching the breach, most were towed howitzers arrayed in a deep security zone 20 to 40 kilometers beyond the berm. The majority of self-propelled weapons remained farther to the rear, intermixed with operational and theater reserves. The Iraqi artillery's eyes, however, were very weak. With the allies in control of the air, observation by aircraft or helicopter was out of the question. To help see deep behind the American lines, the Iraqis erected a series of 40-foot-high towers and manned each with binocular-equipped observers. Because the desert was so flat, these few observers could see as far as 30 kilometers inside American lines on a clear day.[46]

Mostly, however, the Iraqis compensated for poor observation by making extensive use of the Soviet technique of templating fires. Through ground and map reconnaissance, Iraqi fire planners guessed the most likely locations of major US units. Once the Americans began to advance they hoped to use direct fire weapons, such as tanks and APCs, to channelize major forces into previously targeted artillery ambush zones. The Iraqis intended to employ large volumes of fire to make up for imprecise targeting. Using standard Soviet norms to compute expenditures, a templated American artillery battery might be scheduled to receive over 600 rounds whereas a tank company could expect over 1,000. Even with several batteries firing at once, however, such a large volume of fire required at least 30 minutes to deliver. Furthermore, while delivery was in progress, any adjustment or refinement of the fire was out of the question.

Franks's greatest fear was that enough Iraqi artillery would survive the air attacks and raids to deliver chemical munitions on the breaching site. Even if poorly aimed, no one could predict what the effect of chemical fires would be. By all means, Franks wanted the Iraqi artillery destroyed. To prevent his own shorter-ranging guns from falling victim to long-range templated fire, Brigadier General Creighton Abrams, Jr., Franks's Corps Artillery commander, kept them well back in assembly areas. To conduct an effective raid, the American guns were obliged to march to the southern edge of the berm under cover of darkness, fire, and withdraw before daylight.[47]

Brigadier General John Tilelli, the 1st Cavalry Division commander, fired the opening round of the pre–G-Day firepower battle on 7 February. At 2:00 P.M. an artillery forward observer vehicle eased up just behind the berm, raised its distinctive hammerhead sight, and fired its laser designator at one of the observation towers five kilometers inside Iraq. The towers were so small that neither dumb artillery projectiles nor bombs could hit them. A 155-mm howitzer located 10 kilometers to the rear fired a single laser-guided Copperhead projectile. Thirty seconds later the first of seven towers disappeared in a flash of light and black smoke. An adjacent battery followed the Copperhead shot by dropping 400 bomblets around the target, killing anyone near the tower. The already badly nearsighted Iraqi frontline artillery suddenly went blind.[48]

On 13 February, three MLRS batteries, two from the VII Corps's 42d Field Artillery Brigade and one from the 1st Cavalry Division, conducted the first of many well-choreographed rocket raids that systematically eliminated the remaining Iraqi artillery across the berm. At dusk the 27 rocket launchers crept up to the berm. In darkness the crews in 18 launchers punched the data for previously identified and verified targets into their fire-control computers. The huge, boxlike launch pod containers, each holding 12 rockets, slewed toward the targets. At precisely 6:15 P.M., soldiers standing nearby watched as 216 rockets rippled away with successive roars, leaving behind white, smoky fingers pointing northward. A few seconds later, a succession of white puffs on the horizon signaled the release of 140,000 bomblets on top of the Iraqi batteries. Launcher crewmen nicknamed the MLRS the "grid square removal system" for good reason. The third MLRS battery was linked directly to a Q-37 counterbattery radar capable of pinpointing the fires from Iraqi batteries up to 70 kilometers away. Should the Iraqi artillery shoot back, only a few seconds would be needed for the radar to pinpoint the target and the waiting rocket battery to smother it with another 70,000 bomblets. In this engagement, and in all subsequent artillery ambushes executed before G-Day, the Iraqis never took the bait. They seemed to understand that they were no match for the rocket-radar team and would wait to fire until G-Day, when their sacrifice might be purchased at a more lucrative price.[49]

Firepower raids grew increasingly more complex as gunners and airmen became more adept and confident in their ability to synchronize the fires from disparate sources. During the night and early morning of 16–17 February, five battalions from the VII Corps's artillery opened a two-kilometer-square corridor by saturating the Iraqi air defenses with fires. A squadron of Apache helicopters from the 11th Aviation Brigade raced forward through the gap created by the artillery. Five kilometers inside Iraq the squadron fanned out into a thin line about 15 kilometers wide. The Apaches swept slowly northward at just under 30 knots, firing continuously. Each crew worked a specific sector that included towers, vehicles, and communications buildings. After five minutes the Apaches turned back toward the border, reaching it within seconds of the planned recrossing time. The operation was followed in every detail by the corps's deep battle cell through a tactical satellite linkage with the 11th Aviation Brigade. Just before the attack began, an orbiting electronic warfare aircraft hit on an active Iraqi anti-aircraft radar directly in the planned path of the Apaches. A quick TACSAT conversation through the deep battle cell caused an immediate fusillade by 12 MLRS rockets. The radar went off the air immediately. The artillery-helicopter raid on 17 February proved not only successful as a feint but also as a dress rehearsal for a more ambitious and deadly deep attack against major Iraqi armored formations a week later during the ground war.[50]

While successful for the most part, the pre–G-Day raids pointed out problems with targeting, scheduling, and control of fires very similar to those encountered by the Air Force. Wide-area satellite imagery could only locate Iraqi artillery to within about a mile. This level of precision was fine for the Air Force because a pilot had only to be vectored close enough to the target to identify and engage it directly with his on-board delivery systems. However, to hit a distant unseen target reliably with artillery required much greater precision. Although satellite photos were useful, a target identified by satellite had to be further refined by a second, more precise source. Remotely Piloted Vehicles immediately proved their worth as the most responsive, precise, and reliable means for targeting artillery. The RPV platoon was originally intended to perform several intelligence

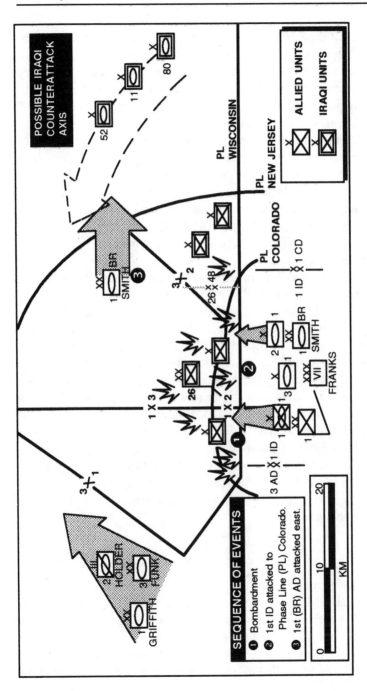

Preparation, Breach and Attack, 25 February 1991

tasks, but the imperative to locate Iraqi artillery became so pressing late in the air war that Franks used the RPVs solely for identifying artillery positions. If a target moved, JSTARS offered great precision. But the communications linkages between the JSTARS aircraft and artillery firing units were slow, convoluted, and uncertain. A great deal of luck and a quick response by rocket batteries within range were necessary to engage a JSTARS target before it moved out of the area. On the rare occasions when an Iraqi battery dared to fire back, radars provided the most precise and timely location data. As with the Air Force, battle damage assessment for artillery strikes remained a nagging problem. Thus, on the eve of the breach battle, Franks's staff still was not sure that enough artillery within range of the breach site had been destroyed.

The layers of European style bureaucracy charged with integrating and controlling indirect fire frustrated early attempts to shorten response times. Too often, important targets such as FROG rocket battalions (the weapon of choice for chemical delivery) moved before they could be targeted. To improve responsiveness, Abrams and his deputy commander, Colonel Ray Smith, pushed responsibility for selecting which targets to fire and when to fire them down to junior officers in artillery brigades and division artilleries. The higher staff at corps set attack criteria and regulated fires by publishing a prioritized list of prospective target types and by allocating specific munitions to each category. Battalion and brigade officers could then order indirect fire strikes themselves without seeking specific approval from higher headquarters for every target engaged.[51]

Firepower at the Breach

General Schwartzkopf's plan to breach the Iraqi forward defenses called for two sequential attacks spaced a day apart. On G-Day, 24 February, at 4:00 A.M., Lieutenant General Walter Boomer's 1st and 2d Marine Divisions crossed the border to breach the Kuwaiti defenses. Boomer's mission was to tie down as many Iraqi frontline divisions as possible and move quickly to liberate Kuwait City. Concurrently, more than 300 kilometers away on the far western flank of the front, General Luck's XVIII Airborne Corps launched the 101st Airborne Division deep into the Iraqi desert in the largest and longest helicopter-borne assault in history. The mission of the Screaming Eagles was to put combat forces astride Highway 8 near the Euphrates River to block withdrawal of the Republican Guard to Baghdad.

Under the original plan, the VII Corps would conduct the main attack a day later on 25 February. However, initial reports from airborne and marine forces were so optimistic that Schwartzkopf ordered VII Corps to begin its breaching operation a day early. This optimism was fueled by reports of little or no resistance from Iraq's third-class frontline troops. Artillery fire was sporadic and, as with Lieutenant Saif's battery, immediately silenced by counterfire. The dreaded chemical attacks never materialized. Many trenchlines and forward positions were discovered to be empty. The challenge was not to kill the enemy but to organize enough POW-handling teams to efficiently control the flood of prisoners of war.

The 1st Infantry Division was charged with cracking the toughest portion of the Iraqi front line. To support the operation by fire, Colonel Mike Dotson, the 1st Infantry Division artillery commander, planned an elaborate three-hour preparation. The last-minute call for the division to breach a day early forced him to compress his plan into half an hour. Working frantically, with only seconds to spare at times, Dotson's gunners reallocated targeting priorities and recomputed the complex firing program. The revised preparation began at 2:30 P.M. on 24 February. After his capture, the commander of the Iraqi 48th Infantry Division later stated, "You attacked us with the same NATO force that was designed to attack the entire Warsaw Pact, and the Earth shook."[52] Even allowing for the Iraqi general's exaggeration, the fires in support of the breaching operation were overwhelmingly destructive. Three field artillery brigades, two groups of division artillery, and 10 MLRS batteries opened up in concert to create a Soviet strike sector, American style. These units fired 11,000 artillery rounds and 414 rockets, dispersing more than 600,000 explosive bomblets into a 20-by-40 kilometer sector. More than 350 howitzers covered the attack for a density of 22 pieces per kilometer of front. The psychological effect of so much accurate firepower landing at once was enough to break the defenders' morale, already lowered considerably by artillery raids, leaflet drops, and 13 B-52 sorties flown against them the previous day. Some artillery was reserved to attack the command and control system of the Iraqi VII Corps to prevent any possibility of the corps's reserve responding to the 1st Division's breach. A single RPV sortie had taken a last look at the battlefield early on the morning of the breaching operation and pinpointed 13 Iraqi artillery positions that were subsequently added to the list of targets to be destroyed later in the afternoon. As a result, the Iraqi will to resist was broken before the breaching operation began. What was postulated to take 14 hours and result in up to 40 percent casualties took only two hours at practically no cost. During the operation the division destroyed the better part of what remained of two Iraqi divisions. No Iraqi artillery fire landed in the breach area.[53]

Assault on the Republican Guard

Once the Iraqi front line was effectively breached, the race was on to close with and destroy the Republican Guard, which was waiting for VII Corps over 160 kilometers to the northeast. The plan of attack was simple. General Franks would strike the Guard one time with a single closed fist consisting of at least three armored and mechanized divisions. By the time Franks was ready to strike, the 24th Infantry Division from XVIII Airborne Corps would have turned east along Highway 8 to close in on and cover Franks's left flank. The 24th would then add its own substantial combat power to the cataclysmic collision with the Guard.

Franks's insistence on a single decisive battle was driven by a desire to end the war quickly at minimum cost. By all means he wanted to avoid any tactical check that might stall the corps's advance and lead to a battle of attrition. He was convinced his corps would win but, from his own experience in Vietnam, he understood that victory at too great a sacrifice in human life would prove Pyrrhic at best. As soon as he located the Guard precisely, he would turn his corps directly to the east with his divisions stretched across an 80 kilometer front from north to south. Northernmost would be the 1st Armored Division, with its left shoulder protected by the XVIII Airborne Corps's cavalry screen. The Third Armored Division would form the middle of the fist, and the 1st Infantry Division, hurrying to catch up from its recently completed breaching operation, would be the southernmost force.[54]

Colonel Don Holder's 2d Armored Cavalry Regiment acted as Franks's lead scout. Spread across a 40-kilometer front, the cavalrymen's mission was to push well ahead of the corps and to search for T-72 tanks, the most distinctive mark of the Republican Guard. The corps's screen was very thin against such an imposing enemy and Holder chose to protect it with ample firepower. An aerial picket line of Cobra helicopters ranged well ahead of Holder's armor. His direct firepower was augmented by three additional battalions from the 210th Field Artillery Brigade, in addition to the regiment's own three howitzer batteries. Eighteen Apaches and 13 OH-58 scout helicopters of the 21st Aviation Brigade, borrowed from the 1st Armored Division, augmented the aerial eyes and killing power of Holder's cavalry aviators. Holder also established an even more distant aerial screen using Air Force A-10s. The aggressive regimental air liaison officer, Air Force Captain Chris Kupko, continually vectored A-10s toward on-call targets. When the lead aerial scouts turned up targets, Kupko directed fighter-bombers to engage, following a drill the regiment had worked out in great detail during training exercises in Germany. Iraqis in the path of the regiment found themselves continually under devastating fire, first from aerial and ground scouts, then from A-10s, and back again to the scouts. Holder's technique replicated VII Corps's model for applying firepower against the Republican Guard on a much smaller scale.[55]

Each armored division marched steadily toward the Guard in a fixed formation commonly called the division desert wedge. The divisions spread themselves across 25 to 45 kilometers of front with columns of armored and wheeled vehicles stretching back 80 to 150 kilometers. As they moved across the flat terrain, the tanks and Bradleys of these huge formations appeared to move like tiny warships preparing to engage in a naval rather than a land battle. Armored and infantry brigade commanders kept accompanying artillery tucked up into the formation to allow the guns to range as far forward as possible, ensuring that, when needed, the brigade commander had his guns nearby. At times the guns had difficulty keeping up with the faster and more agile tanks and Bradley fighting vehicles. In the 24th Infantry Division, which had to move the greatest distance over the most intractable terrain, accompanying howitzers often fell far enough behind to be almost out of range of some supported units.[56]

The techniques of close-in supporting fire common in Vietnam were rarely seen in support of the advance on the Republican Guard. Tanks and Bradleys had enough firepower to take care of all but the most stubborn Iraqi defenses. A moving column would only halt to shoot if a target lucrative enough to justify engagement by at least an artillery battalion was encountered. Normally, missions fired from march column took about an hour to complete and required the expenditure of several hundred rounds of bomblet-carrying projectiles.

Long-range artillery started to fall amongst the columns of the 1st and 3d Armored Divisions when they reached the outpost line of the Republican Guard during the afternoon of 26 February. Most of the Iraqi artillery was, as usual, firing blind in large concentrations. With no terrain to mask its movement, advancing armor halted in place and waited for the strikes to end or simply drove around them.

On 26 February, Major Generals Ronald Griffith and Paul Funk, leading the 1st and 3d Armored Divisions, began to close on the Republican Guard's main line of resistance. There they encountered the Tawakalna Division, supported by the regular 12th Armored Division. Both commanders discovered that the Guard divisions, despite weeks of preliminary aerial bombardment, were prepared and willing to fight. Griffith and Funk applied supporting fires in a similar fashion. Their collective intent was as much to apply psychological pressure with firepower as to cause physical destruction. To begin the process of breaking the enemy's will to resist they layered a continuous carpet of firepower over the

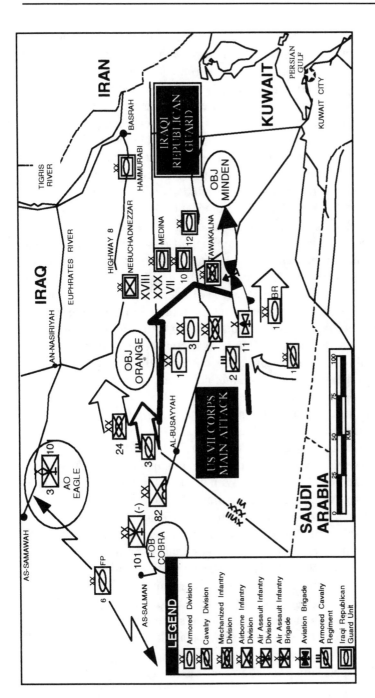

The Great Wheel closes on the Republican Guard, 26 February 1991

enemy. The carpet stretched from the enemy's distant logistic, command and control, and reserve assembly areas to the main line of resistance occupied by dug-in tanks and infantry. The process of application was carefully orchestrated to allow no letup in intensity. When the divisions were approximately 80 kilometers away from contact, low-level air strikes were directed against the entire depth of the Guard. Whenever possible the strikes were observed from fast FACs or light scout helicopters equipped with infrared devices (FLIRS) capable of observing and targeting in all weather. In his more constricted segment of the battle front, General Funk finalized his drumbeat of Air Force firepower with an hour's worth of pinpoint shooting by two Air Force AC-130 Spectre gunships. As close air support A-10s and F-16s appeared over his formation, Funk established informal "airspace coordination areas" (ACAs) along specific grid lines. The ACAs gave aircraft a block of airspace free of friendly artillery fire, and allowed Funk to continue attacking targets outside them. Clever use of ACAs by his division air liaison officer allowed the 3d Armored to keep high performance aircraft in the fight until the last possible moment before tanks closed to direct fire range. Concern for fratricide dictated that no close strikes were to be flown unless aircraft were under positive control by ground observers. When this condition was met, missions were flown safely within five kilometers of friendlies.[57]

On 26 February General Griffith followed his deep air strikes with an aerial attack of his own using the 1st Armored's 3d Battalion, 1st Aviation. With no time for planning or preparation, six Apaches from the battalion's A Company flew over the division's lead elements 100 feet apart just off the deck. The target was a formation of the Adnan Motorized Division discovered just behind and north of the Tawakalna's main line of resistance. The pilots flew in almost pitch-black weather with an unrelenting rainstorm pelting their windshields. Captain Rick Stockhauser led the formation. The night was so dark that at times he had to rely solely on his infrared sighting system to navigate between the Bradleys from his own division and the enemy's T-72s. Well in front of friendly lines he could clearly see through his sight 30 to 40 hot spots sitting six kilometers distant. He used his laser designator to divide the target area into six distinct kill zones, one for each Apache in his formation. As he methodically began to direct his Hellfires into the Iraqis, Stockhauser noticed that the dark night and the very steep angle of the Hellfire missile's trajectory completely surprised and confused the enemy. After 45 minutes on station, A Company returned to refuel and rearm. The battalion made three more circuits through the Adnan during the early hours of the 26th. Later, gun camera video confirmed that the battalion had destroyed 38 T-72 tanks, 14 BMPs, and 70-odd trucks.[58]

While Apache battalions attacked deep, Griffith and Funk continued to apply their carpet of firepower at medium range with MLRS. General Funk kept two MLRS batteries under his direct control to work over fresh targets identified by his aerial and ground scouts or the Air Force, or drawn from preplanned target lists derived from intelligence. In one instance, Funk's rocket batteries were so close that he had to send them seven kilometers back to the rear to get the targets beyond the minimum range of the system.[59] The drumbeat of MLRS and cannon fire on the Republican Guard was continuous. As he drew nearer, Funk divided his supporting artillery into two roughly equal groups that he tucked up tightly behind the lead battalion maneuver task force in his two lead brigades. This permitted two distinct concentrations of artillery—consisting of as many as 50 guns and rockets apiece—to be kept close so that when a worthy target appeared one of these "grand batteries" could be ordered immediately into action. Funk's Division Artillery commander, Colonel John Michitsch, had trained his gunners to employ a "massed-hip shoot technique." Given the signal, entire battalions of rockets and guns would halt in place and orient themselves using GPS or the inertial locating devices aboard MLRS. Then, under the control of the brigade fire support officer, guns of all types and calibers would open fire in unison. The 3d Armored Division Artillery and its supporting 42d Artillery Brigade could execute a massed hip-shoot in less than eight minutes.[60]

Closer in, just before the tanks drew within direct fire range, cannon artillery fires completed laying the firepower carpet. For the most part, as in the case of the 3d Armored, cannons provided massed fires at a distance to take out stubborn pockets of resistance or the few remaining enemy artillery pieces that might still be firing blindly into US formations. During the battle of Medina Ridge on 27 February, Republican Guard guns fired a series of five templated concentrations into an empty space of desert not too far from General Griffith's forward command post. Initially, the Firefinder counterbattery radars were looking in the wrong direction and thus failed to detect the Iraqi batteries. Not long after the rounds began to impact, gunners reoriented two radars toward the north and east and immediately pinpointed a 122-mm D-30 battery firing methodically at a rhythmic four rounds per minute. Colonel V. B. Corn ordered three full MLRS launchers to respond, but, maddeningly, the Iraqi guns were firing from across the 40 Northing grid line that marked the border with XVIII Airborne Corps. Getting clearance to shoot took more than half an hour as the request went back to VII Corps's main command post, then by satellite to the XVIII Airborne Corps command post, then back again. Once clearance was received, however, a subsequent MLRS volley obliterated the offending Iraqis. Corn kept his radars illuminated continuously and within minutes they acquired nine more targets that were silenced by another volley of 12 MLRS rockets. Within two hours Corn had eliminated four Iraqi battalions. In the next 24 hours his gunners destroyed 72 Iraqi field artillery pieces. As each Iraqi battery opened fire, retaliation came less than two minutes later with a minimum of 12 rockets and battalions of 8-inch cannon artillery. Three weeks later Corn walked through the firing positions occupied by the D-30s and counted 13 destroyed guns surrounded by expended MLRS rocket motors, fuses, and warhead shrouds. It occurred to him with gruesome finality that the Iraqi batteries had not had a chance against the effective rocket-radar combination.[61]

If the timing and effectiveness of the firepower carpet was exactly on the mark, the advancing brigades of tanks and Bradleys would close on the Republican Guard and begin to engage without a halt. The M1 tank, in particular, possessed such a dominant overmatch in killing power, protection, and target acquisition that once within about a mile of its target it needed no additional fire support to destroy a defending line of Iraqi T-72s. On only two occasions was VII Corps's armored firing line halted long enough to call in additional supporting fires. In both instances the Iraqi armored defenses were discovered to be intact, unbroken, and particularly daunting.

Late in the afternoon of 26 February, during the 3d Armored's attack on the Tawakalna, Colonel Robert Higgins, the 2d Brigade commander, could see that his lead unit, Task Force 4-8th Cavalry, was having a difficult time punching through an extensive enemy position made up of trenchlines and dug-in tanks and APCs arranged in a pattern almost two miles deep. As darkness fell, Higgins realized that such an enormous defensive position, if left unbroken by firepower, might punish a frontal attack severely. The position was too vast and continuous to maneuver around. He had no choice but to halt in place while MLRS launchers, cannon, and repeated attack helicopter strikes laid an additional five-hour carpet of firepower over the Tawakalna. At 10:00 P.M. the 2d Brigade went in again and by three the next morning had crushed the Iraqi defenses after several desperate hours of close-in tank-to-tank combat.[62]

At dawn the next day, the 1st Armored Division's 2d Brigade collided with unbroken elements of the Medina Division in what would be known as the Battle of Medina Ridge. Colonel Montgomery Meigs, commanding the 2d Brigade, the northernmost unit of the VII Corps attack, spotted a seemingly endless line of hot spots glowing through his thermal sight. As his units crested Medina Ridge, Meigs ordered a halt when he realized the size of the force in front of him. To even the odds, he called for air support. Apache helicopters from the 3-1st Aviation carefully eased up behind his firing line and began to launch a barrage of laser-guided Hellfire missiles toward the distant Iraqi armored formations. The Iraqi artillery responded by dropping rounds behind the line of tanks. As usual, the artillery fired without adjustment and landed harmlessly to the rear.

Both A-10 and F-16 aircraft soon joined the fight, attacking reserves of the Medina Division entrenched a few kilometers beyond the enemy's main defensive line. The crackle of artillery bomblet ammunition dropping throughout the depth of the enemy's position sounded to observers on the scene like an endless fireworks display on the Fourth of July. Meigs's tanks were far enough away to take up the fight without having to close down air and artillery support. Soon, bright orange flashes appeared on the horizon as the tank gunners slammed depleted uranium penetrators into the hapless Iraqi tanks at the remarkable distance of almost 3 ½ kilometers. By then the din of battle was constant. Every available cannon, tank gun, rocket, and missile launcher poured firepower into the Medina without pause. By 3:00 P.M. on the 27th almost everything inside the Iraqi defensive position had been killed or set afire. Meigs's tanks moved forward cautiously through the carnage. Engineer troops occasionally hopped aboard the odd Iraqi vehicle left undamaged and destroyed it with explosive charges. By evening on the 27th the Medina Division had ceased to exist.[63]

A Portent of Things to Come: The Attack into AO Minden

Depth is one of the four tenets of AirLand Battle. From the perspective of a division commander in the Gulf War, deep operations consisted of distant engagements by Air Force aircraft out to about 30 kilometers forward of friendly forces.[64] On occasion, divisional attack helicopters would strike even deeper if intelligence was lucky enough to spot a target large and lucrative enough to justify engagement. Both corps commanders had at their disposal a separate aviation brigade expressly organized, equipped, and trained to conduct true deep operations in the intended spirit of AirLand Battle. Franks's 11th Aviation Brigade had already exercised its deep attack mechanism during the feint and deception phase with a shallow coordinated aerial foray up the Wadi al Batin on 17 February. Based on experience gained during this operation, the deep battle cell at VII Corps headquarters devised a series of more ambitious and much deeper attacks intended to intercept and destroy any counterattack by Iraqi regular army armored formations directed at VII Corps's flanks. Two days into the ground war, Franks and his operations officer, Colonel Stan Cherrie, realized that such a mobile threat was unlikely to materialize. Nevertheless, they were both committed to attacking throughout the battlefield to a depth that would include static Iraqi armored units positioned deep inside Iraq.

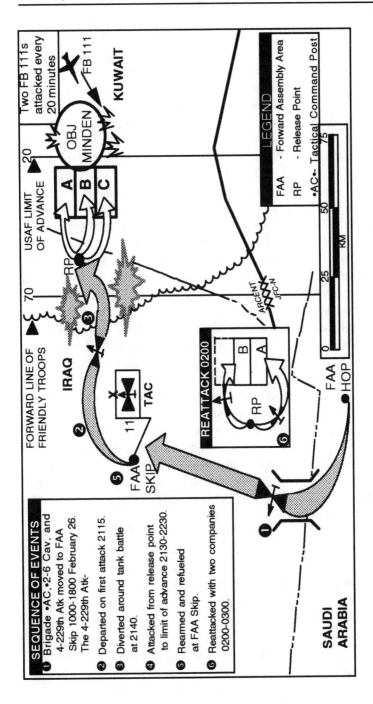

VII Corps Deep Attack into AO MINDEN, 26-27 February 1991

To accommodate Franks's desire to attack deep, the deep battle cell developed a number of contingency plans based on known Iraqi armored concentrations, some of them as far as 150 kilometers inside Iraq. By the afternoon of 26 February, Franks instructed his aviation brigade to activate contingency plan Boot, which targeted the stationary Iraqi 10th Armored Division located astride the main highway from Kuwait City to Basra in Iraq. Colonel Johnnie Hitt, the brigade commander, issued his warning order late on the afternoon of the 26th with a launch time scheduled for nine that evening. Last-minute changes and coordination were made between the flying units and VII Corps via tactical satellite. Colonel Cherrie warned Hitt of the danger of fratricide, particularly when his pilots overflew units in contact. Cherrie also cautioned Hitt to limit his attack to targets within the designated kill boxes and not to fire beyond the 20 north-south grid line, which formed the extreme limit of VII Corps's area of influence. All targets east of that line belonged to the Air Force.[65]

Eighteen Apaches from Lieutenant Colonel Roger McCauley's 4th Battalion, 229th Aviation, lifted off from the forward assembly area at 9:15 P.M. and covered the 100 kilometers to Objective Minden in about an hour. The objective area, located about 80 kilometers behind enemy lines, was divided into three kill boxes. McCauley assigned a company of six Apaches to each. The helicopters spread themselves 150 meters apart and began a slow eastward sweep through the boxes at about 30 knots. The Apaches received small-arms fire as they fired missiles, cannon, and rockets at anything that appeared hot through their thermal sights. In the first sweep McCauley's airmen managed to identify and destroy only about one company of enemy armor. Frustratingly, the pilots discovered when they reached the eastward limit of their advance that hundreds of vehicles, including the great majority of Iraqi armor, were moving untouched toward Basra on the other side of the 20 north-south grid line. Back at the corps main headquarters, Colonel Hitt had received an updated JSTARS readout that showed thousands of moving targets on both sides of the 20 grid line. At 10:30 P.M. he received McCauley's recommendation for a second attack. Hitt immediately approved it.

While McCauley's Apaches were sweeping through Objective Minden, the Air Force was conducting a series of single F-111B strikes east of the 20 grid line. Each aircraft dropped four 2,000-pound laser-guided bombs approximately every twenty minutes. When the air tasking order had been prepared several days earlier, any targets east of this line were safely assumed to be well beyond the reach of the VII Corps commander. The methodical F-111 bombing scheme was never intended to halt the mass withdrawal of several Iraqi armored divisions into Iraq. Even if every laser-guided bomb destroyed a vehicle, only a few of several thousand could have been destroyed using such a slow and methodical technique. When Hitt learned from JSTARS that he had the opportunity to cause great damage to several Guard divisions in full flight, he tried desperately to get permission from ARCENT to attack directly into the Iraqi formations. He realized that just one pass with 18 Apaches could kill more than 100 vehicles in less than half an hour. Unfortunately, once the ATO was in the execution phase, it was almost impossible to change to accommodate last minute tactical exigencies.

A second helicopter attack into the same kill boxes west of the 20 grid line proved more successful than the first. One company discovered a large convoy snaking its way cross-country conveniently spread through two kill boxes. For three minutes the Apache gunners worked the column over continuously. Using classic tactics, they knocked out the lead and trail T-62s with Hellfires, switched to multipurpose submunition rockets, and finished off the remainder with a hail of 30-mm cannon shells in a final pass. The raid on Minden knocked out much of the Iraqi 10th Armored Division. In two separate 30-minute attacks, McCauley's battalion destroyed 33 tanks, 22 armored personnel carriers, 37 other vehicles, and an undetermined number of Iraqi soldiers. Fewer than two dozen Apaches had broken the spirit of an entire division in just over two hours.

Vietnam and The Gulf: A Contrast in Circumstances

More than twenty years separated the employment of American firepower in Vietnam from the Gulf War. The nature of the battlefield and the enemy in both cases greatly influenced how effective a firepower intensive doctrine could be. In Vietnam, thick jungle hid the enemy and allowed him to melt away and disperse before incoming fires caused serious damage. In the Gulf there was nowhere for the enemy to hide. He could be found with relative ease and, once found, tended obligingly to remain in place until destroyed. The Iraqis' inactivity also permitted the United States to keep them beyond arm's reach so firepower could be most efficiently employed while minimizing the chances of fratricide. Whereas the North Vietnamese were tough, tenacious, and stoic under fire, the Iraqis, for the most part, broke and ran, or cowered in trenches and bunkers when exposed to a heavy dose of firepower. In the desert, without benefit of secure hide positions, once broken, the Iraqis never had the opportunity to reform and refit to fight again.

Unlike Vietnam, there was nothing subtle or gradual about the way firepower was employed in the Gulf. From the very beginning of the air war, the firepower onslaught was continuous and overwhelming. Thanks to the technology of the precision revolution, the firepower directed against the Iraqis was several orders of magnitude more lethal than in Vietnam. As a general rule, if an Iraqi target could be located with precision, it escaped destruction only if the allies chose not to engage it. In Vietnam, a practical limit on the destructive firepower an armed force could deliver existed in a war zone in which the insurgent force was dispersed among—and was often indistinguishable from—the civilian population. In the Gulf War, the enemy was easy to spot and was positioned in the open desert far from occupied cities and towns.

Finally, the destruction of the Iraqi war machine and the interdiction of its means of sustainment was sufficient to end the Army's ability or willingness to fight. In Vietnam the enemy's combat capability rested not so much in the materiel strength of the North Vietnamese Army, but in the willingness and ability of its soldiers to stand firm in the midst of overwhelming firepower, suffer casualties, and remain determined to fight. Tough, well-led soldiers are far more difficult to destroy than tanks and artillery. Ultimately, the will of dedicated soldiers is the most difficult commodity to destroy with firepower alone.

7
Firepower in Future Limited War

If the recent past provides any clue to the future of warfare, it seems likely that two themes will recur with unsettling regularity. First, wars in the Third World will flourish as poor but often well-armed states seek to dominate their neighbors or crush internal unrest by force of arms. Second, Western armies increasingly will find themselves involved in such conflicts, often unprepared and often with little real concept of the unseen pitfalls and practical difficulties of fighting limited wars in distant places. Some of the best armies have recently had such experiences. The Israelis, expecting another blitzkrieg-like campaign, invaded Lebanon in 1982, only to discover that their proven skill in armored warfare mattered very little in a war against back-street guerrillas armed with RPGs and Kalashnikovs. What began as a war of intervention became, unexpectedly, a wasteful war of attrition that cost the Israeli Defense Forces more casualties than either the Six-Day or October Wars.

Less than a decade after its withdrawal from Vietnam, the United States again called upon light forces to restore democratic government to the obscure island nation of Grenada. The combat task fell mainly on a lightly armed group of 400 Rangers who parachuted from 500 feet into the midst of the island's Cuban defenders. Victory was quickly won by small groups of well-trained, well-led infantry. Firepower was applied surgically, using helicopter and fixed-wing gunships whenever possible. Just before Christmas in 1989, US forces again showcased their professional competence in a brief campaign against Manuel Noriega and his band of Panamanian thugs. A medley of forces including Army Rangers, Special Forces, and troops from three Army divisions quickly overwhelmed the Panamanian Defense Forces after only a few days of intense urban combat.

In an ironic twist of fate, the once accomplished jungle fighters of the North Vietnamese Army found themselves in the 1980s manning modern Soviet tanks, artillery, and aircraft, attempting to blast and gas guerrillas from jungle enclaves along the Thai border in Cambodia. In a yearly ritual, the Vietnamese regulars attacked, and the guerrillas defended and then dispersed, only to reappear with the return of the monsoon.

The world remains too volatile to predict precisely the next theater of war. But no prudent military planner can deny the real prospect that US conventional forces might be committed against enemies in Central and South America, Southwest Asia, the Middle East, Africa, or elsewhere. The conflicts in Indochina, Afghanistan, the Falklands, and the Persian Gulf offer valuable lessons on the employment of modern firepower in future limited wars. More importantly, these case studies provide useful clues to help in determining how successful firepower systems will be in reducing the human cost of a future campaign.

From a strategic perspective, the single conclusion that seems to grow from all of these recent examples is that the sooner an intervening force can arrive to influence the course of military events, the smaller the chance that the conflict will devolve into a firepower-intensive, wasteful slugging match. In the case of a war of attrition, intervention should come during the earliest stages of an insurgency or overt invasion by a hostile neighbor. Prompt action in the form of military aid and training should make the supported government's forces effective in the field. The objective of such aid should be to help the indigenous army to restrain the enemy and prevent him from escalating the conflict to more lethal levels of warfare. Early arrival in the theater of war is equally essential for an intervening force. The faster a firepower system is assembled in a distant theater, the lesser the risk to the intervening force. In the case of the Falklands, the enemy was effectively isolated and denied reinforcement as the British assembled an expeditionary force at home. In the Gulf, the challenge was to build up an effective firepower system within the theater capable of at first deterring further aggression, and later of defeating Iraq and restoring Kuwaiti sovereignty.

A nation should never contemplate involvement in a limited war without a clear understanding of what firepower and technology can and cannot do. On every occasion, modern nations involved in recent small wars have overestimated the destructive power of their own forces. Inevitably, this overestimate has led to optimism and expectations greater than either men or machines could deliver. Munitions intended to destroy a conventional force may have little or no effect against an elusive, dispersed, entrenched enemy not encumbered by vulnerable heavy equipment or lines of communication. A concentrated bombardment that would shock the life out of a Western unit might have only a temporary effect on the fighting strength of a tough Third World unit inured to hardship and prepared to die for a cause.

From a tactical perspective, the essential principles governing the conduct of modern war remain valid for lesser conflicts. To some degree, though, the unique circumstances of the strategic objective, combined with the prospect of facing a particularly determined enemy in harsh conditions of terrain and climate, have altered the way that these tactical principles are applied. As these five case studies show, an enemy who may appear on the surface to be at considerable disadvantage when facing the onslaught of a more sophisticated force in fact holds certain distinct tactical advantages. His knowledge of terrain and his freedom to move without the restraining tendrils of modern logistics and communications give him unequaled tactical mobility. His familiarity with local regions and people provides him with an insider's sense that makes any maneuver without his knowledge difficult and permits him the initiative to strike at a time and place of his own choosing. More often than not, he has time on his side. To win he merely has to sustain his own existence. He is most likely inured to hardship and resigned to a sustained struggle. Although he might be intimidated by the firepower and technology of his opponent for a while, recent experience seems to indicate that initial uncertainty turns first to familiarity and then often to contempt when the insurgent discovers that napalm is not the atomic bomb, and shells, no matter how destructive, can do little harm when dropped in the wrong place. Finally, a phenomenon of more recent history has been the acquisition of first-rate weaponry by armies formerly possessing obsolescent hand-me-downs. Thanks to the demise of the Cold War, many smaller nations like Iraq can place in the field first-rate armor, artillery, and anti-aircraft weapons the technological equal of those of the intervening force.

There is no question that the American employment of firepower in the Gulf War was a success. Practical application of the precision revolution on the battlefield allowed American air and ground firepower to level Saddam's mountain of first-class war materiel in a well-conceived campaign of attrition by firepower. Victory came quickly—and with few US casualties. Unfortunately, conservative institutions like armies all too often tend to focus on past successes rather than failures when seeking a vision for the future. The Gulf War experience must be treated with great caution. The circumstances that so favored a firepower intensive style of war in the Persian Gulf are not likely to be repeated. A static enemy lying dormant in featureless desert terrain provided an ideal opportunity for precision targeting. The Iraqis were so technically inept and badly led that they did nothing to cope with the surprise of the precision revolution unleashed on them so suddenly and efficiently on such an enormous scale. The Iraqi Army was so morally weakened by poor training, leadership, and motivation to fight that all but the Republican Guard were prime candidates for a program of psychological intimidation by firepower. Open terrain and a static enemy permitted the US firepower system to kill at great distances without having to expose large numbers of soldiers to the horrors of close combat against a steadfast, unbroken foe.

To be sure, superior precision firepower can still give a modern armed force a decisive edge in limited wars. Lethal munitions and precision targeting, unavailable prior to the Gulf War, promise to provide an unprecedented edge to a modern force against any enemy, however well equipped and steadfast, if he can be found and fixed. Control of the air will provide the single greatest firepower advantage to American forces in the future.

Kill ratios and effective control of territory appear to be directly proportional to the efficiency with which aerial assets are coordinated and aerial firepower applied. Limited wars against an insurgent distort the relative importance of traditional airpower missions and serve to blur the distinction drawn between the aerial roles for air forces and armies. Mastery of airspace is not a major issue. The insurgent doesn't need it, and the intervening force possesses it without question. Even in a conflict that takes a more conventional form, such as the Gulf War, no Third World country will seriously be able to challenge the US Air Force's mastery of the air—even if, as in the case of Iraq, it can afford to purchase the most sophisticated weaponry.

However, while air campaigns might be startlingly effective against a mechanized and industrialized enemy like Iraq, such campaigns have proven less effective in other limited wars against less well equipped and more tenacious enemies. It is interesting to note that the Soviets in Afghanistan did not seriously attempt to interdict by air the flow of supplies from Pakistan. The Korean War and both Indochina conflicts have shown that an Asian army can sustain itself even when a sophisticated aerial interdiction effort is directed against it.

Airpower can be decisive in limited wars because it provides mobility (at least to the scene of battle), aerial observation, and close air support. Combat experiences in Algeria, Malaya, Vietnam, and Afghanistan have shown that conventional forces cannot fight an unconventional war without the aid of the helicopter as the primary vehicle for each of these missions. Troop-carrying helicopters have replaced armored personnel carriers for moving squads over long distances in inhospitable terrain; the light observation helicopter has supplanted ground reconnaissance vehicles for observing enemy movements; and gunships provide the very close support to attacking troops once offered by tanks. The Falklands campaign demonstrated in a dramatic fashion that having too few helicopters can risk the success of an entire campaign. Experience in Vietnam and Afghanistan also seems to show that a modern army's combat effectiveness is in proportion to the number of vertical-lift aircraft it can place in the field.

The existing US structure for request and control of Air Force fires is as well designed and efficient as any. The example of Khe Sanh, however, demonstrates that a structure intended to distribute aerial resources with the greatest efficiency does not necessarily provide the most responsive close air support. Flying into an artillery barrage or watching from the ground as aircraft drop weapons of great destructive capacity very close are acts of faith as much as skill and are best done by a team effort in which trust and familiarity between soldiers and pilots give vibrancy to the system and make it work. The experience with air interdiction in the Gulf War suggests that the responsiveness of planned aerial fires has decreased considerably since Vietnam. The ATO, with its characteristic 72-hour cycle, seemed unresponsive to battlefield commanders, particularly to corps commanders seeking to shape the battlefield with BAI. In World War II, Korea, and Vietnam, the preplanned mission cycle against deep targets required 24 hours to complete—one-third the time needed in Desert Storm. The flow close air support system worked well in the Gulf War and provides a model for the future use of CAS. The A-10 in particular was devastating once the ground war began and once the aircraft dropped low enough to provide effective 30-mm cannon support.

The common theme in all five case studies presented here is the recurring inability of the side with the firepower advantage to find the enemy with sufficient timeliness and accuracy to exploit that advantage fully and efficiently. Even in the Gulf, where every technological and environmental circumstance favored the collection of targeting data, the intelligence system consistently came up short. All of the range, precision, and lethality that a firepower system brings to the battlefield cannot be fully exploited unless the eyes of the system can isolate the most lucrative targets within a target array, then pinpoint those targets to within a space smaller than the killing radius of a weapon, and deliver the weapon before the target moves or goes to ground.

To an infantryman seeking to kill the enemy, the source of the ordnance exploding to his front is irrelevant. He must receive the most effective munition when and where he needs it. He must be able to mix firepower from all sources and apply all fires in concert on targets appropriate to the unique capability of each munition. Experience in the Gulf seems to show that armed helicopters and long-range rocket artillery will lessen the problem of integrating aerial close support by assuming many of the more difficult close-in firepower tasks formerly reserved for Air Force fighter-bombers.

True flexibility in the orchestration of firepower will be achieved when a company commander or forward observer can talk routinely to a pilot or gun directing officer aboard a ship just as easily as he can converse with an Apache pilot or artillery fire support officer. Recent experience has shown that unnecessary and inefficient coordination and control slows response time, confuses instructions, denies or diverts essential firepower, and inevitably gets soldiers killed. Limited war experience indicates that a prudent fire support coordinator will array the firepower at his control to cover as much vulnerable and vital territory as possible. A force commander cannot allow too much of his available firepower to be tied down in area control. He must maintain a potent mobile reserve to be applied discretely in types and quantities appropriate to the target. He must be able to mass his firepower quickly if it is to have a destructive effect on an elusive enemy.

The survival of the ground force will be most dependent on a protective aerial umbrella above it during the earliest and most vulnerable phase of an intervention operation. Therefore, FACs and the air liaison element organic to a maneuver force must be particularly well equipped, capable of controlling aerial firepower, and must possess the technical capacity to deliver munitions close to friendly troops. The experience of the Falklands in particular has shown that, to be effective from the opening moments of a campaign, the agencies responsible for controlling and coordinating firepower cannot be last-minute add-ons. A maneuver force must practice with and be comfortable in the presence of air- and sea-delivered munitions. Knowledge of the use of these weapons must be passed to the lowest level within the firepower chain of command.

A fire support coordinator must know how much is enough. He must apply firepower not with the objective of relieving pressure on friendly infantry, but with the single purpose of destroying the enemy's ability and will to fight. He must be extravagant when the enemy is precisely located, exposed, or psychologically vulnerable. He must resist the temptation to fire for the sake of firing when the result clearly does not justify the expenditure. Decisions of this sort demand of a fire support coordinator far more than technical skill and knowledge of the systems at his command. He must study the enemy and his environment intimately, and he must be as aware as his maneuver commander of the intangible factors, the hidden strengths and frictions of battle, which are truer indicators of the types and quantities of firepower he must employ to win.

The balance between fire and maneuver in future limited war will be determined mainly by the specific nature of the war. In a small-scale war of intervention, tempo and speed will dictate that light, highly mobile infantry forces make up the majority of the force. Heavy firepower should come from weapons the infantry have with them: mortars for supporting local assaults and shoulder-fired missiles for taking out isolated centers of resistance. Firepower should be shifted and concentrated audaciously to capitalize on the fleeting but often decisive effect of psychological shock. In wars of intervention on the higher end of the intensity scale, firepower must be used lavishly to win quickly at minimum cost. In previous conflicts, most American casualties occurred in close combat, largely from artillery and mortar fire. In Korea, 82 percent of all casualties from all services were infantrymen. In Vietnam, a war supposedly without fronts, the figure was 65 percent. Close combat deaths were proportionately much lower in Desert Storm because combat soldiers possessed a tremendous firepower advantage. The lesson from the Gulf War is clear: In a high intensity war, firepower must break the enemy's will to resist before close combat begins. Firepower must so weaken the enemy that close-in killing by infantry and armored forces becomes a coup de grace rather than a bloody battle of attrition. We cannot allow the infantry and armor close battle to be a fair fight. Eye-to-eye combat is not a boxing match or a football game. Conflict with both sides evenly matched in firepower will only prolong the horror and cause needless friendly casualties.

Should the Army be obliged to fight another long-term battle of attrition, such as it did in Vietnam, large-scale applications of firepower on the order of Desert Storm would not be prudent and, especially for a low-level insurgency, probably unnecessary. Heavy mortars and helicopters are best suited for day-to-day operations against an unsophisticated insurgent. As the level of violence escalates, the margin of firepower superiority must keep pace, with a rational balance between static firepower for local defense and mobile firepower to support offensive operations. Bold strokes across the map mean little in such wars. Occasional maneuver by battalions is the practical limit. The purpose of supporting firepower should be to amplify the destructive power of a limited maneuver force and to protect it against catastrophic losses in the field.

An infantry force must retain the skill to fight with equal effectiveness in a maneuver- or a firepower-intensive tactical environment. A maneuver commander must be able to sense—from the enemy's character, his weapons, and his dispositions—which of the two will predominate. He must then array his force accordingly. In a maneuver environment, firepower weakens the enemy's will and permits the attacking force to seize the initiative without undue loss. Where firepower dominates, the infantry force finds and fixes the enemy so that firepower can do the killing.

Even should it predominate, firepower must never become such a burden that it keeps the maneuver force on a leash as short as the range of its own supporting fires. Such tactics may create favorable kill ratios, but, if pursued blindly, they may kill the dynamism and elan of the infantry and surrender initiative to the enemy. In future limited wars, air mobility, air-delivered firepower, and the extended killing zone permitted by precision guided missiles offer the greatest potential for allowing the maneuver force unlimited freedom of movement while operating in a firepower-intensive environment. General Kinnard's tactical philosophy, developed in the Carolinas and demonstrated at the Ia Drang, may yet come full circle thanks to modern technology. Fast, powerful helicopters and precision munitions will soon allow airmobile infantry to strike beyond the protective umbrella of fixed fire support, yet carry with it the capacity to destroy the enemy with firepower rather than manpower.

General Kinnard certainly did not neglect the element of maneuver at the Ia Drang. One could argue that the battle waged there, more than any other single event, served to elevate maneuver warfare into the third dimension. The helicopter gave Kinnard the means to leap soldiers over hundreds of kilometers of inhospitable terrain and concentrate them at the decisive point. Equally vital to Kinnard's success was his ability to transport firepower with his infantrymen and provide overwhelming support without inhibiting the flexibility or decisive effect of his maneuver forces. Many years later, when reflecting on the value of firepower to this revolutionary tactical method, General Kinnard emphasized that he never failed to expend all of his available firepower to support troops in combat. "When you have it, you use it. To do otherwise only risks the success of the operation and needlessly gets soldiers killed."[1]

Notes

Chapter 1 *Firepower in the American Way of War*

1. Colonel G. F. R. Henderson, *Stonewall Jackson and the American Civil War* (London: Longman Green and Co., 1978), p. 611.

2. General Dwight D. Eisenhower, *Crusade in Europe* (Garden City: Doubleday, 1948), p. 467.

3. Colonel S. L. A. Marshall, *Men Against Fire* (New York: William Morrow and Co., 1947), p. 191.

4. J. F. C. Fuller, *The Conduct of War, 1789–1961* (New Brunswick: Rutgers University Press, 1961), pp. 103–107.

5. Major General J. F. Maurice, *The Franco-German War, 1870–1871* (London: Swan Sonnerschein and Co., 1900), p. 137.

6. E. W. Lloyd and A. G. Hancock, *Artillery: Its Progress and Present Position* (Portsmouth: J. Griffin and Co., 1893), p. 283.

7. Germany, General Staff, *Drill Regulations of German Field Artillery* (London: H.M.S.O., 1893), p. 132. See also: Major von Rohne. ''Regulations of Fire in Masses of Artillery,'' *Proceedings of the Royal Artillery Institution* (XVI, 1889), p. 16.

8. Colonel H. A. Bethell, *Modern Guns and Gunnery* (Woolwich: Caltermon and Co., 1967), p. 51.

9. Russell F. Weigley, *History of the United States Army* (New York: McMillan Co., 1967), pp. 469–474.

10. Fletcher Pratt, *Eleven Generals: Studies in American Command* (New York: W. Sloan Associates, 1949), pp. 245–262.

11. Ibid., p. 256.

12. Len Deighton, *Blitzkrieg: From the Rise of Hitler to the Fall of Dunkirk* (New York: Alfred Knopf, 1979), pp. 159–169.

13. US Army, HQ VII Corps, *German Artillery: Lessons Learned from the European Theater, 1945* (Ft. Sill, OK: Morris Swett Technical Library), pp. 1–7. (Ft. Sill Library hereafter abbreviated as MSTL).

14. US Army, Ground Forces Board, *German Experiences with Massed Field Artillery Units* (HQ, European Theater of Operations, 1945), MSTL, pp. 2–9.

15. Weigley, pp. 469–474.

16. Ibid., p. 464.

17. Historical Division, HQ US Army Europe, Foreign Military Studies Branch interview with Officers from II Parachute Corps, 6 June–24 Jul 1944, MS B–261; "Operations of the 3rd Falschirmjaeger Division during the Invasion in France, June–August 1944," MS B541. Both documents from the Military History Research Collection, Carlisle Barracks, PA (hereafter abbreviated as MHRC).

18. Weigley, p. 474.

19. Thomas H. Greer, *The Development of Air Doctrine, 1917–1941* (Washington DC: US Air Force Historical Division), pp. 89–101.

20. Joint Staff Task Force, *Close Air Support Study, Phase II, History of Close Air Support Command and Control* Vol. III, Part I, Chapter 3 (MHRC), p. AF14.

21. Kent Robert Greenfield, *Army Ground Forces and the Air-Ground Battle Team* (Historical Section, Army Ground Forces, 1948), Armed Forces Staff College Library, p. 77.

22. Talk by Air Vice Marshal Sir A. Coningham to Assembled British and American General and Senior Officers, Tripoli, 16 February, 1943 (Washington DC: Office of Air Force History Document Collection, hereafter abbreviated as USAF Document Collection).

23. Interview with Brigadier General Laurence S. Kuter, 25 May 1943, a Compilation of Selected Extracts and Quotes, October 1943 (USAF Document Collection).

24. Greenfield, *Air-Ground Battle Team*, p. 81.

25. The best explanation of the streamlined air-to-ground communications system can be found in: AAF Evaluation Board, *Report on Tactical Air Cooperation and Organization; Methods and Procedures of IX, XIX and XXIX Tactical Air Commands and 9th Air Division with Emphasis on Phase III Operations, 31 July 1945* (USAF Document Collection), pp. 116–125.

26. General Omar N. Bradley, *Effect of Airpower on Military Operations, Western Europe* (12th Army Group, Air Branches G–3 and G–2, 15 July 1945) Armed Forces Staff College Library, p. 43.

27. Ibid., p. 44.

28. Ibid., p. 42.

29. Greenfield, *Air-Ground Battle Team*, p. 90.

30. Ibid., p. 47.

31. Ibid., p. 92.

32. Bradley, *Effect on Airpower*, p. 22.

33. Ibid., p. 22.

34. Riley Sunderland, *Evolution of Command and Control Doctrine for Close Air Support* (Office of Air Force History, HQ, USAF 1973), p. 180.

35. Robert F. Futrell, *The United States Air Force in Korea, 1950–1953* (Washington DC: Office of Air Force History, 1983), pp. 471–474. See also: Walter S. Hermes, *Truce Tent and Fighting Front* (Washington DC: Office of the Chief of Military History, 1966), pp. 192–198.

36. Hermes, *Truce Tent*, p. 509.

37. Russell A. Gugeler, *Combat Actions in Korea* (Office of the Chief of Military History, 1970), p. 180.

38. Edward M. Almond Papers, in box marked "Korean War, Army Tactical Air Support, X Corps:" Copy of lecture given to Field Artillery Officers Advanced Course, 1954 (MHRC), p. 8.

39. Ibid., p. 6.

40. Headquarters X Corps, "Army Tactical Air Support Requirements and Trends in Air-Ground Methods, 25 December 1950" (Almond Papers, MHRC), p. 2.

41. Hermes, *Truce Tent*, p. 327.

42. US Air Force, Historical Division, *United States Air Force Operations in the Korean Conflict, 1 November 1950–9 June 1952, USAF Historical Study No. 72*, (Maxwell AFB: Air University, 1953), pp. 201–204.

43. Ibid., pp. 193–196.

44. Sunderland, *Evolution*, pp. 27–30.

45. Almond Papers in box marked "Korean War, Army Tactical Air Support, X Corps:" "The Interval Between Request by Units in X Corps for Air Support and Actual Strike during Period 10 May–12 June 1951," (MHRC).

46. HQ X Corps, *Army Tactical Air Support*, pp. 76–77.

47. Hermes, *Truce Tent*, p. 325.

48. Ibid., p. 385.

49. US Army Combat Developments Command, *Dynamics of Fire and Maneuver (FIRMA III)*, 15 August 1969 (DTIC No. AD857809), p. 17.

50. This short history of early Army efforts to develop an armed helicopter is taken from: LTG John J. Tolson, *Airmobility, 1961–1971, Vietnam Studies* (Washington: HQ, Department of the Army, 1973), pp., 1–16.

51. US Army Concept Team in Vietnam, *Armed Helicopters: Escort of Transport Helicopters, 15 November 1964* (MHRC), pp. 1–48.

52. Tolson, *Airmobility*, p. 34.

53. William A. Becker, "DivArty Fullback," *United States Army Aviation Digest* (July, 1965), pp. 2–5.

54. Interview with LTG (ret) Harry W. O. Kinnard, 16 November, 1984.

Chapter 2 *The First Indochina War*

1. The story of Colonel Piroth's suicide is taken from two excellent sources: Bernard Fall, *Hell in a Very Small Place* (New York: J. B. Lippincott Company, 1966), pp. 151–157; and Jules Roy, *The Battle of Dien Bien Phu* (New York: Harper and Row, 1963), pp,. 170–175.

2. Edgar O'Ballance, *The Indochina War, 1945–1954* (London: Faber and Faber, 1964), pp. 49–54.

3. Ibid., p. 76.

4. An excellent summary of the early days of the war from a tactical perspective can be found in Ronald Spector, *Advice and Support: The Early Years, 1941–1960* (Washington DC: Center for Military History, 1983), pp. 8–90.

5. The Supreme Command, Far East, *Lessons from the Indo-China War,* Volume II (DTIC Number AD 804376L, 1955), pp. 74–97.

6. Colonel V. J. Croizat (USMC Ret.), *A Translation from the French, Lessons of the War in Indo-China,* Volume 2 (Santa Monica: The RAND Corporation, Memorandum RM-5271-PR, May 1967), pp. 81–90. Note: Croizat was commissioned to translate the original French "after-action reports" during the height of the US buildup in Vietnam. His translation contains much of the same material found in the two original translations done by the US Government in 1955 and cited in this chapter under DTIC notations. All three works are available either through DTIC or RAND Corporation.

7. *Lessons from the Indo-China War,* Volume II, p. 82.

8. *Lessons from the Indo-China War,* Volume II, p. 12.

9. US Army Concept Team in Vietnam, *Employment of Artillery in Counterinsurgency Operations* (DTIC Number AD 363667, 1965), p. 1.

10. *Lessons from the Indo-China War,* Volume II, p. 40.

11. Croizat, *Translation,* pp. 69–72.

12. Ibid., pp. 73–74.

13. PK 141 stood for "kilometer post," followed by the number of kilometers between the fort and the point of origin, usually Hanoi. Fall, *Street Without Joy,* p. 177.

14. George K. Tanham, *Communist Revolutionary Warfare* (New York: Frederick A. Praeger, 1961), p. 86.

15. *Lessons from the Indo-China War,* Volume III, p. 93.

16. Tanham, *Warfare,* p. 87.

17. *Lessons from the Indo-China War,* Volume III, p. 92.

18. Ibid., p. 11.

19. Ibid., p. 23.

20. Tanham, *Warfare,* p. 88.

21. *Lessons from the Indo-China War,* Volume II, p. 39.

22. Croizat, *Translation,* p. 343.

23. *Lessons from the Indo-China War,* Volume II, p. 52.

24. Croizat, *Translation,* p. 86.

25. Ibid., p. 275.

26. Fall, *Street Without Joy,* p. 180.

27. *Lessons from the Indo-China War,* Volume II, p. 20.

28. Ibid., p. 20.

29. Fall, *Street Without Joy,* p. 32.

30. Bernard Fall, *The Two Vietnams—A Political and Military Analysis* (New York: Frederick A. Praeger, 1967), p. 115.

31. *Lessons from the Indo-China War,* Volume II, p. 167.

32. Ibid., p. 160.

33. Tanham, *Warfare,* pp. 101–102.

34. Fall, *Street Without Joy,* pp. 61–63.

35. Ibid., p. 59.

36. The details of French firepower doctrine summarized in this section are taken from Commander-in-Chief, Indo-China, Artillery Inspectorate, *Instruction Relative to the Use of Intervention (Mobile) Artillery in Indo-China, 31 January 1953* (DTIC Number AD 804374), pp. 1–41. This document was written by a committee of French artillery officers to provide a uniform regulation for mobile group artillery.

37. Croizat, *Translation,* pp. 244–258.

38. Ibid., p. 245.

39. *Lessons from the Indo-China War,* Volume III, pp. 60–63.

40. Lucien Bodard, *The Quicksand War: Prelude to Vietnam* (Boston: Little Brown and Company, 1968), p. 42.

41. Letter from MG Trapnell to the Secretary of Defense, dated 9 March 1954, contained as an appendix to "The FEAF Staff Study on Indochina" (Washington DC: Office of Air Force History Document Collection).

42. Headquarters, Military Assistance Command, Vietnam, "Strategic and Tactical Study of Khe Sanh," 8 March 1968, Annex A, page 5. (MHRC, Carlisle Barracks, PA).

43. *Lessons from the Indo-China War,* Volume II, p. 295.

44. Ibid., p. 297.

45. Ibid., p. 296.

46. Croizat, *Translation,* p. 341.

47. Ibid., p. 340.

48. *The Use of Intervention Artillery,* pp. 1–5.

49. Ibid., p. 25.

50. Project CHECO, *Close Air Support (In an Environment Devoid of Opposing Airpower) 18 May 1965* (Office of USAF History Document Collection), p. 2.

51. Letter from BG Albert G. Hewitt to the Secretary of Defense, 6 April 1954, contained as an Appendix to "The FEAF Staff Study on Indochina" (Office of USAF History Document Collection).

52. Fall, *Street Without Joy,* p. 35.

53. Ibid., pp. 36–39.

54. Bodard, *The Quicksand War,* p. 246.

55. Fall, *Street Without Joy,* p. 37.

56. Ibid., p. 40.

57. Ibid., p. 38.

58. Ibid., pp. 41–43.

59. Strategic and Tactical Study, p. A5.

60. *Lessons from the Indo-China War,* Volume II, p. 300.

61. *Lessons from the Indo-China War,* Volume III, p. 11.

62. Ibid., p. 20.

63. Fall, *Street Without Joy,* p. 79.

64. *Lessons from the Indo-China War,* Volume III, p. 21.

65. Fall, *Street Without Joy,* p. 105.

66. *Lessons from the Indo-China War,* Volume III, p. 92.

67. Ibid., p. 38.

68. J. R. Lind and K. Harris, *FASTVAL: A Briefing on Implications for the Use of Airpower in Close Support of Ground Actions* (Santa Monica: The RAND Corporation, 1968), p. 8.

69. *Lessons from the Indo-China War,* Volume III, p. 40.

70. Croizat, *Translation,* p. 335; and US Army Combat Developments Command, *Combat Operations Loss and Expenditure Data-Vietnam, Appendix C to Year End Report, FY 1969* (DTIC Number AD 508539), Section A.

71. *Lessons from the Indo-China War,* Volume II, p. 291.

72. Croizat, *Translation,* p. 335; and General William W. Momyer, *Air Power in Three Wars* (Washington DC, Government Printing Office, 1978), p. 310.

73. *Lessons from the Indo-China War,* Volume III, p. 58.

74. Croizat, *Translation,* p. 221.

75. *Lessons from the Indo-China War,* Volume III, p. 220.

76. O'Ballance, *The Indo-China War,* pp. 184–186.

77. Strategic and Tactical Study, Annex A.

78. Ibid., p. A2.

79. Fall, *Hell in a Very Small Place,* p. 480.

80. Strategic and Tactical Study, p. A4.

81. Ibid., pp. D–1 thorugh D–5.

82. Trip Report, "Visit to Dien Bien Phu, 9 March 1954," by Captain Robert W. Hickey and Captain Robert M. Floyd, "The FEAF Staff Study on Indochina" (Office of USAF History Document Collection), p. 8.

83. Strategic and Tactical Study, p. B–4–1.

84. Robert F. Futrell, *The United States Air Force in Southeast Asia: The Advisory Years to 1965* (Washington: Office of Air Force History, 1981), p. 17.

85. Tanham, *Warfare,* pp. 107–108.

86. Fall, *Hell in a Very Small Place,* p. 351.

87. Futrell, *The United States Air Force,* p. 19.

88. Fall, *Street Without Joy,* pp. 263–264.

89. Strategic and Tactical Study, p. A–7.

90. Trip Report by Captain Hickey.

91. Strategic and Tactical Study, p. A–7.

92. *Lessons from the Indo-China War,* Volume II, p. 35.

93. *Lessons from the Indo-China War,* Volume III, p. 38.

94. Futrell, *The United States Air Force,* p. 23.

95. Fall, *Street Without Joy,* p. 264.

96. Fall, *Hell in a Very Small Place,* pp. 377–378.

97. Ibid., p. 368.
98. Strategic and Tactical Study, p. A–9.

Chapter 3 *The Second Indochina War*

1. The narrative of the seige at Plei Me Special Forces Camp is taken from two excellent sources: Major Melvin F. Porter, *The Siege at Plei Me* (HQ PACAF Tactical Evaluation Center, Project CHECO, 24 February 1966); "How Plei Me Survived," *Newsweek*, (8 November 1965), p. 43. The following story of the Battle for the Ia Drang is taken mainly from a personal interview with LTG (Ret) Harry W. O. Kinnard, 16 November 1984. Specific details of the Ia Drang Valley, to include the accompanying illustration, are from Headquarters, 1st Cavalry Division (Airmobile), *The Plei Ku Campaign, December 1965* (Morris Swett Technical Library, Ft. Sill, OK) (Hereafter abbreviated MSTL); Headquarters, 1st Battalion, 7th Cavalry, *After Action Report, Ia Drang Valley Operation, 14–16 November 1965*; LTG Harry W. O. Kinnard, "A Victory in the Ia Drang: The Triumph of a Concept," *Army*, (September 1967), pp. 71–91; Alexander S. Cochran, Jr., "First Strike at River Drang," *Military History* (October 1984) pp. 44–51; "Fury at Ia Drang: Now the Regulars," *Newsweek* (November 29, 1965), pp. 21–24; *Time* (3 December 1965), pp. 30–31.
2. Robert Shaplen, *The Lost Revolution* (New York: Harper and Row, 1966), p.48.
3. HQ, Military Assistance Command, Vietnam, *Operations Report—Lessons Learned No. 6–67: Observations of a Brigade Commander* (MSTL), p. 11.
4. Ibid., p. 11.
5. General William Depuy Papers. Statement by General Depuy contained in Section VI (MHRC), p. 2. See also: HQ, 1st Infantry Division Regulation 350–1, dated 15 March 1966 (MSTL).
6. Ibid., p. 2; see also, Headquarters, 4th Infantry Division, *Battle for Dak To, Inclosure 7, Combat Operations After Action Report, 173rd Airborne Brigade (Separate)* (DTIC No. AD 390643), p.42.
7. LTC William J. Buchanon and LTC Robert A. Hyatt, "Guerrilla Vulnerabilities," *Army Magazine* (August 1968), p. 31.
8. *Observations of a Brigade Commander*, p. 11.
9. LTC Boyd Bashore, "The Name of the Game is Search and Destroy," *Army Magazine* (February 1967), pp. 56–59.
10. US Army Combat Developments Command, *Dynamics of Fire and Maneuver, Final Report, 15 August 1968* (DTIC No. AC 857809),
p. 26.
11. Several excellent examples (both good and bad) of American units assaulting fortified positions can be found in: US Military Assistance Command, Vietnam, *Attack of Fortified Positions in the Jungle, Seminar Report,*

2 January 1968 (DTIC No. AD 844097) pp. 4–16; Also see: *Dynamics of Fire and Maneuver*, p. 26; *Observations of a Brigade Commander*, p.12.

12. Bashore, *Name of the Game*, p. 58.

13. Ibid., p. 57.

14. *Dynamics of Fire and Manuever*, p. II–213.

15. Ibid., p.II–217.

16. Personal interview with Colonel (Ret) C. K. Nulsen, 3 January 1985.

17. LTC Charles K. Nulsen, *The Use of Firepower in Counterinsurgency Operations, Student Essay* (Carlisle: U.S. Army War College, 2 December 1968), p.3.

18. Colonel Charles K. Nulsen, *Advising as a Prelude to Command, Student Essay* (Carlisle: U.S. Army War College, 28 February 1969), p. 18.

19. Ibid., pp. 19–20.

20. Nulsen, *The Use of Firepower*, p. 3.

21. Colonel David H. Hackworth, "Guerrilla Battalion, U.S. Style," *A Distant Challenge* (Birmingham: Infantry Magazine, 1971), p. 258.

22. George McArthur, "Screaming Eagles Sharpen Claws with New Tactics," *New York World Journal Tribune*, (5 February 1967),
p. 23.

23. Ibid., p., 23.

24. Alexander S.Cochran Jr., "First Strike at River Drang," *Military History*, (October 1984), p. 50.

25. *Attack of Fortified Positions*, p. 35.

26. US Army Combat Development Command, *Senior Officer Debriefing Report: Colonel E. F. Gudgel Jr., Commanding Officer, II Field Force Vietnam Artillery, Period 15 June 1970 through 18 January 1971* (MSTL), p. 5.

27. Ibid., p. 5.

28. Information Packet for BG John J. Kennedy, Subject: Heavy Artillery Study, 18 December 1967 (MSTL); See also: Shelby Stanton, *Vietnam Order of Battle* (Washington DC: U.S. News Books, 1981), pp., 95–108.

29. US Army Combat Development Command, *Combat Operations Loss and Expenditures Data, Vietnam, Volume III: Ammunition Expenditures and Losses, FY 1969* (DTIC Number AD 508539).

30. Brief synopsis of artillery doctrine in Vietnam is taken from US Army Concept Team in Vietnam, *Organization and Employment of U.S. Army Field Artillery Units in RVN, October 1969* (MSTL) Volume II, Annex F.

31. Ibid., p. II–17.

32. Department of the Army. *Field Manual (FM) 6–40, Field Artillery Gunnery, 1967* (MSTL), p. 35.

33. *Organization and Employment*, p. II–14.

34. Ibid., p. II–9.

35. Letter from BG William R.Wolfe to BG Lawrence Caruthers dated 24 August 1970 contained in file titled "Responsiveness of FA in the Republic of Vietnam," (MSTL).

36. Headquarters, 1st Cavalry Division (Airmobile) *Lessons Learned, 10 October–30 November 1965* (MSTL), p. 5.

37. US Military Assistance Command Vietnam, "The Forward Observer of the Big Red One," *Operational Report of Headquarters, II Field Force Vietnam Artillery for Period Ending 31 January 1969* (MSTL), p. 33.

38. US Military Assistance Command, Vietnam, *Vietnam Lessons Learned No. 77: Fire Support Coordination in the Republic of Vietnam, 20 May 1970* (MSTL), p. A–6.

39. US Army Concept Team in Vietnam, *Reduction of Reaction Time to Engage Enemy Targets, July 1970* (ACTIV Project No. ACG 68F), pp. VI–1 through VI–4.

40. Ibid., p. V–10.

41. *Organization and Employment*, Annex I: Clearance of Fire—Principles.

42. US Military Assistance Command, Vietnam, *Operations Report, Lessons Learned: Report 1–68.* (MSTL), p. 19.

43. Headquarters, 1st Cavalry Division, *Critique of Operation Clean Sweep, 17–30 December 1965* (MSTL).

44. Headquarters, 101st Airborne Division Artillery, *Operational Report for Period Ending 30 April 1968* (MSTL), p. 9.

45. "The Forward Observer of the Big Red One," p. 33.

46. Military Assistance Command, Vietnam, *Counterinsurgency Lessons Learned Number 58: Operation Happy Valley, 20 June 1966* (MSTL), p. 17.

47. LTC Charles R. Shrader, *Amicide: The Problem of Friendly Fire in Modern War* (Ft. Leavenworth: Combat Studies Institute, 1982), p. 23.

48. US Military Assistance Command, Vietnam, *Operations Report, Lessons Learned: Report 1–67* (MSTL), p. 25.

49. *Operations Report, Lessons Learned: Report 1–67* (MSTL), pp. 1–6; See also *Organization and Employment*, p. IV–36.

50. Undated Memo for Commanding General, I. Field Force Vietnam Artillery titled: "Effectiveness of Artillery," (MSTL). See also: Military Assistance Command, Vietnam, *Operations Report, Lessons Learned, 2nd Battalion, 13th Field Artillery for the Period Ending 31 July 1966* (MSTL), p. 2.

51. Colonel Lloyd J. Picou, "Artillery Support," *Military Review* (October 1968), pp. 4–8.

52. *Reduction of Reaction Time to Engage Enemy Targets*, p. 38.

53. Tolson, *Airmobility*, p. 33.

54. Letter from MG John J. Hennessey, CG 101st Airborne Division to BG Stewart C. Meyer, CG XXIV Corps Artillery, dated 31 October 1970, (MSTL).

55. Picou, "Artillery Support," p. 47.

56. Tolson, *Airmobility*, pp. 32–34.

57. Hennessey letter.

58. The effect of tree blow-down from Air Force bombs is described in isolated combat examples throughout: *The Battle for Dak To*, Enclosures 3–5.

59. Tolson, *Airmobility*, pp. 144–146.

60. David W. P. Elliot, *Documents of an Elite Viet Cong Delta Unit: The Demolition Platoon of the 514th Battalion—Part One: Unit Composition and Personnel* (RAND Corporation: Memorandum RM–5850–1SA May 1969); See also: Richard G. Johnson. *Viet Cong Perceptions of the Relative Effectiveness of US/GVN Aerial and Ground Combat Power* (Student Research Report, Command and General Staff College, 1967), p. 18.

61. In a study conducted by Air Force students at the Army War College in 1970, returning infantry and armor commanders preferred the gunship four-to-one over its nearest fixed-wing competitor: Colonel Walter H. Baxter (et. al.), *An Analysis of Tactical Airpower in Support of the United States Army in Vietnam* (Carlisle Barracks: US Army War College Student Research Paper, 1970), p. 124.

62. US Army Combat Developments Command, *Debriefings of Vietnam Returnees, Command Summary: Statement of an Air Troop Commander* (MSTL), p. 2.

63. Letter from LTG A. S. Collins, HQ, IFFV, to MG Roderick Wetherill, dated 20 October 1970 (Collins Papers, MHRC).

64. LTC William R. Fails, *Marines and Helicopters, 1962–73* (Historical and Museums Division, HQ, USMC, 1978), p. 111.

65. The BDM Corporation, *A Study of Strategic Lessons Learned in Vietnam, Volume VI, Conduct of the War, Book 2* (DTIC Number ADA 096429), pp. 11–58.

66. LTG William W. Momyer, *Air Power in Three Wars* (Washington DC: GPO, 1978), p. 229.

67. US Congress. House. Committee on Armed Services, *Close Air Support*. H. Report. 1965, 89th Congress, 2nd Session, 1965 (Washington: GPO, 1966), pp. 4862–4864.

68. Ibid., p. 4864.

69. US Congress, *Close Air Support*, p. 4861.

70. Personal correspondence with Mr. John Schlight, Chief Historian, Southeast Asia Branch, Center for Military History, Washington, DC, 10 July 1985.

71. Major Rudolf F. Wacker, "Close Air Support: The View from the Cockpit," *Army Magazine*, (July 1970), pp. 17–25. Alfred Goldberg and Lt. Col. Donald Smith, *Army-Air Force Relations: The Close Air Support Issue* (Santa Monica: The RAND Corporation, Report R–906–PR), pp. 30–31.

72. Maj. John p. O'Gorman, "Battles and Bloody Maneuver: A View From the Cockpit," *Air University Review* (vol. 18, No. 6, September–October 1967), p. 25.

73. LTC Ralph A. Rowley, *The Air Force in Southeast Asia: Tactics and Techniques of Close Air Support Operations 1961–1973* (Office of Air Force History, 1976), p. 68.

74. Colonel Robert E. Buhrow, *Close Air Support Requirements: A Study in Inter-Service Rivalry* (Carlisle: US Army War College, 1971), p. 25.

75. Jack S. Ballard, *Development and Employment of Fixed-Wing Gunships, 1962–1972* (Office of Air Force History, 1982), pp. 1–27.

76. Captain Melvin F. Porter, *The Defense of Attopeu* (Project CHECO, HQ PACAF Tactical Evaluation Center, 16 May 1966) statement by Colonel James P. Hagerstrom, p. 10.

77. Ibid., p. 10.

78. Joint Staff Task Force, *Close Air Support Study, Vol III, Part I, History of Close Air Support Command and Control* (MHRC), p. AF 126.

79. Momyer, *Air Power in Three Wars*, p.269.

80. US Army Military Assistance Command Vietnam, *Fire Support Coordination: Lessons Learned Number 77* (DTIC No. AD 509994), p. C–20.

81. Ibid., pp. C3–C17.

82. Momyer, *Air Power in Three Wars*, p. 227.

83. Joint Task Force, *Close Air Support*, p. AF 127.

84. Mr. William Greene, et. al. *Tactical Air Support in South Vietnam, Oct–Nov 1966* (Headquarters, USAF, Combat Analysis Division, AFGOA Report 67–7), p. 3; See also: Army Concept Team in Vietnam, *Reduction of Reaction Time to Engage Enemy Targets* (ACTIV Project No,. ACG–68F, July 1970), p. V–100.

85. Rowley, *The Air Force in Southeast Asia*, p. 63.

86. Edward M. Almond Papers, Document titled: "Time Interval Between Request by Units in X Corps for Air Support and Actual Strike During the Period 10 May–12 June 1951," in box: "Korean War, Army Tactical Air Support, X Corps," (MHRC), p. 1; See also: S. H. Turkel, *Close Air Support, Volume II: Background and Evaluation of Developments and Operations* (Culver City: Hughes Aircraft Company, 1962), p. 80.

87. Office of the Vice Chief of Staff, USAF, *Forward Air Controller Operations, July–August 1968* (HQ, USAF, Combat Analysis Division, December 1968), p. V–12.

88. Headquarters, 173rd Airborne Brigade, *After Action Report, Operation Hump, 15 November 1965* (MSTL), p. 9.

89. Personal interview with LTG (Ret) H. O. Kinnard, 15 November 1984.

90. Thomas C. Thayer, *A Systems Analysis View of the Vietnam War, 1965–1972, Volume 5: The Air War* (Washington: US Army Library, The Pentagon, 1973), p. 118.

91. Raphael Littauer and Norman Uphoff (ed.), *The Air War in Indochina* (Boston: Beaver Press), p. 26.

92. Thayer, *The Air War*, p. 119.

93. *Organizational and Employment*, p. IV–43.

94. Senior Officer Debriefing Report, *Colonel E. F. Gudgel*, p. 2.

95. An early example of the frustration felt by units first in combat as they attempted to coordinate ground and aircraft fires is found in Headquarters, Department of the Army, 173rd Airborne Brigade (separate) *Commanders Combat Note Number 67, 14 July 1965*, (MSTL), p. 3.

96. *Organization and Employment*, Annex I; see also US Army Combat Developments Command, *Senior Officer Debriefing Report: BG Richard A. Edwards, CG, I Field Force Artillery, for the Period 11 August 1968 to 16 March 1969* (MSTL), p. 2; *Reduction of Reaction Time*, Annex I.

97. Letter from LTC Lee Surut to MG Harry Critz, 18 February 1966 (MSTL).

98. Letter from Colonel Edward Grudgel Jr. to MG R. Wetherill, Subject: Responsiveness of FA in the Republic of Vietnam, 7 October 1970, (MSTL).

99. US Army Combat Developments Command, *Senior Officer Debriefing Report: MG George I Forsythe, CG, 1st Cavalry Division (Airmobile), for the Period 19 August to 23 April 1969* (MSTL), p. 54.

100. Ibid., p. 54.

101. Ibid., p. 51.

102. US Army Artillery and Missile School, *Reference Note T 3200,* March 1967 (MSTL), p. 19.

103. Letter from Colonel Richard M. Winfield, Jr. to BG Lawrence Caruthers, Subject: Responsiveness of FA in the Republic of Vietnam, 28 August 1970 (MSTL).

104. *Forsythe Debriefing Report,* p. 55; Colonel Harold A. Dye, "Close Fire Support," *Military Review* (Vol. XLVII, September 1967), pp. 36–43.

105. *Forsythe Debriefing Report,* p. 56.

106. Rene Filipe Larriwa, *The Attack of a Target with the Simultaneous Use of Air and Artillery* (Monterey: Naval Postgraduate School, 1973) p. 8.

107. LTC George M. Shuffer Jr., "Finish Them with Firepower," *Military Review* (Vol. XLVII, October 1967), pp. 11–15; See also: Headquarters, 1st Infantry Division, *Operations Report Lessons Learned for the Period 1 October to 31 December 1965* (MSTL), p. 1.

108. Letters from Colonel John Cooper to Colonel Edward F. Gudgel Jr. addressing Artillery Responsiveness, 30 September 1970 (MSTL).

109. *Fire Support Coordination in RVN,* p. C–33.

110. Letter, Cooper to Gudgel.

111. Personal interview with LTG (Ret) Kinnard, 16 November 1984.

112. Statement by Colonel Mc Allister, Division Artillery Commander, 4th Infantry Division contained in file titled: "Survey of Al McArthur (Dak To)," correspondence received from I Field Force Vietnam Artillery, June 1968 (MSTL), p. 3.

113. Nulsen, Kinnard inteviews; See also: Headquarters Military Assistance Command, Vietnam, *Operations Report, Lessons Learned Number 4–67 "Observations of a Battalion Commander,"* (MSTL), p. 18.

114. Thomas C. Thayer, *A Systems Analysis View of the Vietnam War 1965–1972, Vol IV, Allied Ground and Naval Operations* (Washington: US Army Library, the Pentagon, 1973), p. 208.

115. *Joint Munitions Effectiveness Manual (Surface to Surface),* Effectiveness Data for Howitzer, 105 mm, M101A1 (Army FM 101–60–2) dated 8 March 1978, Section II: Data for Projectile, HE, M1.

116. J. R. Lind, *FASTVAL: A Look at Close Support: A Briefing on the Contributions of Air Power and Artillery in a Fire Fight* (RAND: Santa Monica, March 1968), p. 9.

117. Ibid., p. 8.

118. *Organization and Employment*, p. II–22.

119. Headquarters, 54th Field Artillery Group, *Operational Report, Lessons Learned for Period Ending 1969* (MSTL), pp. 12–15.

120. Headquarters, US Army Vietnam, *Senior Officer Debriefing Report: LTG W. R. Peers, CG, 4th Infantry Division; CG, I Field Force Vietnam, Period 1967–1968* (DTIC Number 502432), p. 6.

121. Information provided by the Threat Branch, Directorate of Combat Developments, US Army Field Artillery School, Ft. Sill, OK.

122. Interview with LTG David Ott, 28 August 1980, as part of the Senior Officer Debriefing Program, US Army War College. (Bound transcript contained in Military History Research Collection Archives, Carlisle Barracks, PA), p. 29.

123. Based on the area coverage provided by a battery of light howitzers fired from a "star" formation. See: *Organization and Employment*, p. II–18.

124. Military Assistance Command, Vietnam, *Counterinsurgency Lessons Learned Number 59: Employment of Image Intensification Devices, 13 July 1966* (MSTL), pp. 1–7.

125. US Army, Vietnam *Operation Report, Lessons Learned 9–66, 27 December 1966* (MSTL), pp. 7–9.

126. Francis J. West, *Small Unit Actions in Vietnam: Summer 1966* (Washington DC: History and Museums Division, HQ, USMC, 1967), pp. 59–67.

127. Thayer, *Ground Operations*, p. 37.

128. Headquarters, 1st Brigade 101st Airborne Division, *Operational Report, Lessons Learned for the Period Ending 31 December 1966* (MSTL), p. 2.

129. W. Scott Thompson and Donaldson O. Frizzell, *The Lessons of Vietnam* (New York: Crane, Russak and Company, 1977), p. 129. Statement by Francis J. West.

130. *Peers Debriefing Report*, p. 6.

131. Ibid., p. 6; See also Thayer, *The Ground War*, p. 37.

132. *Organization and Employment*, p. III–18.

133. Military Assistance Command, Vietnam, *Vietnam Lessons Learned Number 71: Countermeasures Against Standoff Attacks, 13 March 1969* (DTIC Number AD 501615), p. 53; See also: Headquarters, 1st Infantry Division Artillery, *Operational Report, Lessons Learned for the Period Ending 31 October 1968* (MSTL), p. 3.

134. Headquarters, Ninth Infantry Division Artillery, *Operational Report, Lessons Learned Period Ending 31 July 1985* (MSTL), pp. 2–9.

135. Headquarters, US Army Combat Developments Command, *Senior Officer Debriefing Report: MG Ellis W. Williamson: CDC Presentation on Vietnam Experience, Ft. Belvoir VA, 8 December 1969* (MSTL), pp. 2–3.

136. Ibid., p. 2.

137. Headquarters, US Continental Army Command, *CONARC Report— Sensor Program in the Republic of Vietnam, 27 February 1970* (MSTL), pp. 1–3.

138. Ibid., p. 5.

139. Headquarters, II Field Force Vietnam Artillery, *Lessons Learned for the Period from 21 May 1969 to 20 November 1969* (MSTL), p. 3.

140. An illustrative example of such a battle was the Loc Ninh Campaign fought by the 1st Infantry Division October–November 1967. See LTG John H. Hay, Jr., *Tactical and Materiel Innovation* (Washington: Chief of Military History, 1972), pp. 42–56.

141. BDM, *Strategic Lessons*, p. III–95.

142. Ibid., p. III–102.

143. Ibid., p. III–96.

144. Ibid., p. III–110.

145. Ibid., p. III–101.

146. Thompson and Frizzell, *Lessons of Vietnam*, pp. 137–138.

147. Bernard C. Nalty, *Air Power and the Siege of Khe Sanh* (Washington: Office of Air Force History, 1973), p. 93.

148. BDM, *Strategic Lessons, Book 2: Functional Analysis,* p. IX–27.

149. Captain Moyers S. Shore II, *The Battle for Khe Sanh* (Washington: Historical Branch, G–3 Division, HQ USMC, 1969), p. 107.

150. Nalty, *Air Power*, p. 84.

151. Ibid., p. 86.

152. Ibid., p. 88.

153. Headquarters, Military Assistance Command, Vietnam, *Strategic and Tactical Study of Khe Sanh, 8 March 1968, Annex E (Aerial Firepower)*, p. E–2. This study was commissioned by General Westmoreland during The Battle for Khe Sanh for the purpose of comparing Khe Sanh with Dien Bien Phu. The original copy can be found in the Military History Research Collection, Carlisle Barracks, PA.

154. BDM, *A Study of Strategic Lessons Learned*, p. III–102; see also LTG David E. Ott, *Field Artillery 1954–73, Vietnam Studies* (Washington: Office of the Chief of Military History, 1975), p. 151.

155. Shore, *The Battle for Khe Sanh*, p. 93.

156. Nalty, *Air Power*, p. 75.

157. Ibid., p. 73. LTG Momyer disagrees with the nature of the problem. He blames the lack of centralized control. See Momyer *Air Power in Three Wars*, p. 309.

158. Shore, *The Battle for Khe Sanh*, p. 93.

159. Nalty, *Air Power*, pp. 90–92.

160. Shore, p. *The Battle for Khe Sanh*, p. 109.

161. Ibid., pp. 128–130.

162. Ibid., pp. 124–126.

163. Momyer, *Air Power in Three Wars*, p. 309.

164. MG W. R. Peers, "Erosion of NVA Potential," *Pamphlet prepared for Headquarters, I Field Force, Vietnam, 15 April 1968* (MSTL).

165. Thomas C. Thayer, *A Systems Analysis View of the Vietnam War, Volume III: Viet Cong—North Vietnamese Operations, 1965–73* (Washington: Army Library, Pentagon, 1973), p. 16.

166. *Vietnam Lessons Learned Number 71: Countermeasures Against Standoff Attacks*, p. 33.

167. Ibid., pp. 22–32.

168. HQ US Army Combat Developments Command, *Report: Sensor Program in the Republic of Vietnam, 27 February 1970*, (MSTL), p. 5.

169. Thayer, *VC–NVA Operations*, p. 18.

170. MG Spurgeon Neel, *Medical Support of the U.S. Army in Vietnam, 1965–1970. Vietnam Studies* (Washington DC: Chief of Military History, 1973), p. 53.

171. Military Assistance Command, Vietnam, *Vietnam Lessons Learned Number 4–67: Observations of a Battalion Commander, 7 January 1967* (MSTL), pp. 1–3.

172. *Organization and Employment*, p.IV–28.

173. US Mission in Vietnam, *The Impact of the Sapper on the Vietnam War: A Background Paper* (Saigon: October 1969), pp. 14–15. Booklet contained in National Defense University Library; see also: Headquarters, XXIV Corps, *Lessons Learned—Defense Against Sapper Attacks, 14 March 1969* (MSTL), pp. 1–2.

174. David W.P. Elliot, *Documents of an Elite Viet Cong Delta Unit: The Demolition Platoon of the 514th Battalion, Part Four: Political Indoctrination and Military Training* (Santa Monica: RAND Corporation, RM–5851–1SA/ARPA, May 1969), p. 7.

175. F.J. West Jr., *US Fatalities During Vietnamization Part 1: Overview* (Santa Monica: Rand Advanced Research Projects Agency, 1970, Rm–6376–ARPA), p. 4.

176. BDM, *Strategic Lessons*, Vol V1, p. 6–39.

177. Ibid., p. 6–38.

178. Nalty, *Air Power*, p. 88.

179. US Army Combat Developments Command, *Senior Officer Debriefing Report: LTG Julian Ewell, CG, II Field Force, Vietnam, Period 2 April 1969 through 16 April 1970* (MSTL), p. 8.

180. West, *US Fatalities*, p. 5.

181. US Advisory and Assistance Group, II Corps Tactical Zone, *The Dak Seang Campaign, 1 April–8 May 1970* (MSTL), p. 2.

182. Headquarters, US Military Assistance Command, Office of Assistant Chief of Staff J2, Combined Intelligence Center, Vietnam, *VC/NVA withdrawal Tactics, ST 66–45* (MSTL), p. 7, statement of Major Nguyen Van Chuoc.

183. Thayer, *VC–NVA Operations*, p. 149.

184. US Army Concept Team in Vietnam, *Fire Support Base Defense—Final Report, 6 April 1972* (ACTIV Project No. ACG–80F, MHRC), Chapter II.

185. Ibid., p. II–40.

186. Headquarters, 101st Airborne Division, "Preparation of a Fire Support Base," *Operations Report Lessons Learned for the Period Ending 30 April 1968* (US Army Command and General Staff College Library), pp. 5– 28.

187. *Organization and Employment*, p. II–42.

188. Headquarters, 25th Infantry Division Artillery, *Operations Report, Lessons Learned, Period Ending 31 October 1968* (MSTL), p. 9.

189. Ibid., p. 9.

190. *Organization and Employment*, p. II–43–44.

191. The story of the attack on FSB Crook is taken from US Army Command and General Staff College, *Vietnam Monograph: Tactical and Materiel Innovation in Vietnam: FSB Crook* (C&GS Library, 1971); *MG Williamson, Debrief of Returnees from Vietnam.*

192. General Melvin Zais Papers, *Monograph on the Battle of Dong Ap Bia* (MHRC Archives), p.3.

193. Thayer, *Ground Operations*, p. 119.

194. US Army Combat Developments Command, *USARV Artillery Conference, Final Report, 7 September 1967* (MSTL), p. 3; See also LTG Peers Debriefing Report, p. 6.

195. Interview with LTG A. C. Collins as part of the Senior Officer Debriefing Program, U.S. Army War College (Bound transcript contained in MHRC Archives, Carlisle Barracks, PA), p. 364.

196. Statement by Mr. Don Luce, Director, International Voluntary Services, Vietnam; US Congress, Senate Committee on the Judiciary, Civilian Casualties, Social Welfare and the Refugee Problems in South Vietnam, Hearings before a Subcommittee to Investigate Problems Connected with Refugees and Escapees, 90th Congress, 1st Session, 1967, p. 62.

197. Kelly Orr, *The Sunday Star*, Washington, DC, (30 June 1968), p. 4.

198. US Army Combat Developments Command, *Senior Officer Debriefing Report, BG C. M. Hall, CG, I Field Force Vietnam Artillery Period 23 October 1969 to 17 October 1970* (DTIC Number AD 514360), p, A–10.

199. Debriefing Report, LTG A. C. Collins, CG, I Field Force, Vietnam, for the Period 15 February 1970 to 9 January 1971, Collins Papers MHRC.

200. Miscellaneous notes, *Force Feed Fire Support Systems*, 28 May 1969, (MACV File 2020–053, MHRC).

201. Headquarters, I Field Force, Vietnam, *Tactical Note, September 1969* (MSTL), p. 3; Similar sentiment is expressed by MG Williamson in his *Debriefing Report*, tab G, p. 13.

202. For one testimony to the care taken to prevent injury from artillery see LTG W. R. Peers, *Senior Officer Debriefing Report*, p. 6. Similar sentiments can be found in many first-hand accounts. One source devoted entirely to the subject of friendly fire concludes that rules of engagement and safety procedures unduly limited the successful application of firepower in Vietnam. See: LTC Charles Schrader, *Amicicide*, p. 16.

203. Headquarters, US Military Assistance Command, Vietnam, *Vietnam Lessons Learned Number 70: Friendly Casualties from Friendly Fires, 17 October 1968* (MSTL), pp. 5–13.

204. *Organization and Employment*, p. IV–30–31.

205. Letter titled "Artillery Accidents, Lessons Learned," dated 1 November 1968 prepared by Captain Harrison, Assistant Chief of Staff, G–3 (MSTL).

206. *Friendly Casualties*, p. 27.

207. Depuy Papers, Section VI, p. 18.

208. Headquarters 173rd Airborne Brigade, *Combat After Action Report–2/503d Infantry Contact of 19–23 November 1967* Contained as an inclosure to *The Battle for Dak To*, Inclosure 5, p.8.

209. Letter from Colonel Cooper to Colonel Gudgel, 30 September 1970. See also a similar letter from BG Theo Matazas to MG Wetherill concerning FO inexperience, 21 October 1970, all contained in file titled "Responsiveness of FA in the Republic of Vietnam" (MSTL).

210. LTC William L. Hauser, "Fire and Maneuver in the Delta," *A Distant Challenge* (Birmingham: Infantry Magazine, 1971), pp. 227–230.

211. Headquarters, 101st Airborne Division Artillery, *Operations Report, Lessons Learned for the Period Ending 31 July 1968* (MSTL), pp. 3–5.

212. Major Richard Johnson, *Viet Cong Perceptions of the Relative Effectiveness of US/GVN Aerial and Ground Combat Power* (Student Essay, US Command and General Staff College, 1974), pp. 8–20.

213. Futrell, *USAF in Southeast Asia*, pp. 144–146.

214. US Army Concept Team in Vietnam, *Employment of Artillery in Counterinsurgency Operations* (JRATA PRoject No. 1B–153.0, 25 April 1965), pp. 16–26.

215. *The Dak Seang Campaign*, p. 66.

216. Ibid., pp. 4–5.

217. Headquarters, 101st Airborne Division (Airmobile), *Airmobile Operations in Support of Operation Lamson 719, 8 February–6 April 1971* (DTIC Number AD 516603), pp. IV–67 to IV–73.

218. Ibid., pp. I–8 to I–12.

219. Ibid., pp. I–23.

220. Thayer, *The Air War*, p. 291.

221. BDM. *Study of Strategic Lessons, Vol. VI: Conduct of the War*, pp. 4–5.

222. LTC Robert Wagner, "Vietnamization: A Policy—Not a Program," End of Tour Report, Undated, MACV Files, Military History Research Collection, Carlisle Barrackks, PA.

Chapter 4 *The Afghanistan Intervention*

1. The narrative of Mujahideen Commander Haji's ambush is taken from: Dittmar Hack, "Today is Payday for the Infidels," *Der Spiegel* (5 December 1983), pp. 172–185.

2. Joseph J. Collins, "The Use of Force in Soviet Foreign Policy; The Case of Afghanistan," *Conflict Quarterly* (Spring, 1983), p. 20.

3. Mark Urban, "The Strategic Role of Soviet Airborne Troops," *Jane's Defence Weekly* (14 July 1984), pp. 26–28.

4. Ibid., pp. 28–32.

5. "Highlights of Three Years of War Interpreted," *Islamic World Defence* (January–March 1983) in JPRS *Near East/South Asia Report* (17 February 1983), p. 97.

6. David Isby, "Soviet Tactics in the War in Afghanistan," *International Defense Review* (Vol. 4, No. 7, 1983) , p. 689.

7. David Isby, "Soviet Power in Afghanistan: More than Brute Force is Needed," *Defence Week* (14 February 1983), p. 10.

8. Isby, "Soviet Tactics," p. 689.

9. C. N. Donnelly, "Soviet Mountain Warfare Operations," *International Defence Review* (6/1980), p. 826.

10. James H. Hansen, "Afghanistan: The Soviet Experience," *National Defence* (66; January 1982), p. 20.

11.David Isby, "Afghanistan 1982: The War Continues," *International Defence Review* (Vol. 3, No. 11, 1982), pp. 15–26.

12. Isby, "Soviet Tactics," p. 689; Interview with former Afghan Army Colonel A. A. Jalali, Voice of America Building, Washington DC, 23 October 1984.

13. *Christian Science Monitor* (26 July 1982), p. 12.

14. Tahir Amin, "Afghan Resistance: Past, Present, and Future," *Asian Survey* (Volume XXIV, April 1984), p. 387.

15. Rear Admiral T. Gaidar, "A Visit with Soviet Troops in Afghanistan," *Pravda* (3 August 1982), from the *Current Digest of the Soviet Press* (Vol. XXXIV, April 1984), p. 5.

16. Tahir Amin, "Afghan Resistance," p. 373.

17. William Branigin, "Moscow's Troops Show no Zeal for Guerrilla War," *The Washington Post* (21 November 1983), p. 1.

18. Isby, "Soviet Tactics," p. 689.

19. Jalali Interview.

20. G. Kamensky, "Raspredelenic Obiazannoste: Na KNP" (Distribution of Duties in the Command Observation Post), *Voenny Vestnik*: (No. 12, 1972), pp. 69–71.

21. Jalali Interview.

22. Joseph Collins, "The Soviet Afghan War: The First Four Years," *Parameters* (Vol. XIV, No. 2, 1984), p. 59.

23. Jalali Interview.

24. Dissatisfaction among Soviet soldiers is evident in many foreign press accounts. See: *London Daily Mail* (25 November 1983); *Les Nouvelles d'Afghanistan*, (11 December 1982) in *JPRS Near East/South Asia Report* (3 February 1983), p. 166.

25. William Branigin, "Afghanistan: Inside a Soviet War Zone," *The Washington Post* (16–22 October 1983), p. 14; Oliver Roy, "Soviets in Danger of Overextending Themselves," *The Muslim Magazine* (6 June 1984), p. 3.

26. Colonel Glantz's views on the process of doctrinal innovation and reform in the Soviet Army are contained in several excellent pieces. Best

known are his two volumes on the Soviet Manchurian Campaign. Glantz credits many of the more imaginative Soviet tactical concepts such as "forward detachment" discussed later in this chapter to the Manchurian experience. See: LTC David M. Glantz, *August Storm: The Soviet 1945 Strategic Offensives in Manchuria* (Ft. Leavenworth: Combat Studies Institute, 1983); and *August Storm: Soviet Tactical and Operational Combat in Manchuria, 1945* (Ft. Leavenworth: Combat Studies Institute, 1983). Colonel Glantz's views on current Soviet doctrine can be found in LTC David M. Glantz, "Soviet Offensive Military Doctrine Since 1945," *Air University Review* (Spring, 1983), pp. 25–34; and "Soviet Operational Formation for Battle: A Perspective" *Military Review* (Vol. 63, No. 2, February 1983), pp. 1–12.

27. G. Jacobs, "Three Years of Soviet War Operations Evaluated," *Asian Defence Journal* (December 1982) in *FBIS Near East/South Aisa Report No. 2696* (20 January 1983), p. 107.

28. In addition to works by Colonel Glantz, details of the Soviet way of war can be gleaned in bits and pieces from many sources. Major Scott McMichael from the faculty of the Command and General Staff College and Lieutenant Colonel David Glantz of the Army War College provided key insights into Soviet staff procedures and the historical and political roots of the Soviet system for tactical change. Some helpful written sources include Victor Suvorov, *Inside the Soviet Army* (New York: MacMillan, 1982). An academic but equally useful doctrinal source is Malcolm Mackintosh's article "The Development of Soviet Military Doctrine Since 1918," in *The Theory and Practice of War*, ed. Michael Howard (Bloomington: Indiana University Press, 1975).

29. Mark Urban, "The Limited Contingent of Soviet Forces in Afghanistan," *Jane's Defence Review* (12 January 1985), p. 72.

30. Zarin Khan, "Interview in Copenhagen," *Information* (3–4 January 1982), in *JPRS Near East/North Africa Report* (11 February 1981), p. 33.

31. Hansen, "Afghanistan," p. 21.

32. Jalali interview, 25 January 1985.

33. Edward Girardet, "Moscow's Troubles," *The Christian Science Monitor* (4 August 19781), p. 1.

34. Jalali interview, 23 October 1984.

35. Description of Soviet firebases derived from questionnaire written by the author and submitted by Mr. David Isby to Qari Baba, Mujahideen leader of Harket-e-Inqilab-e-Islami at Peshawar, 11 February 1985.

36. Jalali Interview, 23 October 1984.

37. Interview with Dr. Bruce Amstutz, former member of the US Embassy staff in Kabul, 16 December 1984.

38. Interview with David Isby, Arlington, Virginia, 1 March 1985.

39. Yosef Bodansky, "The Bear on the Chessboard: Soviet Military Gains in Afghanistan," *World Affairs* (Winter, 1982–1983), p. 287; and: "Victory Still Eludes the Soviet Army," *Free Afghanistan Report* (Number 5, May 1983), p. 7.

40. "Su–24's, Tu–16's Support Soviet Ground Forces," *Aviation Week and Space Technology* (29 October 1984), p. 40.

41. Hack, "Today is Payday," p. 174.

42. John Gunston, "Afghans Plan USSR Terror Attacks," *Jane's Defence Weekly* (31 March 1984), p. 482.

43. "Highlights of Three Years of War Interpreted," *Islamic World Defence* (January–March 1983), p. 96.

44. Yosef Bodansky, "General of the Army D. T. Yazov: Victor in Afghanistan," *Jane's Defence Weekly* (31 March 1984), p. 38.

45. Yosef Bodansky, "The Bear and the Chessboard," p. 273.

46. Bodansky, "Yazov," p. 38.

47. Ibid., p. 38.

48. "Soviet Air Force in Afghanistan," *Jane's Defence Review* (7 July 1984); a Soviet impression of American airmobile tactics in Vietnam is contained in a fascinating article: Colonel N. Nikitin, "Some Operational and Tactical Lessons from the Local Wars of Imperialism," *Voyenno–Istoricheskiy Zhurnal* (No. 12, December 1978).

49. Lt. Gen. V. Kozehbakhteyer, Chief of Staff of the Central Group of Forces "Soviet Military Art in the Great Patriotic War and the Post-War Period Development of Tactics for Troop Operations in Mountain Wooded Terrain, 1946–1980," *Voyenno-Istoricheskiy Zhurnal* (No. 2, February 1981), p. 42.

50. Bodansky, "The Bear and the Chessboard," p. 283.

51. Mark Urban, "The Strategic Role of Soviet Airborne Troops," p. 27.

52. Isby, "Soviet Tactics," p. 681.

53. Aernout Van Lynden, "Failure of Soviet War Tactics," *Times of India* (28 December 1983), p. 8.

54. "Three Years' of Soviet War Operations Evaluated," *Asian Defence Journal* (December 1982), p. 107.

55. Bodansky, "General Yazov."

56. Dianne Beal Vaught, *Initiative in the Soviet Army and the Afghan Experience* (Library of Congress Research Staff Paper, 1984); Radio Liberty Research, "Soviet Army Places Emphasis on Training for Mountain Warfare," (RL 252/83, 30 June 1983), p. 2.

57. Philip Jacobson, "The Red Army Learns from a Real War," *The Washington Post* (13 February 1983), p. C–4.

58. Vaught, *Initiative*, p. 4.

59. Anthony Hyman, "The Struggle for Afghanistan," *The World Today, Royal Institute for International Affairs* (Vol. 40, No. 7), p. 276.

60. Hansen, "Afghanistan," p. 24.

61. Branigin, "Afghanistan: Inside a Soviet War Zone," p. A–14.

62. Ibid., p. 1.

63. Isby, "Afghanistan, 1982," p. 1524.

64. Douglas Hart, "Low Intensity Conflict in Afghanistan: The Soviet View," *Survival* (Vol. XXIV, No. 2, March–April 1982), p. 62.

65. C. N. Donnelly, "Soviet Mountain Warfare Operations," *International Defence Review* (Vol. 1, No. 6, 1980), p. 826.

66. Douglas M. Hart, "Low Intensity Conflict in Afghanistan: The Soviet View," *Survival* (Vol. XXIV, No. 2, March–April 1982), p. 62.

67. "BTR–70 in Afghanistan," *Jane's Defence Review* (16 January 1984), p. 956.

68. Answer to questionnaire by Sayed Murkhtar Hashmi at Peshawar, 11 February 1985. All questionnaires cited are in the author's possession.

69. Suvorov, *Inside the Soviet Army*, p. 198.

70. Lieutenant General V. Kozhbakteyev, "Soviet Military Art," p. 41. When he wrote this piece General Kozhbakhteyev was Chief of Staff of the Central Group of Soviet Forces. It is a common Soviet practice to disseminate "lessons learned" in Afghanistan to field commands using thinly disguised examples from history or "training exercises." Beginning in 1981 the number of articles in the military press dealing with "exercise in mountainous-taiga or mountainous-desert terrain" increased several fold. Soviet professional soldiers certainly know where the examples come from.

71. Ibid., p. 41.

72. Donnelly, "Soviet Mountain Warfare," p. 832.

73. "A. M. Vasilek Automatic 82 mm Mortar," *Jane's Defence Review* (4 February 1984).

74. *Christian Science Monitor* (22 July 1982), p. 6.

75. Operational Research Office, John Hopkins University, *Effectiveness of Air-burst Artillery Shells on Personnel and Trucks* (ORO T–303); *The Effects of Counterbattery Fire* (ORO, T–284); *On the Accuracy of Unobserved Artillery Fires* (ORO, T–271). (All volumes contained in the Military History Research Collection, Carlisle Barracks, PA.).

76. Very little has been written in English about Soviet fire support doctrine. The best historical treatment is by Marshal of Artillery K. P. Kazakov, *Always with the Infantry, Always with the Tanks*, trans. by Leo Kanner Associates (Moscow: Voyenizdat, 1973). A shorter historical piece more relevant to modern doctrine is Lieutenant General of Artillery M. Sidorov, "Combat Employment of Artillery," *Voyenno-Istoricheski* (No. 9, 1975), translated and reprinted as a Combat Studies Institute article for use by students at the Command and General Staff College. Christopher Bellamy has written several pieces on modern Soviet artillery, among them: "Soviet Artillery and Rocket Forces, 1940–1980," *Jane's Defence Review* (Vol. 4, No. 3, 1983), p. 268. The best "nuts and bolts" treatment of Soviet artillery doctrine is contained in the British Ministry of Defence publication: *Tactics of the Soviet Ground Forces* (MOD: August, 1975).

77. Jalali Interview; Questionnaire from Anwar of Jagdalak, Isby interview.

78. Basil Epatko, *Soviet Air to Ground Troops* (Air Forces Branch, DIA, 1979), p. 17.

79. Victor Suvorov, *Inside the Soviet Army*, pp. 170–173.

80. C. N. Donnelly, "The Soviet Helicopter on the Battlefield," *International Defence Review* (No. 5, 1984), p. 559.

81. Ibid., p. 560; "Soviet Air Force in Afghanistan," *Jane's Defence Weekly* (7 July 1984).

82. John Everett-Heath, *Soviet Helicopters Design Development and Tactics*, (Jane's , 1983), pp. 86–88.

83. No Mujahideen leader answering the questionnaire in Peshawar could recall being attacked from the air by fixed-wing aircraft while in contact with Soviet troops. Su–25 and various MiG aircraft did fly over and occasionally bomb or strafe once the Mujahideen were away from direct combat.

84. Major V. Roklov, "From Different Directions," *Aviatsiya I Kosmonavtika* (No 5, April 1981), p. 5; Hansen, "Afghanistan," p. 21.

85. David Isby, "Soviet Tactics in the War in Afghanistan," *International Defence Review* (Vol 4, No. 7, 19843), p. 681.

86. Epatko, *Soviet Air Support*, pp. 13–16.

87. Colonel B. Nesterov, "Helicopters Over the Battlefield," *Aviatsiya I Kosmonavtika* (No 7, July 1982), p. 9.

88. Frank Steinert and Lieutanant Colonel Kerry Hines,"Afghanistan's Impact on Soviet Military Literature," *Review of Soviet Ground Forces* (July 1982), p. 3.

89. Isby interview.

90. John Gunston, "Afghans Plan USSR Terror," p. 481.

91. Ibid., p. 481.

92. Isby Interview.

93. Yosef Bodansky, "Most Feared Aircraft in Afghanistan is Frogfoot," *Jane's Defence Weekly* (19 May 1984), p. 769.

94. Nesterov, "Helicopters over the Battlefield," p. 10.

95. Interview of former Afghan Major Nabi Wardak by David Isby, Peshawar, 15 February 1985. Wardak's description of Soviet close support tactics is verified in Soviet literature: Major V. Rokhlov, "From Different Directions," *Aviatsiya I Kosmonavtika* (No 5, 1981), p. 4.

96. Gunston, "Afghans Plan USSR Terror Attacks," p. 481.

97. "Su–24's, Tu–16's Support Soviet Ground Forces," *Aviation Week and Space Technology* (29 October 1984), p. 40.

98. Wardak interview.

99. Qari Baba questionnaire.

100. Phillip Jacobson, "The Red Army Learns from a Real War," p. C–4; See Also: Radio Liberty Research Division Archives (Munich), "Soviets Change Tactics Against Afghan Rebels," Washington, 27 December 1982, p. 4.

101. Jacobson, "The Red Army Learns," p. C4.

102. Library of Congress, *Background Information for Members of Congress Alleged Shortcomings in Aid Reaching the Afghan Resistance* (Library of Congress Research Staff Paper, October 1983, p. 2.

103. Major Wardak made this claim. Interview with David Isby.

104. "Su–24's, Tu–16's Support," *Aviation Week*, p. 40.

105. Major Wardak interview. Wardak's description is substantiated in Soviet military journals. See A. Zheltikov, "Both the Pair and Solo," *Aviatsiya I Kosmonavtika* (No 7, 1982), p. 11; Colonel General of Aviation S. Golobev, "With Consideration for the Combat Missions," *Aviatsiya I Kosmonavtika* (No 11, 1982), pp. 4–6; Rear Admiral T. Gaidar, "A Visit

with Soviet Troops in Afghanistan," *Pravda* (3 August 1982), in *The Current Digest of the Soviet Press* (Vol. XXXIV, No. 32), p. 6.

106. "Su–24's, Tu–16's Support," *Aviation Week*, p. 40.

107. Sarchielli Grazians, "Beyond the Snow—Blood," *Il Giorno* (Milan: 13 January 1981), p. 3; Barin Khan, "Interview in Copenhagen," p. 33; *Christian Science Monitor* (19 July 1982), p. 1.

108. Wardak interview.

109. Isby, "Soviet Power in Afghanistan," p. 11.

110. Branigin, "Afghanistan: Inside a Soviet War Zone," p. A14.

111. "Soviet Air Force in Afghanistan," *Jane's Defence Review* (7 July 1984).

112. Isby interview.

113. "Su–24's, Tu–16's," *Aviation Week*.

114. Denis Warner, "Afghanistan, Soviet Union Carving out a New Outer Mongolia," *Pacific Defence Reporter* (Australia: December 1984–January 1985), p. 45.

115. Bodansky, "Frogfoot," p. 769.

116. Christian Science Monitor (22 June 1982), p. 12.

117. Gunston, "Afghan's Plan Terror Attacks," p. 481.

118. Christian Science Monitor (22 July 1982), p. 6.

119. Jalali Interview, 23 October 1984.

120. Nesterov, "Helicopters Over the Battlefield," p. 9.

121. The battle is pieced together from interviews and questionnaires recently gathered by the author, David Isby and Colonel A. A. Jalali, as well as descriptions of similar operations in mountainous terrain found in Soviet military literature: Lieutenant General V. Kozhbakhteyev, "Soviet Military Art" General I Tret'yak "Organization and Conduct of Offensive Combat on Mountain-Taiga terrain," *Voyonno I Istoricheskiy Zhurnal* (No. 7, 1980), pp. 42–44.

122. Bodansky, "The Bear on the Chessboard," p. 278; Oliver Roy, "Soviets in Danger," p. 3.

123. Kozbhbakhteyev, "Soviet Military Art," p. 42.

124. Colonel B. Budnikov, "Helicopters Land an Assault Force, *"Aviatsiya I Kosmonavtika* (No. 7, 1981) in JPRS (17 June 1982(); Bodansky, "Frogfoot," p. 769; Collins, "The Soviet Afghan War," p. 55.

125. Budnikob, "Helicopters Land an Assault Force," Jalali interview, 25 January 1985.

126. "Inside Afghanistan: An Eye-Witness Report Provides Fresh Evidence of Moscow's Relentless Campaign Against the Guerrillas," *Newsweek* (11 June 1984), p. 54; "Highlights of Three Years of War," p. 689.

127. Isby, "Soviet Tactics," p. 689.

128. Van Lynden, "Failure of Soviet War Tactics," p. 8.

129. Kozhbakhteyev, "Soviet Military Art Tactics," p. 8.

130. Hart, "Low Intensity Conflict," p. 63.

131. A. H., "Setbacks for Afghanistan Freedom Fighters—Soviet Encirclement Tactics," *Neue Zuericher Zeitung* (4 March 1982), p. 4; Lieutenant General Kozhbakhteyev, "Development of Tactics," p. 40.

132. Van Lynden, "Failure of Soviet War Tactics," p. 8.

133. *Karachi Jang* (29 June 1982), in JPRS Near East/North Africa Report (7 October 1982),, p. 27.

134. Kozhbakhteyev, "Soviet Military Art," p. 42.

135. Josef Bodansky, "New Weapons in Afghanistan," *Jane's Defence Weekly* (9 March 1985), p. 46. Kozhbakhteyev, "Soviet Military Art," p. 44. Roklov, "From Different Directions," p. 5.

136. Bodansky, "Most Feared Aircraft," p. 769.

137. Isby interview.

138. Author's questionnaire answered by Qari Taj Mohammad. Other guerrilla leaders questioned expressed similar opinions.

139. Donnelly, "The Soviet Helicopter," p. 562.

140. Kozhbakhteyev, "Soviet Military Art," p. 42 and Qari Tay Mohammad inteview.

141. Ibid.

142. Joseph Collins, "Soviet Military Performance in Afghanistan: A Preliminary Assessment," *Comparative Strategy* (Vol. 4, No. 2, 1983), p. 147.

143. Marine Broxup, "Afghanistan Update," *Central Asian Survey* (1983), p. 139; Edward Girardet, "Moscow's Troubles," *Christian Science Monitor* (4 August 1981), p. 1; and: Joseph J. Collins, "The Soviet-Afghan War: The First Four Years," p. 51.

144. Jacobson, "The Red Army." p. C–4.

Chapter 5 *The Falklands Campaign*

1. The narrative of 2 Para at Goose Green is taken from several sources. The best popular account is Max Hastings and Simon Jenkins, *The Battle for the Falkland* (London: W. W. Norton & Company, 1983), pp. 233–253. An excellent analytical study taken in part from personal interviews is Major J. D. Middleton (et al.) *The Falkland Islands: Offensive Attack of Prepared Positions, British Joint Task Force, May 1982* (Ft. Leavenworth Battle Book, Command and General Staff College Library, 1984). The artillery side of the battle, in part, was taken from "Into Action with Black Eight," *Gunner* (September, 1982), pp. 15–17. Additional details from *The Falkland Islands Campaign, The 2nd Battalion the Parachute Regiment History* (Royal School of Artillery Library, Larkhill, UK).

2. Interview with Dr. Richard Holmes, Royal Military Academy, Sandhurst, UK, 22 November 1984.

3. "29 Commando Regiment, RA in the Falklands," *Gunner.* (September 1982), p. 15.

4. *2nd Battalion the Parachute Regiment History*, p. 130.

5. Middleton, *The Falklands Islands*, pp. 7–13.

6. Hastings and Jenkins, p. 177 and pp. 321–323.

7. Inverview with Lieutenant Colonel Michael C. Bouden, Royal School of Artillery, Larkhill, UK, 21 November 1984.

8. Major Gerald R. Akhurst, "A Gunner's Tale," *Field Artillery Journal* (March–April 1984), p. 22.

9. Hastings and Jenkins, p. 252.

10. Lieutenant Colonel M. J. Holroyd-Smith, "The Falkland Islands Campaign-The Perceptions of a Gunner CO," *R. A. Historical Society Proceedings* (Vol. 5, No. 2, January 1984), p. 8.

11. Jeffrey Ethell and Alfred Price, *Air War South Atlantic* (New York: McMillan, 1983), p. 172.

12. Major Jonathan Bailey, "Training for War: The Falklands 1982," *Military Review* (63 September 1983), p. 61.

13. Ibid., p. 62.

14. Minutes of the Conference on the Lessons of the South Atlantic War conducted at the Royal Aeronautical Society, London, on 2–3 September 1982 and published by *Defence and Foreign Affairs Magazine*, p. 3.

15. Major Jonathan Bailey, RA, "Training for War: The Falklands, 1982," *Military Review* (No. 63, September 1983), p. 65.

16. Ibid., p. 65.

17. The details of naval gunfire operations are taken from an interview with Lieutenant Colonel (Ret) Keith Eve, Larkhill, UK, 20 November 1984; *Notes on Naval Gunfire Support* Poole, Dorset, UK, (Document given to the author by LTC Eve; Major M. J. Morgan, RA, "Naval Gunfire Support for Operation Corporate, 1982," *Royal Artillery Journal* (Vol. CX, No. 2, September 1983).

18. Eve interview.

19. Ibid.

20. Ibid.

21. Daniel Kon, *Los Chicos de la Guerra* (London: New English Library 1983), p. 97.

22. Ibid., p. 71.

23. Ibid., p. 117.

24. Major General Donald M. Weller, USMC (Ret), *Naval Gunfire Support of Amphibious Operations* (Headquarters, U.S. Marine Corps, Naval Surface Weapons Center, 1977 (DTIC Number ADA 051873), p. 6.

25. Morgan, "Naval Gunfire," p. 90.

26. Ibid., p. 90.

27. Captain Hugh McManners, *Falklands Commando* (London: William Kimber, 1984), p. 24; also Keith Eve interview.

28. *2nd Battalion the Parachute Regiment History*, p. 128.

29. Middleton, *The Falkland Islands*, pp. 8–18.

30. Lieutenant Colonel Andrew Jones, "British Armour in the Falklands," *Armor Magazine* (March–April 1983), p. 27.

31. *2nd Batttalion the Parachute Regiment History*, p. 128.

32. Interview with Mr. Tony Buxton, Ordnance Design Manager, Royal Ordnance Factory, Nottingham, UK, 27 April 1985; and Middleton, pp. 8–18.

33. "29 Commando Regiment, RA in the Falklands," p. 13.

34. Jones, "British Armour," p. 28.

35. Bailey, "Training for War," p. 63.

36. Bryan Perrett, *Weapons of the Falklands Conflict* (Poole, Dorset: Blandford Press, 1982), p. 79.

37. Hastings and Jenkins, p. 272.

38. Ibid., p. 280.

39. Interview with Major R. T. Gwyn, RA, Ft. Leavenworth, Kansas, 20 January 1985.

40. Jones, "British Armour," p. 29.

41. Holroyd–Smith, "The Falklands Campaign," p. 10.

42. Hastings and Jenkins, pp. 263.

43. Morgan, "Naval Gunfire Support," p. 84.

44. Eve interview.

45. Ibid.

46. Morgan, "Naval Gunfire Support," p. 84.

47. Eve interview.

48. Gwyn interview.

49. Ibid.

50. "29 Commando Regiment RA in the Falklands," p. 13.

51. Jones, "British Armour," p. 29; Gwyn interview.

52. Hastings and Jenkins, pp. 294–296.

53. *The Falkland Islands Campaign: 2 Para in The Falklands* (Royal School of Artillery Library. Larkhill, UK), pp. 144–148.

54. Gwyn interview.

55. Lieutenant Colonel M. I. E. Scott, *The Battle of Tumbledown Mountain* (Royal School of Artillery Library, Larkhill, UK), p. 139.

56. "Notes on the Role of Gunners and Infantry," Manuscript dated 30 July 1982, contained in Royal School of Artillery Library, Larkhill, UK, p. A–2–4.

57. Gwyn interview.

58. Scott, "Tumbledown," p. 139.

59. Akhurst, "A Gunner's Tale," p. 19, Conference on the South Atlantic War, p. 13.

60. Holroyd-Smith, "The Falklands Campaign," p. 12.

61. Akhurst, "A Gunners Tale," p. 21.

62. Bailey, "Training for War," p. 60.

63. Letter from British Army Staff, Washington, Subject: 105mm Light Gun (L118), BASW/73F450, dated 27 September 1983.

64. Holroyd-Smith, "The Falklands Campaign," p. 14 .

65. Bailey, "Training for War," p. 64.

66. Holroyd-Smith, "The Falklands Campaign," p. 14.

67. "The Falklands: An Account of 4th Field Regiment Activities by the Commanding Officer," *Gunner* (August 1982), p. 17.

68. Akhurst, "A Gunner's Tale," p. 20.

69. Bailey, "Training for War," p. 60.

70. Ibid., pp. 67–70; Gwyn interview.

71. Akhurst, "A Gunner's Tale," p. 20.

72. Ibid., p. 18.

73. Bailey, "Training for War," p. 67.

74. McManners, *Falklands Commando*, p. 193.

75. "British Army Equipment in the Falklands," *Defence* (1982), p. 46.

76. Jones, "British Armour," p. 30; *The Falkland Islands Campaign (3 Para History)*.

77. Akhurst, "A Gunner's Tale," p. 21.

78. Jones, "British Armour," p. 29.

79. *2nd Battalion the Parachute Regiment History,* p. 129.

80. Dr. Richard Holmes *The Psychological Effects of Artillery Fire,* Speech given to DRA's Tactical Seminar, June 1983, p. 8; personal interview with Dr. Holmes, Sandhurst.

81. Holmes, *Psychological Effects,* p 8.

82. Kon, *Los Chicos,* p. 33.

83. Holmes, *Psychological Effects,* p. 9.

84. S. L. A. Marshall, *Men Against Fire: The Problem of Battle Command in Future War* (New York: William Morrow & Co., 1947), pp. 145–151.

85. Kon, *Los Chicos,* p. 124.

86. Hastings and Jenkins, p. 305.

87. Akhurst, "A Gunner's Tale," p. 20; 4th Regiment, p. 17,

Chapter 6 *Firepower in the Gulf*

1. The story of Lieutenant Saif's battery is taken from several sources. Classified interviews were derived from ARCENT INTREPs 40-91 and 44-91, 17 and 21 February 1991. To protect his identity "Saif" is a nom de guerre. Iraqi tactics and methods were derived from an interview with Colonel Ray Smith and Brigadier General Creighton W. Abrams, Jr.'s report and briefing, "VII Corps Artillery Commander's Report, Operation Desert Storm," March 1991.

2. Brigadier General Creighton W. Abrams, Jr., "Field Artillery Desert Facts," *Field Artillery* (October 1991), p. 2.

3. Robert H. Scales, Jr., *Certain Victory: The U.S. Army in the Gulf War* (Washington, DC: Office of the Chief of Staff, 1993), p. 9.

4. James P. Coyne, *Airpower in the Gulf* (Arlington, VA: Aerospace Education Foundation, 1990), p. 91.

5. U.S. Army Field Artillery School Study, *Legal Mix II,* 1979, p. 9.

6. Coyne, *Airpower in the Gulf,* p. 76.

7. Third ROKA Air Liaison Report, 8 December 1993, Subject: F-16 LGB Bombing Accuracy.

8. Colonel Donald Kerrick, *ARCENT Military Intelligence History* (April 1991), pp. 6–86.

9. Information on the Firefinder series of radar provided by Mr. Ken Kleypas, Hughes Representative, Lawton, OK, 5 Jan 94. See also: Colonel V. B. Corn, Jr., "Silver Bullets," *Field Artillery* (October 1991), p. 13.

10. Litton Corporation, *Litton Data Systems in Operation Desert Storm,* a poster describing performance characteristics of the lightweight TACFIRE, undated.

11. Donald R. Kennedy and William L. Kincheloc, "Steel Rain: Submunitions in the Desert," *Army* (January 1993), pp. 26–31.

12. 24th Infantry Division, *A History of the 24th Infantry Division Combat Team During Operation Desert Storm: The Attack to Free Kuwait* (January–March 1991), p. 1.

13. XVIII Airborne Corps CG Update briefing slides, 5 November 1990.

14. Coyne, *Airpower in the Gulf,* p. 35.

15. John Romjue, *From Active Defense to AirLand Battle: The Development of Army Doctrine, 1973–1982,* TRADOC Historical Monograph Series (June 1984), pp. 61–64.

16. Richard Davis, *The 31 Initiatives: A Study in Air Force-Army Cooperation* (Washington, DC: Office of Air Force History, 1987), p. 38.

17. ARCENT INTREPs 40-91 and 44-91.

18. Scales, *Certain Victory,* p. 114.

19. Annex D (Fire Support) to VII (US) Corps OPLAN 1990-2 (Operation Desert Saber), p. D-1.

20. Robert H. Scales, Jr., "Firepower, The Psychological Dimension," *Army* (July 1989), pp. 43–50.

21. Coyne, *Airpower in the Gulf,* p. 45.

22. Ibid., p. 40.

23. Scales, *Certain Victory,* p. 174.

24. Interview with General Frederick Franks, Fort Monroe, VA, April 1992.

25. Thomas A. Keaney and Eliot A. Cohen, "Gulf War Airpower Survey Summary Report," draft copy (Washington, DC: 1993), p. 38.

26. Ibid., p. 16.

27. Scales, *Certain Victory,* p. 187.

28. Keaney and Cohen, "Airpower Survey," p. 21.

29. Ibid.

30. Franks interview.

31. *ARCENT MI History,* pp. 21–23.

32. Ibid., pp. 6–74.

33. Scales, *Certain Victory,* p. 192.

34. Keaney and Cohen, "Airpower Survey," p. 20.

35. The story of the first ATACMS mission is taken from an interview with Captain Jeff Lieb, Fort Sill, OK, April 1992.

36. Loral Corporation, *Fact Sheet on the Army Tactical Missile System,* October 1992.

37. Rand Corporation, *Future Army Long-Range Fires: Bringing New Capabilities to the Battlefield* (Santa Monica, CA: September 1993), p. 10.

38. Scales, *Certain Victory*, pp. 168–9.

39. VII Corps Artillery, Operation Desert Storm Briefing, March 1991.

40. Scales, *Certain Victory*, p. 207.

41. Ibid., p. 208.

42. Ibid., p. 209.

43. Ibid., p. 210.

44. Ibid., p. 189.

45. Franks interview.

46. Scales, *Certain Victory*, p. 201.

47. Interview with Colonel Ray Smith, 12 February 1992.

48. Scales, *Certain Victory*, p. 203.

49. Major Mark Jenson, "MLRS in Operation Desert Storm," *Field Artillery* (August 1981), pp. 30–33.

50. Scales, *Certain Victory*, pp. 2–4; interview with Lieutenant Colonel Terry Johnson.

51. Smith interview.

52. VII Corps Artillery Briefing.

53. Ibid.

54. Franks interview.

55. Scales, *Certain Victory*, p. 224.

56. McCaffrey, lecture notes and slides from a "Fire Support in Desert Storm" briefing presented at the Field Artillery Commander's Conference, Fort Sill, OK, April 1991.

57. Interview with Major General Paul Funk, Fort Knox, KY, June 1992.

58. Scales, *Certain Victory*, p. 271.

59. Funk interview.

60. Scales, *Certain Victory*, p. 272.

61. Telephone interview with Colonel V. B. Corn, Jr.; letter, Colonel Corn to author, 13 May 1992.

62. Scales, *Certain Victory*, pp. 276–279.

63. Ibid., pp. 298–300.

64. The story of the deep attack into AO Minden was originally researched and written by Lieutenant Colonel Terry Johnson who, during this action, was deputy commander of the 11th Combat Aviation Brigade. Most of the story is excerpted from *Certain Victory*, pp. 287–291.

65. Franks interview; telephone conversation with Colonel Stan Cherrie, March 1992.

Chapter 7 Firepower in Future Limited War

1. Kinnard interview.

Index

Abrams, Brig. Gen. Creighton, 268
Ad Damman, 243
Aerial rocket artillery (ARA), 91–93, 95, 106, 109
Afghan Air Force, 185–87, 189
Afghan Army Staff College, 163
Airborne Command and Control Center (ABCCC), 264
Airborne units: British, 199–207, 212–14, 216–18, 226, 229, 232; French, 25–28, 38–40, 48, 50, 54; Republic of Vietnam, 150; Soviet, 175–77, 184, 192, 194–95; U.S., 81–82, 102, 287
Aircraft. *See* Aircraft, fixed wing; Helicopters; Remotely piloted vehicles
Aircraft, fixed wing: A–1 Skyraider fighter-bomber, 96; A–4 Skyhawk fighter, 97; A–7 Corsair fighter-bomber, 97, 238; A–10 Warthog fighter-bomber, 236, 253, 257, 275, 281; AC–130 Spectre gunship, 278; An–12 and An–14 transports, 185; An–24 transport, 172; An–26 transport, 172, 185; Antonov transports, 192, 195; artillery light observation, 12–13, 18, 91; B–26 Marauder

medium bomber, 41, 48, 57–58; B–52 Stratofortress heavy bomber, 71, 125, 128, 134–35, 274; B–57 Canberra bomber, 65; C–47 Skytrain transport, 40; C–47 Spooky gunship, 98, 115, 140, 144; C–119 Shadow gunship, 144; C–121 Super Constellation, 123; C–123 Provider transport, 40; C–130 Hercules transport, 22; F–4 Phantom II figh–ter-bomber, 96–97; F–6F Hellcat fighter-bomber, 41; F–8F Bearcat fighter-bomber, 41, 57–58; F–15E Strike Eagle fighter-bomber, 241, 253; F–16 Fighting Falcon fighter-bomber, 239, 253, 281; F/A–18 Hornet fighter-bomber, 241; F–100 Supersaber fighter-bomber, 96–97; F–111 fighter-bomber, 239, 253, 255, 285; Feiseler Storch liaison, 43; fighter-bombers, 239; Harrier jump jet, 207–8, 220; JU–52 transport, 40–41; JU–87 Stuka dive-bomber, 11; L–19 Bird Dog liaison, 91, 96, 255; MiG–21 Fishbed fighter, 188; MiG–27 Flogger fighter, 188;

Morane liaison, 43–47, 57, 91; OV–1 Mohawk light fighter, 20; OV–10 Bronco fighter-bomber, 215; P–47 Thunderbolt fighter, 13; P–63 King Cobra fighter, 41, 187; PB4Y–2 Privateer, 60; Pucara fighter, 215; reconnaissance, 22, 40, 60; Soviet, 172, 183, 185–89, 192; Spitfire fighter, 33; Su–7 Fitter fighter, 188; Su–24 bomber, 195; Su–25 Frogfoot fighter, 188; T–37 trainer, 96; trainers used by FACs, 18; Tu–16 Badger medium bomber, 189, 195

Aircraft, rotary wing. *See* Helicopters

Air Force Frontal Aviation (Soviet), 183–84

Air Force Tactical Control (TACP), 101

Air Force (USAF): advisors and observers with the French in Indochina, 57, 59; advisors to South Vietnam, 96; close support missions, 17–20, 65–66, 97–98, 109, 125–31, 145–46, 259, 263–66; enemy force targeting by sensor, 123–27, 129; landing zone preparation, 111; obtains FAC aircraft, 96; opposes helicopter airlift by Army, 21–22; questions Army use of armed aircraft, 20–21, 91; Seventh Air Force, 123, 127; supporting infantry battalions, 17, 85; tactical air controllers, 18; tactical bombing, 125. *See also* Army Air Forces; Forward air controllers; Gunships

AirLand Battle, 246, 249, 282

Airmobile units: British, 206, 233; Republic of Vietnam, 20, 148–

51; Soviet, 174–75, 184–85, 194–95; U.S., 20–22, 66–73, 81–82, 91–92, 102, 138, 244, 273

Airspace Coordination Area (ACA), 278

Air Tasking Order (ATO), 256, 260, 285

al–Abraq, 260

Algeria, 238

Ali Khel, 155

Al Jabayl, 243

Almond, Gen. Edward, 16–18

American Civil War, 3–4

Andarab Valley, 189

AN/TPQ–4 radar, 242

AN/TPQ–37 Firefinder radar, 261, 269, 280

Anti-Radiation Missile (HARM), 251

An Khe, 66

Antietam, 4, 166

Anti-tank helicopters, 183. *See also* Helicopters

Anti-tank missiles, 203, 239, 279

Anti-tank rockets, 156, 179, 221, 229

Ap Bia Mountain, 140

Arab-Israeli War, 238

Argentine Air Force, 206–7, 215, 218, 220

Armor: armored personnel carriers (APCs), 155, 161, 168, 175–79; ARVN, 65; in combined arms, 103; British, 213; French, 28, 88; German, 9; half-tracked troop carriers, 38; small nations having, 288, 290; Soviet, 155–65, 172, 179, 192–94; US, 10, 13, 75. *See also* Tanks

Army Air Forces (AAF): bombing tonnage of in Pacific, 125; close air support by, 11–15; Ninth Air Force, 12, 15; strategic bombardment by, 11; tactical

bombing in Europe by, 10;
XII Air Support Command,
12
Army aviation units, US: 3-1st
Aviation Battalion, 278; 4-
229th Aviation Battalion, 284;
11th Aviation Brigade, 270,
282–85; 21st Aviation Brigade,
275
Army Central Command (AR-
CENT), 256, 260–61, 285
Army Ground Forces, 9
Army Tactical Missile System
(ATACMS), 259–61
Army War College, 77
Arnold, Gen. H. H., 11
Artillery: airlifted Soviet Army, 21,
40, 66–68, 71, 82, 84–85, 136,
197–200, 206–7, 214; ambush
zones, 268; anti–aircraft, 13, 25,
58–59, 68, 135, 168–69, 179,
207–8; Argentine, 199, 201, 204,
207–8, 214–15, 224, 228–29;
assault, 5; barrages, 8, 72, 121,
128, 181, 239; box barrage, 17,
128–29; British, 199–200, 203,
207, 214–15, 218–20, 223–29,
232; counterbattery fire, 24, 57,
215; fuzes, 7, 138, 215, 225,
228; German, 9–10; harassment
and interdiction (H&I) fire, 118,
141–43, 210–12; light, 244;
mobile, 10; motorized, 10;
position artillery, 31, 57, 84,
169–73; psychological effects
of, 230–33, 249; recoil, 7, 214,
226; self-propelled, 10, 39, 82,
163, 179, 194; star formation,
84; static, 29–31; time-on-
target, 16, 85, 114, 141; towed,
10, 39, 82, 162; used to avoid
contact with enemy, 5. *See also*
Aerial rocket artillery; Cannon;
Firebases; Fire direction
centers; Forward air controllers;

Forward Observers; Ground
Observers; Gunfire spotters;
Guns; Howitzers; Illumination;
Map(s); Mortars; Recoilless
rifles; Rocket launchers;
Rockets
Artillery liaison officers (LNOs),
103–5, 107, 111, 181
Artillery units, US: 27th Field
Artillery, 259; 42nd Field
Artillery Brigade, 269, 279;
210th Field Artillery Brigade,
275; VII Corps Artillery, 237,
260; 321st Artillery Regiment,
147–48
A Shau Valley, 140
Atlantic Conveyor (merchant
ship), 206
Attack Helicopters. *See* Gunships.
Australian forces, 116

Baghdad, 251
Bagram, 158, 161, 169, 195
Basra, 284
Battle Damage Assessment
(BDA), 252, 262, 272
Battlefield Air Interdiction (BAI),
246, 250, 265
Bazarak, 190
Beagle Ridge, 228
Ben Het, 149
Bisko, Sgt. Orest, 116–17
Bluff Cove, 207, 216
Bomblet ammunition, 113
Boomer, Lt. Gen. Walter, 272
Bordard, Lucien, 47
Bradley, Gen. Omar, 11, 15
Bradley Infantry Fighting Vehicle,
245, 263
British forces. *See* Airborne units;
Airmobile units; Royal Air
Force; Royal Army; Royal
Marines; Royal Navy
Burke, Maj. Gen., 95
Bush, President George, 244

329

used by, 12–13, 18, 91, 96; calling fire close to friendly forces, 69, 87, 89, 104; fire clearance problems, 87–88, 100–101; over-estimating the effect of artillery, 51; Royal Artillery, 220–23, 226–27; skills needed by, 86, 88–89, 104, 111; training of, 104; use of telephones by, 7. *See also* Ground observers; Gunfire spotters; Radios

Forward Looking Infrared (FLIR), 278

Fragmentation bombs, 41, 71, 195

France, 12–15

Franco-Prussian War, 5–6

Franks, Lt. Gen. Frederick, 250, 257, 266, 272, 274

Fratricide, 258–59, 265, 278, 284

French forces: Air Force, 40–43, 46, 52–53, 57–58, 60; Foreign Legion, 40, 50, 53; Groupments Aerien Tactique (GATACs), 41–42, 44; mobile groups (GMs), 29, 31, 35, 38–39, 47–50, 52–53, 150; naval aviation, 41, 48, 58, 60; 6th Colonial Parachute Battalion, 48; 6th Light Armored Division, 248

French Fort, 118

Funk, Maj. Gen. Paul, 276–77

German Air Force, 9, 11, 15, 43

German Army, 9–11, 21, 43

Ghazni, 195, 197

Giap, Gen.: anti-aircraft defense by, 134–36; attacks Dien Bien Phu, 58–61; attacks Khe Sanh, 120–21, 130; attacks US support troops, 132–34, 136, 140; besieges Hanoi, 47–49; conventional warfare by, 36–37, 41, 52, 54; guerrilla warfare by, 49–51; use of forest bases, 28;

use of manpower against firepower, 32; war aims of, 74

Girardet, Edward, 189

Glantz, Col. David, 166–68.

Global Positioning System (GPS), 241, 279

Goose Green, 199–208, 211, 213–15, 229, 232

Grand Batteries, 279

Grenada, 235–36

Grenade launchers, 179, 213. *See also* Rocket-propelled grenades; Smoke

Griffith, Maj. Gen. Ronald, 276, 280

Ground observers, 44, 69, 73

Gunfire spotters (RN), 208–10, 220–21, 224, 228

Guns: 3.7-inch, 31; 4.5-inch, 199, 212, 220; 12.7-mm "Gatling," 183; 14.5-mm AA, 68; 23-mm AA, 179; 25-pounder, 31; 75-mm mountain, 50; 130-mm, 150, 170; 155-mm "Long Tom," 10, 31; development of, 8; number used by NVA, 154; siege, 5–7

Gunships: air strikes by, 96; close support by, 71, 93–95, 143–44, 149; in Grenada, 236; preparing LZs, 79, 111; Soviet helicopters as, 155, 170, 183–88, 192–97; transports as, 98, 115, 140, 144; US helicopters as, 21, 66, 71, 76, 92–96, 152. *See also* Aerial rocket artillery; Close support missions

Gurkhas, 204, 214

Ha, Sr. Col. Vi Tung, 63–68, 71–73

Hagerstrom, Col. James, 100

Haji, Comdr., 155–58, 197

Hall, Brig. Gen. C. M., 155–58, 197

Isabelle, 61
Israeli Defense Forces, 287

Jackson, Gen. "Stonewall," 3
Jacobson, Philip, 187
Jalali, Col. A. A., 163, 190
Japanese, 10, 15, 76, 174
Jefferson, Thomas, 3
Jellied gasoline. *See* Napalm.
Joint Surveillance Target Attack
    Radar System (JSTARS), 261,
    272, 284
Jones, Lt. Col. "H.," 199–201, 204,
    213

Kabul: Afghan Army Staff College
    at, 163; highways leading to,
    160, 197; minefield around,
    169; operations north of, 185,
    189; Soviet 40th Army at, 158,
    184, 187
Kalergis, Brig. Gen., 142
Kamal, Babrak, 158, 196
Kasserine Pass, 11
Keeble, Maj. Chris, 201–3, 216
Khafji, 258, 265
Khe Sanh, 106, 111, 117, 120–31,
    149
Kill box, 255, 285
Kinnard, Brig. Gen. Harry, 21–22,
    66–68, 72, 81, 138, 295–96
Koh Bani, 195
Korean War: artillery observer
    aircraft (L–19), 91, 96; aviation
    on station times, 102; Combat
    Commands and RCTs, 38;
    divisional artillery (105–mm
    howitzer), 82; effect of artillery
    and bombing, 51–52, 85;
    firepower doctrine affected by,
    15–20, 180; gun–infantryman
    ratio, 84; "meat grinder"
    operations, 51, 141; multiple air
    arms employed, 41; napalm
    bombs used, 48, 51; recoilless

rifles captured by the Chinese,
    36; retreat under fire, 231; value
    of vertical envelopment
    demonstrated, 19–20
Krulak, Lt. Gen. Victor, 95
Kuhestan, 195
Kupko, Capt. Chris, 275
Kuwait, 244, 251–2

Lai Khe, 109
Landing zones (LZs): Albany, 73,
    81–82, 93, 141; armed helicop-
    ters escort transports to, 20;
    artillery registered on, 150;
    Columbus, 71–72; Falcon, 68–
    69; "hot," 112; in Afghanistan,
    184, 194–95; "preparation" of,
    79–81, 100, 111–12; X-Ray,
    68–72
Laos: air strikes in, 116; as an
    NVA/VC sanctuary, 133;
    French operations in, 55;
    gunships used in, 96; infiltra-
    tion routes through, 120; US/
    ARVN operation into, 149–50;
    Viet Minh operations in, 49
Laser-guided bombs, 285
Lebanon, 287
Lieb, Capt. Jeff, 259
Light infantry, 78–80, 244–46
L–19 Bird Dog, 255
Luck, Lt. Gen. Gary, 251, 273
Luftwaffe, 9, 11, 15
LZs. *See* Landing zones

Manchuria, 15, 174
Manning, Col. Edsel, 65
Mao Tse-Tung, 25
Mao Khe, 48–49
Map(s): artillery fire by coordi-
    nates, 7, 10, 86, 116, 212;
    inaccurate, 88, 153; exercises,
    163; location errors by FOs, 33;
    reconnaissance, 216, 223; of
    troop and civilian locations, 87;

Nuayriyah, 244
Nulsen, Col. C. K., 78–81

Ott, Maj. Gen. David, 114

Panjsher Valley, 160–61, 170, 185, 189, 195
Paktia Province, 158
Pakistan, 189, 196
Parachute bombs, 188
Parachute flares, 34, 47
Parachute troops. *See* Airborne units
Pave Tack laser designation system, 239
Pearson, Brig. Gen. Willard, 91
Peers, Gen. W. R., 113–14, 130
Persian Gulf War, 235–6
Philippines, 58
Phuoc Yen, 147
Pike, Col. Hew, 223
Piroth, Col. Charles, 23–24, 57
Plei Ku, 65
Plei Me, 63–66, 68, 76
Port Stanley, 203, 206–7, 210–11, 214–33
POW-handling teams, 273
Precision revolution, 238
Prussian General Staff, 3
Pyrotechnics, 9, 111. *See also* Flares

Qandahar, 172
Quang Duc, 149
Quebec, 37
Quesada, Gen., 15

Radar: beacon guiding air strikes, 17, 101, 111, 128, 141; control of AA guns, 135, 208; counter-mortar, 117; ground surveillance, 117–19, 123, 139
Radios: aircraft VHF in ground force vehicles, 12–15; air support without use of, 34–35;

Argentine, 230; for artillery fire requests, 34, 73, 92, 116, 162; British, 220; deceptive transmissions, 134; in FAC aircraft, 18, 43–44, 100–102, 147; in Hind helicopters, 185; linking ground units, 85; linking sensors to FDCs, 118; Soviet backpack, 161; transmission intercepts, 59, 66, 123, 134; used by ARA, 92, 106; used by FOs, 10, 12, 86, 104, 106; used to call for air strikes, 116, 172; as Viet Minh targets, 34
Recoilless rifles: 75-mm, 40; Argentine use of, 223; French use of, 32, 40; NVA use of, 65; US, captured by Chinese, 36; US use of, 138; Viet Minh use of, 25, 34, 36, 49–50
Red River delta, 35–37, 61, 136. *See also* Delta (Hanoi)
Red River Valley, 28
Remotely piloted vehicles (RPVs), 241, 261, 270, 274
Republic of Vietnam forces: 1st Armored Brigade (ARVN), 150; 1st Division (ARVN), 151; 22nd Division (ARVN), 149, 152; Air Force, 65; Marines, 150; popular and regional forces, 63, 73; Rangers, 78, 150–51. *See also* Airborne units; Airmobile units; Armor; Montagnards
Rifles, 5, 8, 166
Riyadh, 256
Rocket launchers: 66-mm, 200; 122-mm multiple, 132, 170, 172, 192; hand-held, 224; Soviet, 36, 181–82, 196; used by NVA, 132–33, 136, 139–40; used by Viet Minh, 31, 36, 60. *See also* Multiple Launch

Tumbledown Mountain, 218, 223–24, 227, 229
Turkey, 245
Two Sisters, 218, 221

U–2 reconnaissance aircraft, 260
Union Army, 3
United Arab Emirates, 245
United Nations Command, 16, 18
US Air Force. *See* Air Force (USAF)
US Army: 1st Armored Division, 276, 280; 1st Cavalry Division, 22, 66–73, 81, 91–92, 102, 138, 266; 1st Infantry Division, 75, 107–9, 115, 119, 145, 237; 2nd Armored Cavalry Regiment, 275; 3rd Armored Division, 275–77, 279–80; 4th Infantry Division, 95, 142; 5th Cavalry Regiment, 72; 7th Cavalry Regiment, 68–73, 81–82, 93, 141; 9th Infantry Division, 80, 118; 11th Air Assault Division, 21–22; 24th Infantry Division, 244, 248, 274; 25th Infantry Division, 77–78, 118–19, 139; 39th Infantry Regiment, 80–81; 82nd Airborne Division, 244, 248; 101st Airborne Division, 81, 116, 140–41, 147–48, 244, 273; 173rd Airborne Brigade, 102; 196th Light Infantry Brigade, 78–80; Combat Commands, 38; Eighth Army, 16, 18; XVIII Airborne Corps, 244, 248, 258, 264, 266, 273; Fifth Army, 12; I Field Force, 95, 113, 143; Rangers, 177; Regimental Combat Teams, 38; II Field Force, 104, 142; VII Corps, 237, 244, 246, 250, 256, 260–61, 263–64, 266, 274, 282, 286; Special Forces, 63, 68, 115–16, 177; II Corps

Tactical Zone, 65, 149. *See also* Airborne units; Airmobile units; Army Air Forces; Artillery units, US
US Marine Corps (USMC): 1st Marine Division, 272; 1st Marine Force Reconnaissance Company, 116–17; 2nd Marine Division, 272; 26th Marine Regiment, 121, 128–29; aircraft, 18, 65, 91, 95, 127–28, 131; Fleet Marine Force, Pacific, 95; Force Reconnaissance Company patrols, 115–17; tanks, 121. *See also* Khe Sanh
US Navy (USN): aircraft provided to French, 41; aircraft used by USAF, 96–97; air strikes by in Vietnam, 65, 97, 127–29; gunfire supporting infantry, 88, 148

Van Fleet, Gen. James, 16, 18
Vaux, Col. Nick, 221
Verdun, 51, 53
Vertical envelopment, 19–20
Viet Cong units: 9th Division, 118; 33rd Division, 67–68
Viet Minh 351st Heavy Division, 36–37
Vietnamese in French Army, 29, 40, 53
Vinh-Yen, 47–49, 51, 55, 120

Wadi-al Batin, 266, 282
Waring, Lt. Mark, 199–200
War Zone "C," 107
War Zone "D," 78
West, Francis J., 116–17
Westmoreland, Gen. William, 66, 125, 131
White phosphorus (WP): rocket-propelled, 185; shells, 71, 86, 88, 111–12, 147
Williamson, Maj. Gen., 118